ECONOMIC CHANGE IN RURAL INDIA

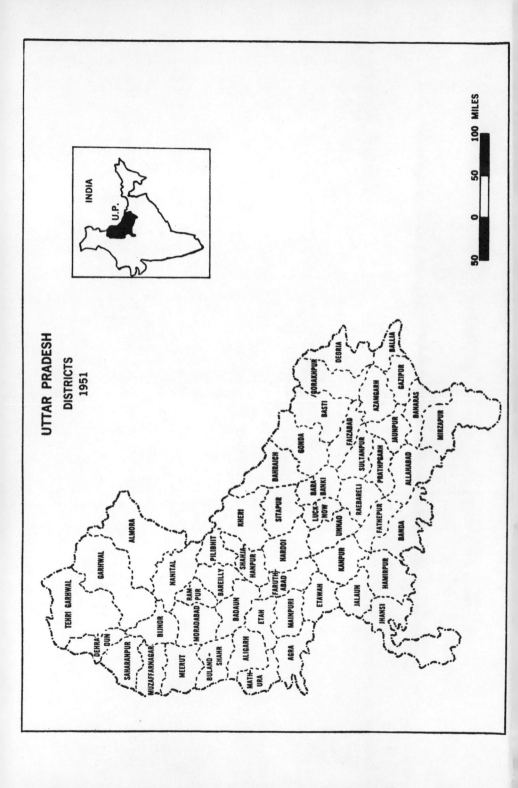

UTTAR PRADESH
DISTRICTS
1951

INDIA

U.P.

50 0 50 100 MILES

Economic Change in Rural India

Land Tenure and Reform in Uttar Pradesh, 1800–1955

by Walter C. Neale

KENNIKAT PRESS
Port Washington, N. Y./London

ECONOMIC CHANGE IN RURAL INDIA

Copyright © 1962 by Yale University
Reissued in 1973 by Kennikat Press by arrangement
Library of Congress Catalog Card No.: 72-85284
ISBN 0-8046-1704-X

Manufactured by Taylor Publishing Company   Dallas, Texas

To Walter Neale, Karl Polanyi, and Vera Anstey

Acknowledgments

Since the inception of this work at the London School of Economics in 1951–52, many people and organizations have been very helpful in furthering its completion.

During my two years as a Fulbright Fellow at the London School of Economics, Vera Anstey was a most encouraging supervisor, and to her I owe my introduction to the subject matter. Since that time both Dr. Anstey and Harold H. Mann of the Woburn Experimental Station have given advice and, above all, encouragement. The historical approach and method of analysis stem from years of association with Karl Polanyi, formerly at Columbia University.

Daniel Thorner of the Sorbonne and Maurice Zinkin of Bombay, and Karl Pelzer, John E. Sawyer, John Perry Miller, and Henry J. Bruton of Yale University have read earlier drafts of the work and have given much constructive criticism. It is to Dr. Thorner and to Professors Sawyer and Pelzer that I owe the line of revision adopted since submitting the original as a doctoral thesis to the London School of Economics. McKim Marriott of the University of Chicago made a number of helpful suggestions about the argument in Section 3 of Chapter 10.

Further research and the revision of the manuscript were made possible by funds granted by the Carnegie Corporation of New York through the Yale–Carnegie Fund. The Corporation is not, however, the author, owner, publisher, or proprietor of this publication, and it is not to be understood as approving by virtue of its grant any statements made or views expressed therein.

I acknowledge with appreciation and thanks permission from Macmillan Co., Ltd., London, to quote from *The Little World of an Indian District Officer*, by R. Carstairs; from Harcourt, Brace and Company, Inc., New York, and Faber & Faber, Ltd., of London, to quote from Penderel Moon's *Strangers in India*, published by Reynal & Hitchcock; and from Ernest Benn, Ltd., to quote from *Indian Village Crimes*, by Sir Cecil Walsh.

I am also indebted to Anne Granger for typing the manuscript through two revisions. Winifred Thorne and the staff of the India House Library and S. C. Sutton and the staff of the old India Office Library were most helpful with my research and must have saved me a year of work. Harpal Singh and Jai Pal Singh of Panjab University kindly contributed the maps. Others, particularly in India, have helped me with particular problems, and to all of them I offer my thanks.

To my wife and children I owe two years of quiet, coffee, tea, and the warm room, while writing the original draft, and aloof patience thereafter.

Walter C. Neale

June 1961

Contents

List of Tables

ECONOMIC CHANGE IN
RURAL INDIA

PART I

CHAPTER 1

The Problem

Land reform is the chant of the times. In the present struggle
of former colonial areas to raise their standards of living it has
become axiomatic that land reform is a prerequisite to any advance, while the present tenurial systems are often blamed on the
colonial powers. Land reform has been supported by interests as
diverse as scholars, U.N. committees, American ambassadors, independence movements, and Marxist revolutionaries. Countries as
different as Guatemala, India, and Hungary have undertaken to
redistribute the land and change the systems of tenure. The purpose is always to assure the agriculturalist security, prosperity, and
a "fair share." Behind the reforms lie an interpretation of history
and an assumption about peasant motivation. Land reform rests
partly upon a theory of exploitation: a belief that a small group
of landlords has lived parasitically on the labor of the cultivating
"masses," and that as a rule the landlord has secured his position

by force, fraud, special privilege, or some other devious means contrary to public morality. With reform, however, the cultivator will have the security and incentive to change his ways and improve his land. With security and his "fair share" the cultivator will strive to achieve prosperity and to enjoy it.

The history of land tenure does not always support the accepted historical doctrine, and in fact the difficulties facing agriculture are not always those presumed by the reformers.

The poverty of underdeveloped regions is striking, and so is the importance of agriculture to these areas. It follows that the organization of agriculture must contribute to development, and development to the welfare of those on the land. It does not follow, however, that these areas are backward because there are landlords or because the colonial powers pursued particular policies, nor does it follow that the abolition of landlords will remove the obstacles to development. The major force acting upon the societies of underdeveloped areas during the past century and a half has been market capitalism. Enough Western elements were introduced to disrupt the old society, but not enough to bring the rapid economic advance enjoyed by the West. The roots of poverty lie in the lack of capital, the incomplete introduction of the market, the social hierarchy of the village, and the lack of respect for the processes of secular government.

This is a story and a study. It is the story of land tenures and the market for land in Uttar Pradesh from the British conquest to the present. It is a study of how that history has conditioned present policies and of how present conditions may be expected to affect the welfare of agriculturalists and others under the newly reformed system of land tenures. It covers a full cycle of history from the advent of the British upon the north Indian scene at the end of the eighteenth century to the reconstitution of the Indian system of tenures in the middle of this century immediately after the nation achieved independence.

It is well known that Rome fell on account of size, sin, sex, and soil erosion. Certainly the latter two are largely responsible for many of India's present difficulties. In India nearly three-fourths of the people live on and by the land. India desires to industrialize, to modernize its techniques of production, and to raise the standard of living of its peoples. The government of India and the governments of the constituent states have set themselves enormous tasks of irrigation, flood control, power generation, agricultural improvement, industrial expansion, and social legislation. Conditioning all these efforts, in fact the person for whom many of them were devised, is the "man behind the plow," and sometimes his wife in front of the plow. The seriousness and constancy of his problems keep him in a condition of chronic crisis. Starvation, debt, and insecurity have been the lot of the Indian ryot. If he is to be helped, the programs of economic development must be consistent with the way his life is organized on the land, or his life must be reorganized to make it consistent with the programs. Since all schemes for improvement must work through the mechanism governing the activities of the ryots, the system of land tenure—how the land is held, how it is managed, how its produce is disposed of—is central to an understanding of how the economy may be modernized and the living conditions of the Indians raised.

The entire Far Eastern area has been characterized by self-sufficient village economies in which money and markets were conspicuously lacking.[1] The self-sufficient village of almost self-sufficient households looked to tradition and religion to justify itself and was so organized that capitalist ways had no place in it. Certainly in the past, and even to a surprising extent today, this is true of the village economies of India, including Uttar Pradesh. In India, in addition to the joint family and village, there is a caste system and together they are the foundation of Indian social organization.

The economy of India was built upon the joint family, which was generally able to satisfy its own needs. When the aid of a craftsman or a special service such as that of a watchman was required, the village provided it. Cutting across village lines, but nonetheless regulating the activities of their members within each village, the castes provided a code of behavior governing the relationships between the members of the various castes.

Above the village level economic integration was achieved through the rulers and the land revenue system. The rulers took a share of the harvest and used their share to support their families, cohorts, servants, armies, and administrative officials. There was no need for regional economic integration from the point of view of the villages. The need arose on the political side, from the state, which needed material resources to maintain itself.

Motives were phrased in terms of family duties and religious principles rather than in terms of material gain. "From the beginning India believed in the indivisibility of life. Spirituality . . .

must permeate our actvities domestic and social, political and economic." In India this also meant that endeavor was not directed primarily toward material welfare, but that success and approbation were earned through meditation and saintliness, which were embodied in the forest recluse or the "super-social man" who had released himself from the ties of family and possessions. On a more mundane plane there was a strong emphasis upon the temple, which marked the center of the village and served as a meeting point for many purposes. "Rule and ceremony, rite and injunction, pageant and symbol are devised to prepare the variety of human souls for an approach to the realization of the highest goal."[2]

India was organized socially around the family, the village, the caste, and the temple, and politically around the village and the state, whether the state was a great empire or a minor raja ruling over a few square miles. The source of values was religion. This was as true of the villagers' personal lives, reflected in the tribal laws of equal inheritance and the desire for sons to perform rites after death and carry the family's debts, as it was the spiritual strivings of saints and seers.

This long-lived system was shaken by Western civilization, with its constantly growing industry regulated by a market mechanism completely foreign to Indian tradition. The present position of the Indian agriculturalist is the outcome of the impact of British rule and, through British rule, of Western capitalism, Western industry, and the Western state and laws, upon the indigenous system existing two centuries ago. Policy today is devoted to altering this position, especially by legislative measures to change the system of land tenure and to place a new group in possession of the rights over land and its produce. All over India the economic impact of British rule has been the impact of market organization and Western ideas of rationality upon an indigenous system *which did not organize its productive and distributive activities around buying and selling and the concept of economic efficiency.*

Market capitalism spread in Great Britain in response to the developing Industrial Revolution.[3] A society already relying on contract and commerce extended these techniques to industry. Markets for the factors of production were established, and the human and material resources of the nation were directed by contracts made on these markets. Neither status nor custom, religion nor family, locality nor birth determined a man's means of livelihood, his place of abode, or his activities. He sold his working life and all pertaining thereto upon a market which valued him only for his marginal productivity. He was no longer John Sykes of Holborn, C. of E., sturdy yeoman, son of William Sykes, but· a productive unit equivalent to so many pounds of capital or acres of land. This highest compliment to the individuality of man was also a threat to the amenities, ceremonies, and anchors of security which a man regarded as *his* life.

At the same time that the West, under England's leadership, adopted the *market* in order to absorb *industry*, it accepted industry which had requirements all its own. The world of industry is the world of matter-of-fact, face to face with the laws of the natural world, and requiring at every turn a relating of means to ends. The problem of organizing inputs and outputs is simply a means–end problem, and consequently industrial society is a highly rational one.

At the same time-and-place juncture of history there entered another highly significant element, the scientific or utilitarian value scale. Never has it proved satisfactory even to its most ardent proponents, who must always differentiate the higher from the lower order of wants, but it has yet to be superseded in the West in any major area of life where it has taken hold, and it is continuing to spread its sway, particularly into the confines of the family. Birth control in urban areas is a clear case in point.

Here are the three leading aspects of the capitalist organization of society. All three have been lumped under the term "capitalist rationality," yet only modern technology is, properly speaking, "rational." The activities of the successful businessman or consumer upon the market are rational, for the businessman and consumer relate means to ends, but the market mechanism itself is not rational. Similarly, given utilitarian ends one can pursue them rationally, but of themselves ends cannot be rational any more than they can be green. The social history of the past century and a half has, however, led us to speak of pursuing rational ends in a rational fashion upon a rational market, and this in turn has led us to use indiscriminately the word "rational," which in fact has three distinct referents: the means–end relationship, the market environment in which means and ends are related, and the utilitarian value scale which has been employed in selecting the ends.

It was this three-pronged rational capitalism that the West

brought to India. India did not have a market mechanism or a
rational technology. To be sure means and ends were related in
India, as in every society which perforce extracts a living from
nature, but there was no preoccupation with this relationship to
the exclusion of all nonrational elements, nor any constant drive
to "rationalize" production. And finally India did not have a utilitarian value scheme. Western capitalism had a twofold impact
upon India: the impact of the market and the impact of indus-
trialism. On the market side two aspects may be distinguished:
the effects on internal organization and the effects of a new kind
of external tie. The capitalist was interested in buying and selling
and making contracts. The Englishman who wanted tea, cotton,
or silk wanted to buy at such a price that, after transporting the
goods to England, he could sell it for more than the costs he had
incurred. He could hardly pay the Indian with gleaning rights
and so many rupees every time one of his daughters married. The
Englishman also wanted liquid means of defraying his costs of
administration. The English solution was to introduce contract
law and a monetarized economy. In point of fact the British did
much less than one might have expected. They established planta-
tions outside the villages on lands previously uncultivated. Whereas in England the country people were dispossessed by enclosures
and in consequence formed an unattached army of workers, in
India the English made no such assault upon ties to the land. The
British built their own centers at Calcutta and Bombay. But if
England did surprisingly little to turn India into an Asiatic England, still it did enough to undermine the old system; a contract
was a contract, the man, not the joint family, was the factor in
which the entrepreneur was interested, and prices and wages were
the means of organizing English economic interests in the area.

Another internal effect was the weakening of local industry by
competition. Power driven machinery and factory organization
can turn out goods more cheaply than any weaver with his loom or
blacksmith with his forge and hammer. By providing cheap goods
to the Indian villager the Westerner put a strong downward pressure on the returns to the artisan. Only so long as the position of
the artisan was protected by the traditional village structure had
he no need to fear competition. But as money earnings were in-
jected into the village and as the external economic relations of
the village were monetarized, an alternative presented itself to
the other members of the village. While the self-contained charac-

ter of the village was losing its purity, the artisan was not gaining that essential quality of the perfect factor of production: mobility. He was still bound by caste, by tradition, and by ties to his joint family. If he gave up these links, he had no new way of life which he understood, nor did the transformation of the economy proceed far enough to provide him with an alternative life.

The new external tie was with the world market. Instead of producing for the village, a number of Indians were asked to produce for the whole world. A market place in front of the temple and a supply–demand network of information and bids without fixed abode are two very different things. Since the Indian cultivator had no contact with or understanding of the world market which was demanding a new kind of behavior from him, an immense body of middlemen grew up to connect him with it. To the dangers of an erratic monsoon the villager now had to add the dangers of an apparently nonsensical and erratic market.

The market buys food crops, but when industry enters the market, it demands industrial crops which, like food crops, bring in a cash income but which, unlike food crops, are no earthly use to the grower if he cannot sell them. A village engaging in any sizable production of sugar, cotton, jute, or tobacco depended on the international market, and the growing industry and standard of living of the West were constantly bringing pressure to bear to increase the output of the industrial crops which they needed.

Despite the dislocation caused by the introduction of Western capitalism, the high material productivity of industry offers an attractive future to those who have seen how it can raise the material welfare of those peoples who adopt it. This means that the problems created by the impact of the West cannot be solved by rejecting wholesale the society to which India has been subjected these past two hundred years. There are many who will not accept a return to the past at the expense of a richer future.

Such are the issues central to this case study of Uttar Pradesh; a study that will review the pre-British system of land tenures, the system established by the British and the reforms made therein, the effects of the system upon agriculture and the rural economic structure and the reasons therefore, the reforms the Indians have undertaken since independence, and the relationship between the Western systems of law and economy and those of India which have been subjected to the Western systems for two centuries.

The argument in the following pages divides into four parts: a description of the agrarian system in the later years of Mohammedan rule; a history of the agrarian system created and modified by a century and a half of British rule; an analysis of the effects and failures of the British system; and lastly a description and analysis of the new agrarian system introduced immediately after independence. The historical narrative of Part II may appear at first too detailed, especially in respect to legislation, and the sociologically inclined reader may find the argument in Chapter 3 and Section 3 of Chapter 11 extended. In defense of the historical narrative it may be said that in the literature on tenure the documentary evidence of British reforming zeal during the nineteenth century has not been properly appreciated, and much of the argument in Part III will carry conviction only if the reader has been closely acquainted with the legislative measures of the last forty years. Much of current literature appears to be founded upon misapprehensions of British policy, and since the plea for reform is in large part a plea for change in policy and legislation, it becomes crucial to the argument for (or against) land reform to establish exactly what has been attempted in the past. To assert that the British did attempt many reforms will not persuade unless the evidence is clear, and therefore much space has been devoted to a reconstruction of British policy. Experience of briefer arguments has shown that unless chapter and verse are cited the modern student of reform remains skeptical of the intentions of his forebears. For similar reasons, the sociological argument has been presented at length. Assertions of the importance of social institutions and attitudes seldom impress economists, so it seems worthwhile to set forth in detail the relationship of these institutions to the functioning of the rural economy, especially for the benefit of those not yet acquainted with the administrative literature of the nineteenth century and the anthropological literature of the twentieth.

CHAPTER 2

The Place

The constituent state of the Indian Union known as Uttar Pradesh is a boot-shaped area about the size of Italy with a present population of 63 million. The boot lies over the upper Ganges, extending from an ankle in the Himalayas in the northwest to a toe in the middle Ganges in the southeast. Along its northern side are the Himalayas and along its southern side is the mountainous Deccan region. To the east is the Gangetic plain of Bihar, and to the west the dry plains of the Punjab. The north and south are thinly populated and not at all suited to primitive techniques of agriculture, but the area of the central valley is one of the most populous in the world.[a] The present area fell to the British piece

a. The three natural areas of U.P. had the following population densities per square mile:

	1891	1941
Himalayan Tract	90	123
Central Indian Plateau	207	232
Gangetic Basin	550	651

M. D. Chaturvedi, *Land Management in the United Provinces*, pp. 3, 6, 10. By 1950 the most densely populated district, Meerut, had 984 people to the square mile; *India: A Reference Annual 1958*, p. 573.

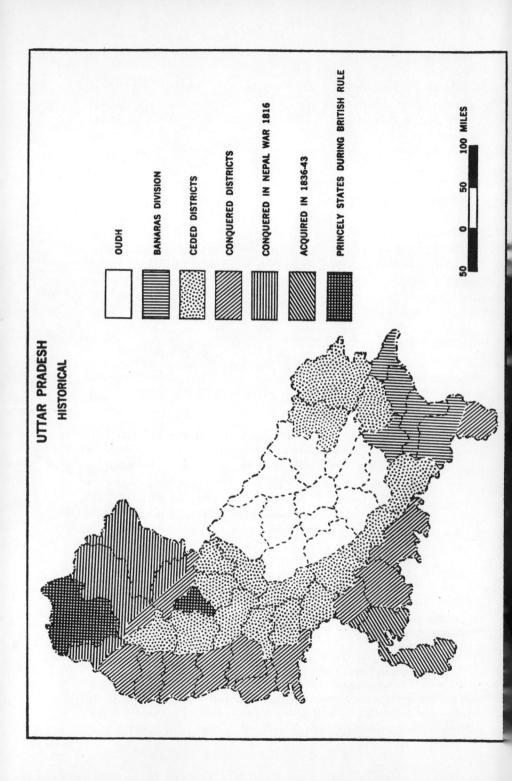

UTTAR PRADESH
HISTORICAL

OUDH

BANARAS DIVISION

CEDED DISTRICTS

CONQUERED DISTRICTS

CONQUERED IN NEPAL WAR 1816

ACQUIRED IN 1836-43

PRINCELY STATES DURING BRITISH RULE

50   0   50   100 MILES

by piece over eighty-six years, but the accretions fall into three groups when classified according to the British land policy pursued at the time. In 1775 Banaras came under the East India Company and in 1795 was "permanently settled" in accordance with the policy in Bengal at the time. In 1801 the "Ceded Districts" were given to the Company by the king of Oudh; in 1803 the "Conquered Districts" fell to the Company; and by 1817 Bundelkhand had also fallen to military action. Together from southeast to northwest, Banaras, Ceded Districts, and Conquered Districts formed a crescent moon facing north, with Bundelkhand forming a bump under the shallow. Together they were collectively administered after 1835 as the North-Western Provinces. Policy during the first half of the nineteenth century turned away from permanent settlement, and these areas went through all the difficulties involved in that change of policy. By 1856, when Oudh acceded to the Company and filled in the moon to make the boot, the lines of land policy were taking shape.

Oudh's unique problem stemmed from the Indian Mutiny and the peculiar talukdari tenure rather than from shifts in British policy. Until 1877 Oudh was separately administered by a chief commissioner. Thereafter until 1902 the lieutenant-governor of the North-Western Provinces also served as the chief commissioner of Oudh. In 1902 the North-Western Provinces and Oudh were amalgamated under the name United Provinces of Agra and Oudh, usually referred to as U.P.; the initials are still used for the area since the name Uttar Pradesh (which means "northern state") was adopted when it became a constituent state of the Republic of India.

The formation of the United Provinces by slow accretion was the outcome of British imperial policy. Having established itself in Bengal at the mouth of the Ganges, the East India Company faced the problem of unstable borders to east and west. The strategic frontiers of India are the Burmese mountains and Tibetan plateau in the east and north, and the Afghan and Iranian mountains and plateau in the northwest and west. The push toward these frontiers is the story of British expansion in India and today underlies the relationships of India with Pakistan, with Burma, and with China. In the early years of British domination of the subcontinent the Company desired buffer states to protect itself from the depredations of the warring Marathas in the west, the Sikhs in the northwest, and the Afghans to the north of the Sikhs.

However, one buffer requires another—weak states often ask protection in exchange for suzerainty—and so the Company found itself accepting Banaras from its raja and then protecting Banaras from the marauding Maratha expeditions from the Deccan by taking over the Ceded and seizing the Conquered Districts, allowing the kingdom of Oudh to the north to remain independent. The North-Western Provinces were subordinate to the Presidency of Bengal, not only in administrative structure but also in the importance attached to them. In fact, only with the growth of the independence movement and the advent of political democracy has the area become central rather than peripheral to Indian politics.

The year 1857 marks a turning point in Indian Imperial history, for this was the year in which the sepoy troops and the declining local rulers took up arms against the East India Company and turned all north India into a theater of war. The Mutiny (sometimes called "The First War of Independence" in India, but still commonly known as "The Indian Mutiny") ended the administration of the East India Company; it created a gulf between ruling Englishman and subject Indian not healed until independence; and it destroyed the possibility of a revival of Indian society in its traditional political, social, and economic form. The immediate cause of the Mutiny was the annexation of Oudh by the Company. Oudh had been in such turmoil for half a century that it was ineffective as a buffer against Afghan or Pathan incursions; and it had been so badly administered that the English felt they could no longer tolerate the corruption, violence, and torture to which the Nawabs, their agents, and their opponents resorted.[b] In 1856 the Company took over the administration of Oudh, announcing that it intended to settle land titles on the cultivators. Understandably, this enraged the talukdars who had ruled small principalities under the leading members of their various lineages, and in a way not fully understood even yet, the talukdars and officials of Oudh combined with the dissatisfied sepoys of the Company army and the other remaining independent rulers of north central India to wipe out the British administration in the area and start one of the world's most infamously vicious wars.

b. O. K. H. Spate, *The Geography of India and Pakistan*, p. 510–11, remarks that "it must be admitted that the Nawabs of Oudh have had a bad press; but all allowance made, their private morals, their public administration, and their taste seem to have been all on one level, and that depraved."

The Mutiny was so violent that it was not until 1885 that the British India Association, the predecessor of the Indian National Congress, was founded. There was in fact a period of half a century during which the subcontinent remained politically quiescent. Reform and revival movements within Hinduism spread, and around the turn of the present century Indians began to turn to politics as the means of asserting national consciousness. After the First World War the Congress under Gandhi united the Hindu and some of the Muslim population in an independence movement which eventuated in national sovereignty in 1947. It was during the twenties that U.P. rose to prominence in Indian political history. It became the stronghold and the testing ground of the Congress, the scene of campaigns of refusal to pay rent, and supplied the Congress with a disproportionate number of its leaders.ᶜ In the tale to be told in this book, the early date and the radicalism of land reform legislation in U.P. owes much to the strength of the Congress party, and especially of its more radical wing, from the early twenties.

The northern part of the Himalayan tract is snow-covered, but as one proceeds south there are forests, first in the bhabar areas and then in the tarai. The bhabar is waterless because the rainfall sinks into the porous deposits of boulders and debris brought down from the mountains. The water oozes out at the foot of the hills to form a very moist and malarial area called the tarai. The area of the Central Indian Plateau is laced with rivers the valleys of which provide rich soil, but by and large the sandstone soil of the Vinhya-Kaimurs and Satpura ranges is poor.[1]

The vast body of the state lies in the Gangetic Basin. The basin comprises 72 per cent of the area and holds 90 per cent of the population—more than 60 million at the close of British rule. It consists of three great river systems: the Ganges, the Jumna, and the Gogra. The eastern districts drain into the Gandak system. Starting in the Himalayas and flowing south, then turning east and finally joining, the Jumna, the Ganges, and the Gogra roughly parallel each other and form three smaller basins within the main basin. The western part of U.P. is less fertile, has less rainfall, has been overcultivated, and is badly eroded around the Jumna. Partly

c. Today there is a feeling throughout other parts of India, but particularly in the south, that the country is dominated by people from, and the interests of, U.P.

as a result of higher rainfall, partly as a result of a higher water table, partly because it is geologically younger, and partly because cultivation has been less intensive, the eastern region is the more fertile. The west is almost treeless and probably always has been, while the east is well wooded and consequently cooler, and the lower temperature brings more rainfall. In this basin 87 per cent of the people are classified as rural and live in villages averaging a little over one to the square mile. It is this rich alluvial basin of the upper half of the Ganges that forms the intensively cultivated, highly agricultural state of Uttar Pradesh.[2]

There are five cities with a population in excess of a quarter of a million, of which only three are centers of manufacturing activity, and there are another eleven cities of over a hundred thousand, all of which are primarily administrative headquarters of districts.[3] Of the five large cities Banaras (355,000) is both a Buddhist and Hindu religious center and the seat of an old kingdom, while Allahabad (332,000) derives a religious importance from its situation at the confluence of the Ganges and Jumna, and because it is the site of the Kumbh Mela or religious fair held every twelfth year and attended by as many as a million people. Kanpur, the largest city (705,000), is second only to Ahmedabad in Gujarat in industrial output. It is the major center of the woollen and leather goods trade, a major center of the cotton textile industry, and has many establishments engaged in flour milling, processing of vegetable oils, sugar refining, chemical production, and many other minor industrial enterprises. Lucknow, in addition to being the capital of the state, supports its 496,000 people in railway shops, cotton and paper mills, sugar refineries, and the light consumption trades. The modern economy in Agra (375,000) is represented by cotton mills, woollen carpet factories, and large hide and wool markets.[4] In terms of number of jobs and value of output, the industries of U.P. are primarily agricultural processing and textiles. While 40 per cent of the glass factories and 50 per cent of the glassworkers in India are situated in the state, the total number of glassworkers amounts to only 5,000. In the cotton mills of Kanpur and western U.P. there are jobs for only 56,000 workers.[5]

The soils of U.P. vary from heavy clay through loams to occasionally sandy patches, the clay being the best for paddy cultivation. The soils are alluvium, newer as one moves eastward. Rainfall varies from an annual 60 inches in the north and northeast to 30 inches in the south and west, with an average of 45 inches. In

the extreme southwest of the state toward the Rajasthan desert
rainfall averages less than 25 inches a year. In the eastern districts
very heavy annual flooding occurs during the monsoon.[6]

Somewhat over three-fifths of the land is cultivated in the western two-thirds of the state, and the proportion is higher in the
east. Less than a tenth of the land is under forest, current fallow,
or fodder crops. Wheat is grown on almost a fourth of the land,
the lesser millets (bajra and jowar) on a fifth, and rice and gram
each occupy a little over 10 per cent of the arable land. As one
moves eastward in U.P., rice becomes more common until in the
eastern districts there is about twice as much land devoted to rice
as to wheat. Ten per cent of the land is given to barley, while
maize, sugar cane, oil seeds, and cotton in the ratios 6:5:4:2 cover
about a sixth of the land.

In the west and north wheat is an irrigated rabi (winter) crop,
while to the south and east rice is an unirrigated kharif (summer
or monsoon) crop. Wheat is irrigated primarily from canals, but
more recently power-driven tube wells have been sunk in the
wheat growing areas. These wells, the construction of which is one
of the major agricultural measures of the Five Year Plans, can
each irrigate about 1,000 acres of cultivated land. At the time
India became independent, over 11 million acres of U.P. were irrigated, but almost none of this irrigated acreage was to be found
in the eastern districts.

The agricultural year begins with the arrival of the monsoon
in June. By the end of July the kharif crop has been sown. August
and September see tilling in preparation for the rabi crop. During
October and November, after the monsoon has passed, the kharif
crops are harvested and the rabi sown. From December to mid-
February there is irrigation and weeding of the rabi, which is
harvested during March and April and threshed and sold during
April and May. The month from mid-May to mid-June is devoted
to the cultivation of sugar cane on irrigated lands.

There is some rural industry. Aside from the usual village maintenance trades one finds tanning, carpentry, pottery works, and
about a quarter of a million people engaged in handloom weaving.
Forty to fifty thousand people find seasonal employment in the
sugar refineries scattered about the northern and western districts.

CHAPTER 3

Before the British

1. INDIAN TENURES

The tenurial system of pre-British India has been a subject of dispute since the British first entered upon the administration of Indian territory, but to some propositions there has been general consent since Holt Mackenzie's famous Minute.[1] In his Minute Mackenzie showed that the native Indian tenures were not at all like those in Britain but were governed by complicated systems of customary law. Half a century later Sir Henry Maine gave the term "status societies" to the ancient Roman and Hindu systems of law, pointing out that they were not organized around nor did they contain a system of contracts. Prices, as we understand them, and therefore rents and the sale of land, did not exist. "What," asked Maine, "in a primitive society, is the measure of Price? It can only be called Custom," for "men united in these groups out of which modern society has grown do not trade together on which I may call for shortness commercial principles."[2]

If "it is in the highest degree improbable that the various layers of the little society were connected by anything like the systematic payment of rent,"[3] how did pre-British India organize its rural economy? The answer to this question appears less simple today than it did when Maine wrote, for we are more fully aware of regional differences, of differences in the rates of change,[4] of differences within more or less homogeneous areas, and of the paucity and incompleteness of our sources of information.

In the greater part of the world the right of cultivating particular portions of the earth is rather a privilege than a property; a privilege first of a whole people, then of a particular tribe or a particular village community, and finally, of particular individuals of the community. In this last stage land is partitioned off to these individuals as a matter of mutual convenience, but not in unconditional property; it long remains subject to certain conditions and to reversionary interests of the community, which prevent its uncontrolled alienation, and attach to it certain common rights and common burdens.[5]

The Roman idea of ownership as the power of absolute disposal in perpetuity never prevailed in India.[6] The two principal ideas of landed right were that the person who first cleared the land and made it productive had a first claim on the land, expressed as a share in the product, and that he who conquered the area had a claim to the product. A claim to hold land, to enjoy its produce, to alienate it, or to inherit it could be based only upon these grounds, and throughout the East the strongest connection with the soil was an ancestral holding. The ancient custom of India as expressed in the "Institutes of Manu" clearly recognized a right in the land, but although Manu speaks of "an owner" it is equally clear from the body of the "Institutes" that the right is a family right devolving by joint succession. The right attached to the individual as the head of the family, the manager, or the representative. A daughter could not inherit or could do so only until her marriage; if she could inherit unconditionally, the land would pass from the family.[7] Mohammedan law was in principle a law of joint inheritance,[8] for only a third of a Mohammedan's estate could be bequeathed, the rest passing to "sharers," "residuaries," and "distant kindred," with males always receiving double the share of females. Because many Mohammedans followed the Hindu custom of living in joint families, this system of inheritance was in effect the same as the Hindu system. The Mohammedans also recognized the right of pre-emption for persons intimately associated with the holder of a right.[9] Many Mohammedan tribes engaged in agriculture followed the same customs of succession to property as the neighboring Hindu tribes.[a] There was sometimes a slight concession to the idea of primogeniture, as in Gonda where the eldest son received a slightly larger share than the others,[10] but there was never a power of testamentary disposition in the "ancient usage,"[11] and in the middle of the nineteenth century wills were "not known at all" in Oudh.[12]

The Mohammedan legal authorities were agreed that a conquered person who paid jaziya (head tax) and land revenue retained the right to sell or dispose of his land. They further recognized the right derived from first cultivation, and like the Hindus claimed unoccupied land for the prince, who could grant the waste to others. The U.P. Zamindari Abolition Committee held that zamindars (see Glossary) "both in theory and in actual practice were regarded as mere tax gatherers or state officials; they were not held to possess an indefeasible right of property."[13]

The Indian village economy was organized around two institutions, the family with its dependents, and the castes, which cut across the lines of loyalty between the heads of the leading families in the village and their dependent laborers and artisans. Sometimes there were several leading families descended from the founders or latest conquerors of the village, each managing its affairs separately; and sometimes the leading groups in the village were united in a brotherhood descended from a putative founder or conqueror. These villages were known as "severalty" and "bhaiachara" respectively. The cultivators of a village were joined together under a headman, and the villages in turn were united

a. B. H. Baden-Powell, *The Land Systems of British India, 1*, 24–26 (hereafter referred to as "Baden-Powell," with volume number and page citation). He cited the following instances: "In the Punjab so strong is the feeling that land belongs to the family, that a childless male proprietor is, in many tribes, not allowed to alienate any ancestral land without necessity, nor can he will it away; his power to disappoint natural heirs by *adopting* a son, is, in some tribes, limited by custom."

under a raja, "the basis of the whole society being the grain heap, in which each constituent rank had its definite interest." There was "no trace of private property, whether individual or communal, the rights which bear the nearest resemblance to it being the essentially state rights of the Raja." This state of affairs was still found "in many places" when Bennett conducted his settlement operations.[b]

The solution to what we would consider the problems of property rights, rents, wages, prices, and taxes was a system of interdependent rights and duties made effective through a complex series of operational devices which assured each party to the village economy, from the raja down to the slave-plowman, a share in the produce. The descriptive elements in the analysis which follows are taken from Bennett's *Settlement Report on District Gonda,* except as otherwise noted.

The village did not hold its lands in common. What it did have in common were its officials and its servants. The officials were the watchman, and, where the raja took his share from the village, a headman, and a patwari (village scribe). The blacksmith, the carpenter, the herdsman, the washerman, the barber, the priest, the potter, and sometimes a kahar servant to the headman were the village servants. All of these received their remuneration in a share of the grain heap.[c]

---

b. *The Final Settlement Report on the Gonda District,* by W. C. Bennett, pp. 48, 49. In the settlement report literature there is information on the state of affairs in the district at the time of the settlement, but the full reports on settlements in the N.W. Provinces did not start until 30 years after occupation by the British so that the officers did not have direct observational evidence on previous conditions. The settlements in Oudh were made within 10 to 20 years after the occupation, and for the preceding 50 years the British had a Resident at the capital at Lucknow, so much more is known about native practices in that area. However, I have found an attempt to portray the pre-British system as a whole only in Bennett's *Settlement Report,* and shall cite from that frequently. A difficulty even with the Oudh *Reports* is that the kingdom was under British influence for a long time before the occupation and cannot be considered a "pure" Indian society. Gonda was probably untypical of Oudh as a whole, since the other settlement officers did not find such complete lack of monetization in their districts.

c. Baden-Powell, *1,* 253; Bennett, pp. 45–46. A similar list from Phillip's "Tagore Lectures, 1876" is given in Z.A.C. *Report,* p. 67: headman, registrar (patwari), policeman, crop-watcher, water-distributor, astrologer, blacksmith, carpenter, potter, washerman, barber, silversmith.

The assignments of the harvest in favor of the various members of the community were of three kinds: first on the standing crop before it was cut; second on the whole grain heap before the main division; third on the raja's or cultivator's separate share after the main division was made. The exact arrangements varied from place to place. Biswa, the right to cut one twentieth of a bigha (about six-tenths of an acre) of each cultivator's land before the rest was touched, was generally enjoyed by the watchman of the village site, the watchman of the outlying fields, the blacksmith, the carpenter, the herdsman, the priest, and frequently the culti-vator himself. When the cultivator took part in biswa there was a partial equalization of incomes which we can liken to a depend-ent's allowance under a modern income tax. The cultivator re-ceived the fixed biswa share before his outturn was divided with the raja, with the result that smaller holdings paid a smaller pro-portion of outturn to the raja than larger holdings. From another district it is reported that "the smaller the size of the holding, though the yield as a rule is greater, the proportion of the land-lord's share is less" because the cultivator retains a minimum amount in any case.[14]

From the harvested crop the slave-plowman[d] took his share, which varied from one-seventh in the populous districts to one-

d. Higher castes frequently had a slave-plowman who bound himself and his descendants to labor for the landholder in exchange for a loan of Rs. 100 to Rs. 200. Each year the plowman received a share of the crop which he helped to cultivate. The share was normally too small to provide subsistence for him-self and his family. The extra food given to him by his master was added to the debt, so that instead of releasing himself from his obligation a plowman ran more deeply into debt. It was, however, easy for him to change masters by borrowing from a new master in order to liquidate his obligation to the old. In later days members of an enslaved family sometimes absconded to the English and saved enough to buy freedom for the other members of their family. The slave-plowman was "usually of the dregs of the population of the Kori or Cha-mar castes" (Bennett, pp. 46–47). This was a local variation of the historically and geographically widespread institution of debt-slavery or debt-serfdom. Ba-den-Powell (2, 247–49) reports that the system also existed in Bahraich where the slave-plowman was called a sawak. Debts were from Rs. 30 to Rs. 100 and the sawak received one-sixth of the produce, which was reported to be insuffi-cient to support a family of four, but food was so scarce that every second man in the plains of Hisampur was a sawak. The system was legally unenforceable under the British since the laborer had no reciprocal right to maintenance in case of crop failure, but it survived "by the consent of the parties and the force of the custom." The system was not confined to Oudh, for even in the 20th

fifth in the hill area, and added to this one panseri.[e] The whole village joined in the cutting and threshing, and the cutters and threshers took a sixteenth of the rice and the "fattest sheaf in thirty of the other crops." As each man helped his neighbor and recovered from the latter's heap, the real burden fell upon the raja's share of the produce, since his division followed the other deductions. This too amounted to an income-equalizing operation, for the sixteenth share given up by the small peasant was more than counterbalanced by his share from the larger farmers. Next the carpenter, blacksmith, barber, washerman, and watchman each took twelve panseris of threshed grain from each cultivator for each four-bullock plow owned by the cultivator, and six panseris for each two-bullock plow.[15] There could only have been very rough "economic justice" in this process, for although the size of the plow would have affected the amount of work required of the blacksmith and carpenter, and might have roughly represented the relative size of fields the watchman guarded, the size of the plow must have had little direct relation to the amount of work done by the barber and washerman. It was really a matter of the well-to-do paying a larger share for a public service. The herdsman's six panseris for each bullock left in his care was the closest approach to payment of a *quid pro quo*.

The above deductions were called bhatta and preceded the division of the grain heap into halves, one for the cultivator and one for the raja. Then one seer[f] in every maund of the raja's heap was returned to the cultivator, another seer was given to the patwari, a double handful to the priest, and finally a tenth of the raja's share went to the village headman. A few payments were made from the cultivator's share: the blacksmith and carpenter each received an additional three panseris, the herdsman another panseri, the priest a handful, and one or two seers went to the patwari.[16]

---

century it was found in Madras Presidency where the plowmen were called *padiyals* and kept their contracts because of the respect in which ancestral debt was held and because there was no obvious alternative employment (see P. J. Thomas and K. C. Ramakrishnan, *Some South Indian Villages: A Resurvey*, p. 350). W. H. Moreland (*India at the Death of Akbar*, p. 115) doubts that there were any laborers in Mughal India free to choose their employers.

e. A *panseri* is $\frac{1}{22}$nd of a maund, which is now about 82 lbs., but was probably between 50 lbs. and 60 lbs. before the British standardized its weight.

f. There are 40 seers in a maund, about 2 lbs. today.

The raja was the sole owner of the waste. The cultivators were allowed to graze their animals on the waste, to collect fuel from it, and even to get their building lumber from it. Houses escheated to the raja if the occupant moved. Fish and wild rice belonged to the raja, who allowed a fixed deduction for the gatherer. Throughout the kingdoms of Oudh the raja levied tolls on outsiders wishing to cut wood on his waste.[17] He also granted leases to those wishing to clear land for cultivation.[18]

Bennett says that this or something similar in all essentials was the method followed throughout Gonda wherever rents were paid in kind. The produce of the land was "the common property of every class in the agricultural community, from the Raja to the slave. No one was absolute owner more than the others, but each had a definite and permanent interest."[19]

> There were few classes not included in the agricultural community, and of these the principal were the Raja's servants, the grain and money dealers, and the keepers of shops for the sale of brass pots, ornaments, and stuffs. The staff maintained for the realization of the Raja's dues and the superintendence of the cultivation was paid on terms freely agreed to, by either cash wages or arbitrary assignments on the Raja's rights, and formed no necessary or integral part of the community. The relations between the grain dealers or shopkeepers and the rest of society were regulated by the ordinary principles of commerce, not differing essentially from those in force in Europe. It will be seen that they had nothing in common with those which governed the remuneration of the blacksmith, the carpenter, the ploughman and the shepherd.[g]

There is evidence in other settlement reports that the system employed in Gonda was not rare. In Saharanpur "the cultivator generally in the district is the Zemindar himself; in each village, a little land beyond the means of some individuals of the body of Zemindars is found in the cultivation of other persons who pay rent in kind. Also in the comparatively few Villages, in which the

---

g. Bennett, p. 44. See also Sir Henry Sumner Maine, *Village Communities in the East and West,* p. 127: "the Grain-dealer is never a hereditary trader incorporated with the village group. . . . The trades thus remaining outside the organic group are those which bring their goods from distant markets."

tenure is what is termed Zemindaree, the cultivators pay in kind; money rates are rare, as are cases, where the Mouzah (the village landholding) is underlet. The rent received by the Zemindars is divided in their accounts into Government share, the Sereenea of the Zemindar, which is always one seer of the maund of gross produce, and the mulha or sum to meet Village expenses, which is about as much as the Sereenea." Cash returns were found only on land growing sugar cane, cotton, and churree.[20] In another district, where only 28 thousand acres paid a rent in grain at the end of the nineteenth century, 113 thousand had paid in kind in the 1860s.[21]

The importance of the operational devices to the villagers was that they made it unnecessary to evaluate or even to total the gross produce and that they assured every member of the community a minimum share so long as the whole village was not suffering from famine. The devices made it unnecessary to develop a concept of ownership in the Roman sense, for the land never came into the allocative system but only its produce. The system of interdependent rights and duties was expressed in the allocative system in the form of definite operations which resulted in each person getting his share, and these operational devices filled the function performed in Western society by prices, wages, rents, and taxes.

Fair Shares

Further evidence of the absence of a concept of ownership is to be found in systems for reallotting burdens in accordance with local ideas of equity. These were instances of the "one for one principle," which is merely to say that in any exchange each person gets the equivalent of what every other person gets, and in a division each person gets one. It is the obviously fair way to divide, as any child will be the first to tell you. In bhaiachara villages where the rents and sayar profits (from village waste lands) were insufficient to meet the revenue, the village owners each had to contribute a share of the deficit. In Banaras each measure of land, called a bigha, had to contribute an equal amount—one bigha, one share. To keep the shares fair, the bighas were large and each bigha included some of each kind of land. In Banda each bigha contributed the same amount, and to overcome inequalities in the quality of the soils the bighas were of varying size—the poorer the soil, the larger the bigha. Similar devices were used elsewhere.[22]

From a larger administrative viewpoint, different size bighas in each village, to say nothing of different size bighas in the same village, must have been disturbing. If one doubts that a bigha can be called a unit of measurement, the answer, of course, is that it did not change. A bigha was one share at all times and in all places. The idea of a universal measure for land had no significance for the villager, while the idea of a "fair share" was of the utmost importance.

A similar system was to divide the land into "plows." A "plow" of land was subdivided into two "bullocks," which in turn had eight "legs" or "wells" of land which might be divided into "runs" (an area watered in a given length of time), and the "runs" split up into "bullocks" and "legs." This system was more common in the Punjab, where it seems to have been based on what each of the original settlers brought to the establishment of the community.[23] The "plow" of land, like the bigha, was not a uniform quantity, but rather a share in the community.[24]

The bhej-berar system was an answer to extremely heavy revenue assessments, and for this reason was found in ancestral share as well as bhaiachara villages. The revenue burden was periodically readjusted, and with this readjustment went a redistribution of the land. Whenever a shareholder became insolvent, his arrears were distributed among the others according to their share of the burden. The inducement to the underassessed to compromise with the overassessed was the fear that the revenue burden could not be borne without mobilizing all the resources of the village.[25] The original system of redistributing the lands had been given up "in civilized parts of the country," but inequalities were still adjusted by redistributing the burden.[26]

When a landlord body owned several villages it was common to give each co-sharer an allotment in each village and to allot him fields of different quality within each village. Periodic exchange of the lands had been given up in the United Provinces by 1892 except where floods might wash away a field. These alluvial lands were divided into strips at right angles to the river so that each strip contained some flood, some moist, and some upland land.[27]

The same procedure was adopted when a group of families owning jointly decided to divide their holdings and settle with the government by individual family. Each family would take a plot of each kind of soil in each village, and in this manner every family was treated fairly.[28]

The British recognized the existence of these systems of "fair shares" in their legislation. Regulation VII provided that where the share of the revenue payable was based on a co-sharer's land by measure and it was customary to adjust the shares, the collector might do so at the settlement. He was also empowered to repartition the land,[29] and settlement officers could redistribute land or readjust the revenue burden where it had been customary if the co-sharers asked him to do so.[30] Baden-Powell says that in fact the redistribution was left in the hands of the local panchayat of co-owners subject to interference by the settlement officer.[31]

The various systems of "fair shares" and their long continuance under British rule illustrate the force of village custom and community through the nineteenth and into the twentieth century. Under a Westernized system of land law it should not have been difficult for a person to opt himself out of the system if he thought he would benefit, but in fact the villagers continued to follow the "one for one principle" long after the market had presumably provided a more accurate system for measuring and allocating burdens.

Mughal and Post-Mughal "Deeds" and "Sales"

Although a number of transactions before 1856 look like sales of land with title deeds, they were really transfers of rights and powers to talukdars, zamindars, jagirdars, and birtyas[h] designed to formalize a *de facto* shift of power or a grant of court favor.

The only property the Muslims recognized was a revenue-free grant for a particular purpose. These "milk" grants were given in perpetuity in form, but in fact they were frequently resumed by the grantor. In the period immediately preceding the British, the downfall of dynasties and the attendant confusion presented subordinate officials with many opportunities to make such grants on insufficient authority, while in other cases grants were founded upon plain fraud. These were all claimed as property when the British moved in.[32]

Another element of indigenous land organization having certain attributes of property and the appearance of a sale was the institution of "birts" or grants from the raja. Powerful families in Oudh grew into positions intermediate between the raja and the cultivator and rajas granted similar intermediate positions to

h. See below. Birtyas eventually merged with talukdars and zamindars.

others.[33] The birt took the form of a sale, but sometimes the sum paid was so small as to make it apparent that the "sale merely recognized the raja's loss of power to the vendee." The price of the birt depended upon the wealth and position of the buyer; the price was not even mentioned in the birt, nor was any receipt given. The price was in the nature of a complimentary offering; or, in anthropological terminology, the price was a counter-gift. The prices contrasted "strikingly" with the prices at real sales of waste made by the British a short time later. Although the holder of a birt took the place of the headman of a village, his grant did not include "the peculiarly zamindari attributes of manorial rights and transit dues."[34]

In grants to talukdars the words of old Persian deeds were used. The deed specified a sale of every kind of proprietary right and explicitly included the sale of the trees on the land, yet the old proprietors in reality retained full rights in their trees and "any interference would have been considered as an unpardonable usurpation." Also, the rights in land cultivated by the old proprietors were never disturbed. In fact "the only right incontestably conveyed was that of engaging for the revenue, and representing the village in its transactions with Government." Bennett says that only the raja could be considered a proprietor in the Western sense, and that he cannot find a single instance where a raja sold or mortgaged land to another raja. Another transaction called "bai" resembled the sale of real property "in that some kind of consideration was paid, and some kind of right transferred; and differed, in that the consideration, it may be said, never bore any relation to the real value of the property and never transferred an absolute right of ownership in it."[35]

Communities exercised a veto over transfers of land so that a man could not alienate his land without his neighbors' permission. Since popular feeling prevented a permanent alienation of land, there arose a kind of usufructuary mortgage redeemable upon repayment. Thus land could not in fact be sold and was transferred only to a limited extent by mortgage. "The seizure and sale of land for private debt was wholly and utterly unknown—such an idea had never entered into the native imagination."[36]

There was also a class of "tenant" who may well be regarded as a kind of owner. These tenants held their land absolutely, independent of any contract with the landowner. They were called tenants of khudkasht, and their claim was usually based upon some past superior status which had been lost in the series of conquests, usurpations, and grants.[37]

Land Revenue

The process by which the grain heap was divided throws light on the question whether the raja owned the land and on the question whether the raja's share, called land revenue by the British, was a tax or a rent. The actual division of the produce of the soil can be made an excellent case for arguing that the state was indeed the owner of the land. As we have seen, every member of the community was in some sense an owner, with the exception of soldiers, officials, and merchants. However, there seems to be general agreement that local rulers managed, certainly in the years just before the British, to take for themselves whatever could be called a surplus. Baden-Powell cites a Colonel Briggs to the effect that "the weight of taxation on ordinary lands prevented the existence of real property in them," while he himself says that the demands on the land had so risen "that no *valuable* property in it remained."[38] For centuries the land revenue had been so high as to absorb all the rent, and in a real sense the state was the proprietor, but the *state never let land competitively or interfered in its management.*[39] From the British point of view a decision that the raja owned the land would mean that the East India Company, as heir to the raja's position, would own the land and could then legitimately charge a rent—in effect, charge as much as possible by letting the land competitively. On the other hand, if the raja did not own the land his share was to be interpreted as a tax, and the canons of taxation required a minimization of the burden. The question of who owned the land before the British period arises from applying the logic of a market system to a nonmarket society.

The fact of the matter was that the revenue was neither a rent nor a tax in the Western sense, just as the raja was neither an owner nor not-an-owner in the Western sense. If we think of the owner as the person who oversees the use of the land, the state was not the landowner, for the state only tried to maximize its exactions after the economic return on the land had been determined by others: what was planted was the villagers' affair. The raja was one of a large number of people in the rural hierarchy who had rights over the produce of the land, and although he was often the most powerful person, his share did not differ in principle from any one else's share. The entire difficulty of interpretation arose from the attempt to force Indian institutions into the mold of British ones.[40]

From the earliest times the division of the crop or an equivalent money payment was the principal revenue of the ruler, and the organization of the territory was devised to secure the realization of this revenue.[i] Whether under Rajputs, Mughals, Marathas, or Sikhs, the revenue organization was essentially the same. The lowest level of revenue administration was the village headman and the village accountant. Above the village there was frequently a small grouping of villages under an officer and staff, and still higher there was always the district—the pargana or taluka—with its headman and accountant known as the kanungo. Districts were grouped under a diwan or nazim who was responsible to the emperor for the revenue of his province.[41] Sometime long before the entry of the British upon the Indian scene the ruler's share was fixed at as little as an eighth or twelfth in some places, at as much as a third or half in other places. The share varied depending upon the ability of the ruler to exact more or less, while the share going to the central authority varied with the position of the center vis-à-vis the people on the spot. At the height of their power the Mughals brought all the land revenue from a large area directly under their control at Delhi, but later the emperor lost control of the revenue. Many local people in authority were not really revenue collectors but rather petty princes in tributary status to whomever was the most powerful overlord.

The share depended upon the kind of crop and the way in which it was cultivated rather than upon the value that could have been extracted from the land by the peasant. There was uni-

---

i. Baden-Powell, *1*, 179. The land system has been called feudal, but this is incorrect. George Campbell ("Tenure of Land in India," in the Cobden Club, *Systems of Land Tenure in Various Countries,* p. 148) says that the pre-Mohammedan invaders had established a system similar to the European feudal system but that the Mohammedans swept it away, except for a few remnants in Rajputana. Daniel Thorner ("Feudalism in India," Chap. 7 in Rushton Coulborn, ed., *Feudalism in History*) argues that Rajputana was not feudal, as Tod has asserted, but tribal with an incomplete feudal superstructure which might have developed further had it not been superseded by a kinship system (pp. 138–43). Following Moreland, Thorner also says that the Muslim and Mughal systems were not feudal, but rather bureaucratic: a typically Asiatic slave bureaucracy as found, for instance, among the Ottomans.

versally a "capital development" allowance in that irrigated lands
were taxed a smaller proportion of the produce than unirrigated
lands, on the ground that a portion of the product was due to the
cultivator for the extra capital and labor he had invested.[42] The
assessments were high but were seldom exacted in full, for in poor
years there was immediate easing of the demand upon the land.[43]

Innovations in the traditional system of dividing the grain heap
were made by the Mughal emperor Akbar, and the effect of these
innovations has been to confuse the issue. The traditional system
of landholding involved the payment of a share of the produce
in kind to the ruler, who in turn protected the cultivator.[44] Akbar
did not attempt to alter the principle. In fact, his aim was to eliminate the various intermediate layers of petty chiefs and rajas who
had grown up between the emperor and the cultivator. What he
and his chief minister Todar Mal did was to substitute money
payments for the share of grain. The average yield of crops in a
normal year was determined by his officers, and one-third of this
yield was valued at the average of ten years' prices in order to arrive at revenue rates. These rates were then used in assessing each
cultivator's liability for revenue on the basis of the acreage of each
crop grown. While cash was substituted for kind, the principle
remained the same, for the annual payment by the cultivator was
not a fixed tax upon his land, but depended on both the area
cultivated and the crops sown. Confusion arose because, when the
British officers later went into the area in which Akbar had carried through his reforms, they often found cultivators paying cash
to superiors and understandably thought this was evidence that
the Indians paid rents and not the grain share, embedded in the
social and political institutions of Indian society. One officer concluded that "where rents in kind prevail, custom regulates them,
but that rents in money are established to get rid of custom, which
is unfavourable to improved agriculture in the province; consequently, where rent in money prevails, custom does not regulate
it."[45] The results he attributed to money rents can as easily be
attributed to British influence in the area for half a century. Another officer was surprised to find that "a general opinion has prevailed in the District, that rent must naturally be paid in kind,
and that substitution of a money rate is contingent, on the consent of the cultivator." He explained to the local zamindars their
right to eject tenants who would not agree to money rates, and
was even more surprised to find "This simple process had not

been understood even by the most noted of men, who had been accustomed to purchase at Government sales." Yet he himself indicates what the system had been when he says that tenants reacted to high rental rates by growing the worst grains and renting land from neighbors for the best crops.[46] This is a rational procedure only if the rent is a customary share of whatever is grown, regardless of the potentialities of the land.

In principle, Akbar's system allowed for revision of the revenue demand, but after a while, instead of revising the revenue, the sum assessed upon the land was left constant while cesses, dues, and benevolences were added, and in time these too acquired the dignity of custom.[47] Here, perhaps, is the solution to the apparently contradictory statements found in different sources, some to the effect that the state share was permanently determined by custom and some to the effect that the cultivator sometimes suffered from extremely heavy exactions. The revenue assessment proper was a specific, customary share, or so much money, but the actual exactions varied upward with the ability of the rulers to add to their demands under the guise of variously named additional dues, and downward as a result of the rulers' willingness to overlook principle when the land revenue could not be extracted.

With the decline of Mughal power, the centralized system of land revenue collection gave way to farming the revenue and holding the farmer responsible for a given contribution to the treasury, presumably everything in excess of his costs of collection, but often the farmer could realize a larger sum by abusing his position. Akbar's successors, Jehangir and Shahjehan, were extravagant and turned to farming out the revenue to officials in an effort to increase receipts.[48] This farming of the revenue was done on a large scale, and grew with later emperors, but with the Marathas and Sikhs the process had extended down to single or small groups of villages which became the talukas found by the British. The agency for revenue farming was the local raja or talukdar, or the local officers of the nawab. The system was oppressive, as it delegated the ruler's function of revising assessments to the revenue farmer. Since the revenue farmer obtained his position by virtue of striking a bargain with the ruler, he had to offer a goodly sum, and was thus compelled to raise the assessments upon the cultivators.[49]

Campbell said that the real value of land during the Mughal period and later went to the rulers, and that there was no margin of profit to permit systematic subletting. The value to the cultivator was a matter of sentiment, affection, and habit.[j] In places the older system had deteriorated to the point where there were no rights. In Saharanpur cultivators other than zamindars were "simply tenants at will" and there were few "cultivating communities."[50] In Pilibhit the zamindari tenure arose because there were no village communities left by the early nineteenth century, but to argue that the tenants' willingness to leave a village if the zamindar mistreated them indicates the existence of freedom of contract would be to ignore the probability that movements from village to village were flights from the gross exactions current in Oudh.[k]

As a result of the cash payment system and the deterioration in public administration it was difficult to find evidence of the principles governing the division of the grain heap among the welter of different local rates and practices.

We have seen how everyone had a claim to a share in the grain heap and how no one could claim to "own" the land in the sense that he could dispose of it and its produce as he chose. If all the claimants bundled their rights together, then indeed there would have been an owner—a complete landlord. It is sometimes implied that the "republican" communities of Indian tradition existed until the British era, but whatever was the case millennia ago, there were no republican communities in U.P. in the centuries before the British occupation. On the other hand, there were some self-governing communities, and there were communities newly founded on waste land or in the jungle. They were "republican" only for the founders or those permitted to engage in self-government. An analogy might be drawn with the ancient Greek republics where many residents were not citizens, for attached to the Indian communities there were servile tribes. These might cultivate small plots but were not considered to have any proprietary rights in them. There were also "new" cultivators who did not have a voice in the management, but whose economic position was similar to that of full-fledged members. "It is certain that, as a rule, such cultivators were not dispossessed so long as they wished to hold

j. Campbell, p. 165. *Report on the Settlement Operations of the Rái Bareli District*, MacAndrew's Appendix (p. 11), says that the government demanded all the produce, allowing nankar (a subsistence allowance) to the cultivator.

k. *Report on the Settlement of Pillibheet*, by Elliot Colvin, p. 19. Colvin cites a "Report of 5th January 1818" by Sir E. Colebrook, arguing for rental contracts, but takes the opportunity to refute the position.

their fields, but it may equally well be asserted that if any individual were for any reason dispossessed, there was little chance of any remedy available to him."[51] The revenue was almost equal to the rent which could be asked, so that "new" cultivators contributed about the same amount as the proprietary members.

After a time the distinction between the two groups became shadowy. The relationship between old and new occupants in the village was never that of landlord and tenant. Old families did not let land at a profit. Whenever there were payments made by the new occupants, the dues were regarded as perquisites to the headman and not as rent. New cultivators were needed when a village became depopulated. The ruler had no intention of allowing the remaining old villagers to play dog-in-the-manger or to use their status to engross the profits of new cultivation. In consequence old and new villagers were on more or less the same economic footing. When a new tribe conquered a village, the old villagers would lose control of village management, but due to the shortage of cultivators would retain their old economic position.[52]

Occupancy Rights

When the British began to grant cultivators of long standing "occupancy rights," which is to say, the right to hold land without fear of ejectment as long as the rent was paid, it was obviously in the interests of those whom the British had recognized as owners to deny the existence of any such right under the Indian custom from which the British derived the occupancy status. An endless debate ensued. Some among the British administrators claimed that there was no such thing in the Indian tradition as an occupancy right, others admitted the right in principle but insisted that such rights had been lost in fact long before the British entered upon the scene. Others held that the rights existed and that any lack of direct evidence was a result of the absence of written records, and of the very nature of the right, which could find expression only when denied. Within a system of interdependent sharing one would not expect to find the occupancy right articulated in a modern form.

Although MacAndrew, in handling hundreds of petitions of sepoys from Oudh, never heard of a right accruing "to the mere cultivator," he believed "At the same time the genius of the people is averse to change, and as a matter of fact, they remained on the land and cultivated from generation to generation. Their rents were regulated neither wholly by competition nor custom, though traces of both are to be found. They were sometimes raised by the landlord in consequence of the arbitrary pressure of the 'nazim', but one certain and sure cause of enhancement was an increase of the population."[53] In Shahjehanpore the *Settlement Report* says that "Rents throughout the district generally . . . are low and inadequate, as they are regulated more by custom than competition" and have risen by only a sixteenth while prices have almost doubled.[54] Even if the occupancy right was not made explicit, the practice clearly recognized it. Thus when Thornton criticized the deputy collector for listing as occupancy tenants "all who had held the land for ten or twelve years, although they had not urged that the zemindar could not turn them out," he was confusing the cultivators' way of looking at the matter with English legal forms. He made the same mistake when he stated that the rent-paying cultivators only claimed an occupancy right "subject to payment of fair rent, and no right was urged to hold at low rates,"[55] for the right the cultivators did claim is meaningless unless the "fair rent" refers to a level of rents established independently of negotiations with the zamindar—that is, to customary rents.

On the other side of the issue, we find explicit statements of the right. In the tarai area those recorded by the British as landlords referred to themselves as revenue farmers, and in Rampoor the settlement officer found "no recognized private landlord" and "no tenant with an admitted right of occupancy."[56] The Western classifications simply did not apply.

In reference to occupancy rights, Sir C. E. Trevelyan pointed out that "the Settlement Officers in Oude have, under every disadvantage, said enough to show that the prevailing impression among them is that such rights do exist."[1] Strachey remarked that "as everybody admitted, so-called tenants with the rights of occupancy in the North-Western Provinces—and he [i.e. Strachey] supposed that there must be several millions in those provinces—were in fact co-proprietors of the land with the superior land-

1. "Minute," by Sir C. E. Trevelyan, 23 August 1864, in *Papers Relating to Land Tenures and Revenue Settlement in Oude*, p. 217. "Every disadvantage" was pressure from the Chief Commissioner of Oudh, who thoroughly disbelieved in both the existence and the desirability of occupancy rights. See below, Chap. 5, Sec. 1, "The Oudh Compromise."

lord."[57] During the debate on the Punjab Tenancy Bill, Sir Henry
Maine went to the heart of the issue:

> But what was the problem before the first Settlement
> Officers? To discover whether tenants were occupancy-
> tenants or tenants-at-will—whether they could be evicted,
> and their rents enhanced at pleasure—and this discovery
> had to be made in reference to a state of society which in-
> cluded neither eviction nor rent. Really, Sir, the customary
> mode of doing that which is never done—the customary
> mode of dividing the non-existent—strike one as belonging
> to that class of questions on which it is best to decline giv-
> ing a confident opinion.[58]

Earlier in the debate he had attacked the very idea that the tenants
were tenants:

> Rights over land or any valuable commodity are either
> rights arising out of contract or proprietary rights. This
> distribution of rights is considered by the best jurists as ex-
> haustive; if then the occupancy-ryot does not hold (and it
> is clear he does not hold) under contract, it follows that he
> has some sort of property in the land.[59]

The solution to this much vexed question is that there were no
occupancy rights, because an occupancy right by its nature is an
exemption from the sphere of free contract. Until a market arises,
the question of whether certain rights are exempt from contract
on the market does not arise, nor does the question whether
twelve years continuous occupancy creates the right. If the cultivator was primarily a member of a village community, then the
particular lands he cultivates at any one time may not be a matter
of concern. It becomes a matter of concern when each plot is
owned in perpetuity by a specific individual. But if occupancy
rights could not exist in the absence of a reason for their existence,
it is nonetheless true that the former status of the cultivator could
be preserved only by exempting him from market forces by the
creation of occupancy rights.

2. POLITICS AND ECONOMICS

In Western thought we have carefully divided the fields of economics and politics. We regard ownership as a bundle of rights

in the economic sphere and political power or official position as a bundle of rights and powers in an entirely separate sphere. To see this clearly we need only think of how we disapprove of the use of political power to achieve economic gain.

In the kingdom of Oudh in the eighteenth and early nineteenth centuries there was no such dividing line. It was not possible to say that this man was a political leader, and that that man was an owner. Nor was it possible to say that this man was the owner and that that man was the manager. It was not even possible to say that this man was the employer and that other man the employee. One man had a certain bundle of rights and duties. Another man had another bundle. One man had a lot of power, another man had very little power. Thus the question whether the land was owned by the raja, the talukdar, the zamindar, the cultivator, or the king of Oudh was not a real question. Each had claims based upon custom or upon grants by the king or a raja, or upon grants made by a talukdar or zamindar. But in addition to these claims, each did or did not have the power to enforce his claims or to enlarge his claims. There was no appeal if a usurper had the power to usurp.

Keeping in mind that there was no dividing line between the exercise of political power and economic claims to control of the use of the soil and the distribution of its produce, it is possible to see in the organization and history of Oudh in the century and a half before the Company's occupation the origins of those claims to ownership which the British recognized when they established a framework for the management of the land and the security of the revenue from land.

The political situation in Oudh in the hundred years before the Company became the ruler was confused and unstable. The area which became the North-Western Provinces was ruled by a series of conquering tribes between 1750 and 1801, each of which in turn established what purported to be a government and administration, but was replaced by another victor within a few years. The administration was farmed except when plundering seemed better.

The territory that became the province of Oudh was a successor kingdom to the Mughal Empire, with a king at the capital at Lucknow—a Muslim who had been the Mughal nazim of the province but had usurped the title of king at British instigation. The king of Oudh had an administrative service of officers ranging from nazims of small provinces down to revenue collectors in the dis-

tricts. Alongside this official Mohammedan hierarchy there was
an older administration deriving from the Hindu rajas, who maintained minor kingdoms within and about the greater kingdoms.
These rajas also had a claim to the revenue to be collected from
the villages. In the trans-Gogra area of Gonda these petty kingdoms varied in size from one hundred to one thousand square
miles. The authority of the raja would have been despotic, Bennett asserted, if it had not been bound by a custom having the
sanction of religion, so that the raja never dared to take a larger
share of the crop than custom prescribed for him. The Mughals
had taken only the land revenue and a few cesses out of his hands
and had left the miscellaneous taxes and the enforcement of
law and order to him. "The Raja was as necessary a representative
of the temporal as the Brahman was of the spiritual side of the
community, and the sanction of the national creed and affection
of national feeling attached themselves equally to either institution." Civil disputes were handled by the caste panchayats and
decisions were enforced by caste penalties, but the raja tried major
cases and held an appellate authority. "The Rajas of Gonda and
Utraula, when dispossessed of the direct collection of the revenue
in nearly every one of their villages, used still to spend hours daily
in kutcherry as judges in the villagers' disputes." The raja could
call out his militia, and it was an almost daily practice to do so. If
any able-bodied man failed to respond to the call he could be sure
his house would be burned over his head at the raja's first opportunity. This tradition and the importance of the raja in the life of
the kingdom was so strong that although it was sixty years since
he had enjoyed full sovereign powers, the whole militia of Gonda
followed the raja to Lucknow in the Mutiny.[1]

There were two other political authorities in Oudh: the zamindars and the talukdars. The former were persons or groups of
persons who were the leaders in village affairs. Sanads (grants)
from the raja permitted them to collect and keep the revenue and
delegated to them the raja's judicial functions. The talukdars
operated on a larger scale over several villages. They derived similar rights from the Mohammedan ruler in Lucknow who, unable
to manage affairs through his own officers, delegated revenue and
judicial powers to the talukdars. The talukdar might have been
an officer of the king at Lucknow, a court favorite, a revenue
farmer, or a local leader or rich man. It was quite possible that he
was several of these at the time he received his sanad of a taluka

(district). He might also have been a raja himself so that he might in any particular case combine the political attributes of several different positions; a zamindar who was also a court favorite would have behind him, in addition to the terms of his sanad, the administration of revenue and justice in his own village, the delegated prerogatives of a raja, and the favor of the king of Oudh. If a raja were made a talukdar, he would combine virtually all the attributes of sovereignty although he was at the same time a grantee of the king of Oudh.

This confusion existed because there was no one person capable of concentrating all the attributes of government in his own hands. The actual division of governmental functions depended in each case upon the relative power of the people involved. Each of these, the king at Lucknow, the raja, the talukdar, the zamindar, and even the royal officer and village headman, was only too willing to take as much power as he could get. In legalistic terms, it would be possible to say that the sovereign power was the king of Oudh, that his officers—the headman of villages and the talukdars—derived their power from him according to the terms of their grants or offices; that the rajas ruled their small kingdoms on the authority of tradition and age-old custom, subject to an allegiance to the king of Oudh; and that the zamindars derived their powers from the terms of the grant from the raja. But such legalistic reasoning would be misleading because the law derived from existing conditions rather than the existing conditions from the authority of the law. To say, for instance, that a talukdar was only a particular kind of revenue officer or revenue farmer completely overlooks the fact that he might have become a talukdar because it was only on those terms that the king at Oudh could prevent him from revolting. Similarly, an officer could usurp the powers of a talukdar or even a raja, and to say that he had no authority to do so ignores the fact that there was nobody who had the power to stop him.

Landlords, Zamindars, and Talukdars

Baden-Powell lists four ways in which landlord villages—that is, villages owned by a joint family or group of joint families— grew up. It might be by the grant of a prince to one of his dependents; the dependents might seize a village when the prince's estate became disrupted or divided; a revenue farmer or auction purchaser might acquire an estate; or a clan might conquer and settle an area, dividing the land in equal shares "by custom of the brotherhood." In the last possibility lies the origin of bhaiachara villages. In all the cases the descendants of the original claimants multiplied so that shortly there was a large body of landlords.[2]

There were a number of ways in which an official could transform his position into a landed estate. When the authority of the state weakened, the lives and property of the subjects were endangered and the villagers came to look to the local officials and chiefs for protection. Dependence led to encroachment upon the villagers' rights; "the extent of this encroachment varied from one part of the country to another and from time to time, but it never amounted to a surrender of the cultivator's rights of property in land, or to the acquisition by the local lord of the status and privileges of an English landowner." The headman could become a zamindar. As trustee for the group he had rights stemming partly from his inheritance from the founder of the village, partly from his semi-elective position as popular leader, and partly from his position as the ruler's revenue collector. By extending these rights at the expense of the other members of the community he could transform his status from that of a leader to something like that of a Western landlord. The jagir, or revenue-free grant, was designed to support troops, police, and officials; in the early days the jagir included only the revenue from the land, not the land itself, and only for the lifetime of the grantee, but once it became hereditary there were ample opportunities for turning it into a proprietary right in the land. Some ryotwari villages—villages where each family owned its own land and where there was no ownership bond common to all the village families—became landlord villages as the leading men gained concessions and were then granted additional powers by the state.[3]

In the North-Western Provinces there were originally two kinds of villages: the zamindari and the bhaiachara. In the zamindari village the landowners claimed the land jointly and their respective shares were determined by the laws of inheritance. In the bhaiachara village each family owned its own lands separately. As a rule each of the original settlers or conquerors received an equal share of land. Whether the division of the land was equal or not, the succeeding generations divided the land on the same principle as the founders did, and not on the principle of inheritance. As time went on, and particularly after the British conquest, the line between the two types became blurred and the variety of organization in the villages became greater. Whether because of internal dissension or some other reason, zamindari villages would allot specific plots to each family to hold permanently. If all the land were so divided the village was known as "perfect pattidari," while if some land continued to be held in common by the village landlords the arrangement was called "imperfect pattidari." On the other hand, a bhaiachara village might decide to hold some land in common, in which case it was known as "imperfect bhaiachara." The "imperfect bhaiachara" and the "imperfect pattidari" were almost indistinguishable since in both cases some land was held in common and some by individual families. After a time the actual holdings in a pattidari village ceased to correspond with the ancestral shares as a result of transfers, accidents, and decisions to divide otherwise. During the nineteenth century many bhaiachara villages became "perfect" or "imperfect" pattidari, for when a man died his heirs divided his land, and ancestral shares replaced the former tribal rule of custom. Thus, as custom, possession, and ancestral inheritance, along with partial and complete division of the land, were mixed within villages, the historical origins of the two kinds of village lost their significance.

The British officially recognized three types of village: zamindari, with a single landlord, or with the whole village jointly owned by several persons; pattidari, with shares based on inheritance; and bhaiachara, with the shares of the co-owners based on a customary allotment. The official descriptions, while historically inaccurate and indifferent to the principles of village organization, were probably justified administratively by the mingling of types during the nineteenth century. There were also villages where a joint claim to a common area never existed at all in any form, each man or family individually claiming his or its holding. These were classified as bhaiachara because of the absence of ancestral shares, although there was no "custom of the brotherhood." Villages recently founded or conquered and villages in which an officer or local personage had seized possession and set himself up as a zamindar shortly took on the appearance and attributes of the older villages as the descendants multiplied and divided the land. The same thing occurred when kingdoms broke up and the raja's descendants became zamindars.[4]

A peculiarity of the zamindari system of ancestral shares was that the burdens were allotted without any regard to whether one share had become much improved while another had deteriorated, perhaps washed half away by a river. The general system in the pattidari villages was to let the land held in common and use the proceeds to pay the land revenue. Other revenue from waste, forests, and dues, called collectively sayar, was added to the rents. If the total was more than sufficient to pay the land revenue the excess was divided according to the ancestral shares; if insufficient to pay the land revenue each zamindar had to contribute to make up the deficit in the same proportion.[5]

The term "zamindar" was found throughout India. The exact meaning has varied from time to time and place to place, but in general meant an intermediary between the ruler and the cultivator. In Bengal his position was rather like the position of the talukdar in Oudh. He was an official revenue agent over a large area and exercised many tax and judicial powers. The Bengal talukdar was a grantee of a smaller area over which he exercised the powers of an agricultural manager and in which he behaved in many ways like an English landlord.[6] In what is now U.P. the positions were reversed. The talukdar was the large-scale revenue farmer and semi-independent political chief, while the zamindar was a local political power and the manager of a few villages, a single village, or a part of a village.

The talukdars arose because the king of Oudh was not able to manage his affairs. The economic history of Oudh in the century ending in 1856 was largely a history of the struggle between the king of Oudh, the rajas, the talukdars, the zamindars, and the officers of the king. Each tried to increase his power and his share of the land revenue at the expense of the others. Where the local raja or zamindar was strong, Lucknow settled for a lump sum payment in lieu of the rights, but where the local power was weak, Lucknow took nearly all the rights, leaving only nankar (a subsistence allotment from revenue) to the raja.[7]

The king's nazim found that the difficulties in the way of direct collection of the revenue were enormous. Rajas went into revolt, zamindars stopped cultivating, the court officers appointed to collect the revenue did not know the localities to which they were assigned, while the nazims were not appointed on merit.[8] In 1837–39 the villages of southern Oudh were cannonaded in order to force the villages to pay the revenue.[9] The nazim's only recourse was to delegate his position to people on the spot who knew how to use authority to raise the revenue, and who were willing to pay the nazim enough so that he could remit the required revenues to the center and still retain a profit for himself. The people

who could exercise the nazim's authority successfully at the local
level were either rajas or the local "capitalists." The raja combined his own powers with those delegated by the Mohammedan
government, while local "capitalists" regarded the purchase of authority from the king as an investment whose fruition they could
await. The villages in such a contract were known collectively as a
taluka, while the local "capitalist" farming the revenue was known
as a talukdar. In principle the "capitalist" was merely a contractor
for the revenue, but in realizing the revenue he actually exercised
the powers of a raja, "was bound by the same rules, and worked
on the same principles."[10] The local "capitalists" were drawn
from many sources: local zamindars, relatives of the king, court
favorites, or speculators. Sometimes, as happened in the district
of Bahraich, an ordinary co-sharer in a village rose to be a talukdar by virtue of his great "courage and prudence." First his own
co-sharers recognized him as a protector against the exactions of
revenue officials and of talukdars trying to extend their talukas.
As he proved successful in protecting the interests of his own village, surrounding villages committed themselves to his care. In
this way he built himself an estate and was recognized by all as
the talukdar of his own taluka.[11]

When the rajas became talukdars their dominions did not sur-
vive intact. "The effect of mutual jealousies, family feuds, and so
forth was to break up the old 'Raj' territories into subdivisions
and smaller groups, so that in the end the actual taluka estates
were by no means coterminous with the former Hindu [Rajput]
Kingdoms."[12]

The Mohammedan claim that the king was the sole zamindar
gave rise to a conflict of claims between the talukdars and the
zamindars. The talukdar derived his claim from the sanad of the
king of Oudh, who in turn had derived his claim to all the revenue
from his denial of the rights of the zamindars. "There were many
cases where the village zamindars preferred the more intelligent
collections of the contractors to the extortions of an official . . .
but, as a rule, the transfer only took place on the agreement of
the talukdar and the Nazim, was met with every resistance in their
power by the zemindars, and not unfrequently ended in the total
annihilation of their rights, except so far as they extended to the
sir in their own cultivation."[13] From 1798 to 1814 Sa'adat Ali
Khan enforced direct management of the revenues from Lucknow,
but from 1814 to 1837 revenue management reverted to the taluk-

dars. Again, this time with the support of Company troops, direct
collection of the revenue was attempted by Mohammed Ali Khan.
He could not control his officials, who were more rapacious than
the talukdars. The effort had failed by 1842, but had further altered the boundaries of the rajas-become-talukdars' dominions.[14]

The talukdar's right varied from almost absolute ownership
where he founded and managed the village, to receiving a quit-
rent, somewhat larger than the revenue he had to pay, while granting complete control to a lessee. The talukdar might grant or fail
to seize rights up to what amounted to a zamindari position just
beneath his own. A talukdar whose original claim stemmed from
his position as a raja might also administer justice and settle disputes.[15] The rights of the talukdar also depended upon the
strength of the rights he found existing in the villages. If zamindari families already existed in the villages, they were likely to
become underproprietors with varying degrees of independence,
perhaps having a right over the whole village, or perhaps only
over certain plots.

In Gonda zamindars were common in the areas where cultivation was old, and almost unknown in the recently cleared regions.
They were branches of old raja stock who had been granted state
rights in groups of villages and jagirdars who were granted similar rights in payment or reward for heroic service in war. The
zamindar took the place of the raja in the village, and in Gonda
was exempted from paying land revenue. In the plots which the
zamindar cultivated personally—his sir land—the zamindar combined all the rights of the cultivator and of the raja. Sir land was
therefore the closest approach to absolute private property to be
found in Gonda. However, the zamindar did not escape free of
obligations, for he had to furnish soldiers to the raja and contribute to the treasury sharakatana, an arbitrary gift to defray expenses, and bhent, complimentary offerings exacted according to
fairly regular rules. The zamindar differed from the raja in two
important respects. He never possessed the full rights of a ruler,
and his law of inheritance was tribal (equal division among sons)
whereas primogeniture marked the raj, since the raj was indivisible, and in fact the raja tended to reabsorb rights that had been
given away.[16] The village zamindars were so numerous, cultivated
so much land themselves, and could so easily prevent the cultivation of land, and thus deprive the Mohammedan king of Oudh
of any revenue at all, that the Mohammedans assessed the total

value of the rights possessed by the zamindars, deducted a dehi nankar (allowance for the zamindars), and required that the rest be delivered to the king.

It was very difficult in Oudh for a village to remain independent of the talukdars. Only villages that were militarily strong and very determined could stay out of a taluka. Of the villages that were not forced by armed might into the taluka of an ambitious talukdar, some joined to avoid oppression by another talukdar, some to avoid the exactions of the nazim's officers, who were often worse oppressors than a local talukdar who had some feeling of *noblesse oblige* toward his villages.[17] Bennett thought that in Gonda the talukdari system was a "palliation of the intolerable anarchy which would have prevailed without it," and "it was not on the whole a bad thing for the inhabitants of a district generally."[18]

The Golden Age

In current literature there is a myth that before the British arrived in India there was a Golden Age. Its exact dates are vague, so one cannot be sure whether it included the post-Mughal period, or that period itself, but it is quite clear that modern authors hark back to a day when everything was better than it has been since. The myth is just not true. The rich were rich, the poor were poor, and people ran around chopping each other up. There are, however, enough elements of fact and enough misreading of the facts to keep the myth alive, outside of its obvious advantages as propaganda for independence and as an explanation of the present poverty of India.

Pre-British India had a workable and working system based on the village. The villages survived—not individually, but as a type —for hundreds of years, their characteristic features remaining unchanged.[19] These villages were communally organized, but the view that because communal villages worked they were happy, cooperative ventures is a misreading of history, and upon it a wonderful superstructure of what conditions were, or would be, has been built. In fact, the lower strata in the village communities do not seem to have been in an enviable position at any time, and the villages and the villagers certainly did not fare well at the hands of local rulers or of empire builders. The Indian system was very like those of Egypt or Mesopotamia, where agricultural com-

munities flourished off and on for thousands of years, but which
show little change from their first appearance in history to the
present day. They too were successful systems in that they worked,
but they never produced the magnificent flowering of adaptation
to the modern world implicit in the mythology. Nor would one
attribute to these systems the virtues of kindliness.

It is written of the post-Mughal upheavals and British conquest
that

> Except in the theaters of war, these kaleidoscopic changes
> affected the countryside very little. Away from the scene of
> conflagration, the average peasant continued to concern
> himself with his agricultural pursuits blissfully oblivious of
> the political vicissitudes of empires and kingdoms. Dynas-
> ties rose and fell. The cataclysmic events which engulfed
> the rulers of the day left little, if any, impression on rural
> areas.[20]

While the succession of grand and petty monarchies did not affect
the village organization nor the traditional way of life, the upheavals did affect individual villages and peasants. Villages were
burned down, lands were thrown out of cultivation, and a great
many peasants were killed. The quotation should be amended to
leave out the "blissfully." Perhaps one-half to two-thirds of Bengal
was uncultivated at the time of the Permanent Settlement.[m] In
U.P., wars and oppressive "taxation" had impoverished the countryside during the second half of the eighteenth century. Cultivated lands had gone to waste. Abject poverty was everywhere.

m. Baden-Powell, *1*, 208 n. Another, and very bad case of this sort of reread-
ing of history is to be found in the Z.A.C. *Report:*
> Hindu society had from very early times perfected an organization for
> the harmonious adjustment of the interests of the community. Individ-
> ual ownership of land or other means of production was recognized, but
> the economic and social organization of the village was so strong and
> perfect that it prevented economic conflicts between individuals and
> classes. Private property was to be regarded not merely as an opportunity
> for private profit but also as a service. The efficient cultivation of land
> was a means of living to the cultivator, but it was also his duty to the
> community.

Aside from the obviously emotive effect of "perfected harmony" and so forth,
one simply doubts the implication that there was no greedy gain, and that any
ultimate efficiency had been reached. As for the emotive use of words, one
could just as well say that the village was so perfectly organized that the lower
classes never had a chance. Both statements are equally true and equally false.

In the forty years before the British conquest the territory had been a battlefield for Sayyids, Pathans, Jats, Gujars, Rohillas, Sikhs, and Marathas. Each succeeded the other as plundering conquerors and each was driven out after a few years by the next.[21] In 1807 a Special Commission was appointed to find out whether the existing level of land revenue was high enough to be perpetuated in a permanent settlement. The commissioners doubted that it was, so they asked the collectors:

> The local officers, in reply to the Commissioners, deprecated a permanent settlement as the country at that time was impoverished and depopulated. Almost all the early collectors deplore the depopulation of their districts and refer to extensive tracts of desolate waste lands. There is abundant evidence that this was the case. In Cawnpore, Mr. Welland, who was the first revenue officer appointed to the district, wrote: "The subjects in this part of the country are in the most abject poverty." Let the face of the country be examined and there will hardly be a manufacture found, or an individual in such circumstances as to afford the payment of a tax. The whole is one desolate waste, in which tyranny and oppression have hitherto permanently prevailed.[22]

The type of village is ancient, but actual villages have had short histories in the constant process of founding, conquest, destruction, and depopulation.

Many recent suggestions for reform seem to look to the re-establishment of a fine society by the repeal of the history of British India, in which history is included all undesirable elements. It must therefore be pointed out that the British did not ruin a beautiful society. What they did was to pull the props out from under a functioning society without replacing the props or building a new society on other foundations. It is impossible to re-establish pre-British India. It would also be undesirable.

PART II

CHAPTER 4

The Years of Company Rule:
From the Conquest to the Mutiny

1. OWNERSHIP

The Early Settlements of 1801 to 1822

When the British came to India it never occurred to them that cultivated land could belong to no one, or, if one prefers, to a large number of people, each owning in a different way. Consequently, they insisted there were landowners when no such persons really existed, and they actually created landlords. "Even if the zamindars had been less like landlords than they actually were," wrote Baden-Powell, "it was almost inevitable that a system should have shaped itself in the minds of our legislators, by which some one person would be recognized as landlord. So strong was the effect of prevalent ideas, that years afterwards, when the tenures

of village bodies in the North-West Provinces, and their peculiar
constitution, were discovered, our public officers could with difficulty realize this state of things; and they kept on writing as if
some one person in the village must be *the* proprietor."[1]

The sources of British misconceptions were twofold: Adam
Smith's view of the economy, and the socioeconomic structure of
rural England. The first provided the rationale of British policy
and the second a picture of the institutions through which the
market forces portrayed by Smith worked themselves out.

The views of the classical economists were accepted completely
by most of the administration of the East India Company. Ben-
tham himself had trained many of them. There was no doubt in
their minds that the road to a wealthy country was along the
track laid out by Adam Smith: the search for profits would lead
to the accumulation of capital and the most productive organization of economic activity. This was the rationale for freeing the
economy from traditional restraints which the British assumed
were merely an overlay on the "natural" state of the economy. But
the customary restraints were not a peculiar Hindu–Muslim auto-
cratic addition; they reflected the very content of native life, and
by ignoring these restraints because they were not a part of man's
"economic" nature, the British ignored and thus disrupted the
whole pattern of Indian culture.

The British went beyond the lifting of restraints. They had a
positive picture of how an agricultural economy was organized
in its "natural" state, and this picture was the organization of the
English countryside.[2] The Ricardian analytical divisions of income into rents, profits, and wages were matched in the England
of 1750–1850 by the country gentry of landlords who let to large-
scale tenant farmers who in turn hired the agricultural labor. The
gentry undertook the functions of land management and of local
government. The farmers organized the farm work and supplied
the stock and working capital. The hired work force did the manual labor. The gentry led the countryside in agricultural improvements, working with and through their tenants. At the same time
they supplied the social and political leadership and the local
administration. The tenant farmers were men of business ability
and they operated on a scale sufficiently large to justify calling
their earnings the profits of management rather than the wages of
labor. While divided by class, although not always by level of income, there was a high degree of cooperation between landlord

and tenant. The farmers' legal security of tenure under freely negotiated leases varied from one to seven years, but in practice
farmers stayed for much longer periods and rents were raised with
apologies. It was under this system that England's revolution in
agricultural techniques was carried on.

It was this scheme that the British visualized when they set forth
the rules governing land tenures in India. Today we would say
that it is naïve to expect to export successfully a whole system, and
even in those days a blind eye must have been turned on experiences in Scotland and Ireland. Furthermore, an analogy more appropriate than the tenant farmer of southern England would have
been the small yeoman farmer who was being dispossessed by the
enclosures of the late eighteenth century. Nevertheless, the model
was founded upon everyday observation and the logic of classical
economics.

Starting with the premises of English classes and of classical
economics, the British had to decide whether private individuals
owned the land or whether the state owned the land. The question
arose because there was a school of thought which held that in
India the state was the owner. If this were the case, the East India
Company as successor to the Mughal Empire had become the
owner of the land in India.

Prior to the break up of the Mughal Empire the state had never
claimed to be the sole owner of the land, but when that empire
split into a number of principalities, the Mohammedans used the
claim in an effort to take power from the local zamindars. When
the viceroys of Oudh, Bengal, and Hyderabad insisted they were
the owners of the soil, it was the first time such a claim had been
heard.[3] To understand why the rulers claimed to be sole owners
we must understand that they were usurping the government from
the Mughal Empire on the one hand, while on the other asserting
their authority over the petty chiefs who were as willing to usurp
from the new rulers as the new rulers were from Delhi. The economic foundation of any Indian state was the revenue from the
land, so that any person hoping to wield power had to engross as
much of the revenue as possible, and a claim to own the land
helped to justify the ruler's exactions. To the Indians a claim to
the land was a means of consolidating political power, whereas
to the English such a claim had logical implications for the distribution of income. "If it were determined that Government
might be justly regarded as owner of the land, then of course what

it took from the actual cultivator might be regarded as *rent;* and Government was further entitled to take the whole of the remaining produce of land, after allowing the cultivator the costs of cultivation and the profits of his capital."[4] On the one hand, if the government did not own the land, the land revenue must have been a tax, and this conclusion carried with it an obligation to minimize the tax burden in accordance with the economic canons of the nineteenth century. There were immediate financial advantages for the Company if it were the owner. On the other hand, it was felt that there might be even greater long-run financial advantages in the creation of an economically prosperous and socially stable countryside.

Today we can look upon the question as a false one. The limitation of the choice to "tax" or "rent" is valid only as long as we confine ourselves to the axioms of the market. Nature provides no such limits, and in fact the only proper way to treat land revenue is as the share of the product of the land which went to the government, just as other shares went to artisans and priests. In a market system with absolute private property, the earnings from production must be rent, interest, profits, or wages. It is possible to look at any other system and say that we would call this return "rent" and that return "wages." But it is not necessary, nor if used exclusively is it apt to be helpful, in analyzing a system different from that in which the terms were devised. When the premises of the market are dropped, the facts of the matter are clear: a system of shares for everyone, divided as custom and power dictated—land revenue, the zamindar's share, the cultivator's share, the plowman's share, the carpenter's share.

It is no wonder that the early British administrator had trouble. It was not a question of his honesty, nor of his objectivity, nor yet of his intelligence. His premises were simply inapplicable to the situation he faced. When the Zamindari Abolition Committee of the U.P. legislature took the view that the controversy "had great practical importance in the early days of the British rule and misconceptions of theory led to great injustice, to the disintegration of the most important social institutions of India, the village community, and to the oppression of the vast masses of the people,"[5] it undoubtedly believed that the land belonged to the cultivator or to a corporate village community. The position is as tenable as the position that the land belonged to the landlord or to the government, but the committee was equally in error since it assumed a kind of ownership that did not exist. If the land belonged to anyone, it belonged to a large number of people, and not least among them were the rajas and the zamindars. .

In 1793 Bengal, under whose jurisdiction the North-Western Provinces fell during their formative years, adopted the system of permanent settlement in fixing the assessment of land revenue. The zamindar or landlord contracted with the government to pay a yearly sum fixed in perpetuity, and in exchange became the owner of the land. It was presumed that the zamindar, to whom any improvements in the productivity of the land would accrue, would expand into surrounding waste lands, employ the best agricultural methods, and invest. The government reserved the right to protect the interests of those under the zamindars, but it was thought that the latter would reach a fair understanding with their tenants since it would be to the zamindars' interest to encourage tenants to increase the productivity of the land. The large areas as yet uncultivated seemed to provide protection to the tenants, for it was felt that the zamindars would have to compete among themselves to attract tenants. The Company believed that a permanent settlement would create a prosperous and highly cultivated Bengal. Things did not turn out that way, but it was a reasonable expectation at the time. Banaras, having come under Company control in 1775, was permanently settled at the same time.

Since the settlement in Banaras had little effect upon the general development of U.P., we need only touch on it lightly. Settlements for the land revenue had been made in 1789 for four years; the settlements were extended for ten years in 1790, and then in 1795 the highest previous settlement was made permanent.[6] The settlement was made with the landlord or joint village community. In the latter case the headman was treated as a superior landlord and the other members of the community as his inferiors, but the whole community was responsible for the revenue. A few settlements were made with talukdars. Since Banaras shortly became part of the North-Western Provinces, its further revenue history was that of the rest of the province except that, the revenue being fixed in perpetuity, by the end of the century the revenue from Banaras was only one-third of what it would have been had assessments been changed from time to time, as happened in the rest of U.P.[7]

Whereas in Bengal the position and powers of the zamindars

had become so firmly established that no plan which ignored their
rights was feasible,[8] in the North-Western Provinces the zamindars, despite the existence of rajas who had become "revenue
zamindars" and talukdars, had not "grown into the very nature
of things," and the village bodies retained a good deal of vitality.
The element that distinguished the settlements in the North-Western Provinces including Banaras was that they were made with
bodies of village co-sharers.[9] As early as 1795 the British began to
recognize the complexity of Indian land tenures, although it was
many years before there was real understanding of the native
system, and by that time it was too late to do anything about it.

If the conditions that greeted the British in the Conquered and
Ceded Districts were chaotic, the results of early policy were dis-
astrous. The settlements between 1801 and 1822 were marked by
mismanagement, overassessment of the revenue, forced sales of
land in arrears of revenue, revenue farming to the highest bidder,
and settlement of the revenue with the wrong persons. Negligence
and understaffing on the British side were matched by fraud and
deceit on the Indian side. In the preceding period the chaos itself
had given the cultivators a fighting chance to protect their holdings and reduce revenue collections, but the conscientious inelasticity of the British permitted no escape. Where a purchaser at a
sale for arrears of revenue could not be found, a revenue farmer
free to abuse his position was found. Settlement officers lacked
knowledge of the communities with which they were dealing, and
their duties were so numerous that they had no time for any but
the most cursory enquiry into existing rights in the land. They
would look at the local records, but these had been falsified when
they were not already inaccurate. A settlement officer would ask
the kanungo (chief record-keeper of the district) with whom the
settlement should be made. If the kanungo were honest, the answer might or might not be correct, and if he were dishonest, the
officer could not help doing an injustice.[10] The tahsildar, or native
revenue collector, was paid a commission on the amount realized.
It is obvious that he was no help in arriving at fair or correct decisions. Furthermore, even the honest kanungo who knew his area
could not state that this or that man was the rightful owner, for
quite possibly there was no owner in the English sense. He would
make an approximation, naming a former cultivator whose claim
might be as good but no better than that of his successor—or naming the village headman. Actually every member of the village

community should have been named. The rights of vast numbers were swept away in the process, while a large number of lucky winners acquired rights to which they had never thought to aspire. The ignorance of the British conferred exaggerated rights upon the person with whom the settlement was made even in those cases where the most appropriate man had been picked. A revenue farmer or talukdar might be in possession of the land in one sense, while a zamindar or cultivator might be in possession in another sense, but in selecting the superior interest of the talukdar the British made him a complete owner. Co-owners signed for their groups, and then used this record later to substantiate claims to be sole owners, and the same thing could be done by someone who had purchased a share from a co-owner and could convince the settlement officer that he had "bought" the property. He too became landlord of the whole, reducing the co-sharers to the status of tenants. The first settlements "entirely obliterated all customary rights whether zamindari or occupancy."[11]

The demands for land revenue in the Ceded and Conquered Districts were so high after 1801 that the evils of erroneous entitlement to land were increased by forced sales. The result of such sales was to extinguish completely the rights of all the occupants.[12] Events from the period are revealing. It was thought at the time that the nawab of Oudh had shown revenue returns as high as possible in order "that the British authorities might be amused with an exaggerated estimate of their acquisition," yet the first British settlement was for a higher total than the nawab's estimate. Within the year the settlement broke down and one-sixth of the revenue was remitted.[13] In Kanpur the collector assessed by calling for bids from those who had taken contracts in past years. The bids were invariably higher than the general estimate of gross produce. One-fifth of the district was sold for arrears of revenue in 1802.[14] The next year revenue officers paid Rs. 85,638 to acquire property that was supposed to pay a revenue of Rs. 171,000.[15] There was obviously more than ignorance at work here. In the first triennial settlement of Allahabad district the revenue was farmed to those who could find someone to stand security, with the result that the farmers were at the mercy of their sureties who seized the opportunity to oust old proprietors and obtain possession of land assessed to more than Rs. 600,000 annually. In Muzaffarnagar district the Sayyid clan had acted as nonmanaging protectors of the villages. The Gujars, Rohillas, Sikhs, and Marathas

had driven them out and kept them out, but they returned with
the British, who, instead of giving them a talukdari status, which
they might have been expected to claim, made them proprietors
of two-thirds of their claims and abolished all other rights in those
lands. Immediately the Sayyids lost a half to two-thirds of their
new acquisitions to tradesmen and moneylenders and so became
occupancy tenants instead of proprietors. There were a large number of talukdari estates in Gorakhpur. Beneath the talukdars
there were persons holding a proprietary interest in the form of
birts granted to support younger relatives of rajas, to reward
services, to support religious persons, and to encourage the clear-
ing of waste. In every case the holders of birts were made sole
proprietors while the talukdar, actually a minor raja, became a
proprietor only of the lands he personally cultivated.[16]

Without trying to minimize the injustice done, it is nevertheless
to be noted that not all farmers of revenue lived on the borderline
of criminality. At the opening of the nineteenth century, landholding was not as profitable as it has since become, and the risks
were much greater. Many farmers of revenue resuscitated derelict
villages or brought waste under the plow at considerable expense
to themselves.

> Where *usurpation* happened [writes Baden-Powell], it was
> not so much the process of revenue-farming of our earliest
> settlements as in the unhappy application of the *sale laws*.
> The *only* idea of recovering arrears—and this was the law
> derived from Bengal—was . . . to put the "estate" up to
> auction. The purchaser would then become the absolute
> owner, and the village became "zamindari" for him and his
> sons after him. . . . Invited by the system, speculators would
> procure, by fraudulent means, evidence that a village was
> in arrears, and it was sold, perhaps without the real owner
> knowing.[17]

Regulation VII

The period of disruptive settlements lasted for two decades.[18]
After the unsuccessful first settlements, it was decided in 1803 to
have two successive three-year settlements, followed by a four-year
settlement, and then permanent settlement. By 1806 the revenue
had risen 19 per cent, so the next year a special commission was

appointed to examine whether the extent of cultivation and the size of the revenue would justify a permanent settlement. The commission reported against immediate fixing of the land revenue. The government in Bengal did not like the report, but in 1811 the Court of Directors of the Company in London came out against permanent settlement until more was known about the area. The debate over permanent settlement for the Provinces continued; meanwhile the revenue was assessed at five-year intervals and the law of sale for arrears applied. In 1818 the Board of Commissioners (the revenue authority of the North-Western Provinces) recommended that the settlement be made permanent, but the Court of Directors continued to oppose it, and the government in Calcutta had shifted to supporting temporary settlements.

During this period doubts about the applicability of a doctrine of sole proprietorship for each estate or village grew. First there was a minute by Sir Thomas Munro describing the ryotwari tenure of Madras, where single families each claimed their own land. The special commission report of 1808 on the North-Western Provinces added to the doubts, which were further strengthened by studies made in Madras and Bombay between 1814 and 1818. These doubts were turned to certainty in 1819 when Holt Mackenzie described the tenures of northern India in a minute which became the basis of policy in the North-Western Provinces for many years.[19] Mackenzie's Minute was an analysis of the settlements already made and was filled with citations from the reports of officers in the various districts of the Provinces. He argued that the British should not think in terms of *one* owner of any given property, and particularly that the British should not confuse the *representative* of a group of owners or of a village with the *owner* of the property or village. He furthermore insisted that local records and the assurances of the tahsildars could not be accepted, and that only a survey and a record of rights made under the direct supervision of a European officer would make sure that rights were correctly recorded.[20] It is interesting to note today that Mackenzie was protecting the zamindars against the encroachments of rajas and revenue farmers, and that the problem of protecting tenants against the zamindars had not arisen. In 1821 Regulation I established a special commission to reinvestigate every private and public transfer of land in the preceding eight years and gave it the power to annul any such transfers that it considered to contravene the precepts of equity. Every act of the revenue officers was thrown open to revision, and there were many alterations in ownership as a result.[21]

The authorities had realized by this time that the administration of land revenue, and in consequence the justice of the system of land tenure, left much to be desired. Regulation VII of 1822 was therefore promulgated, and from this Regulation flows the tenure system of the North-Western Provinces.

Regulation VII established the market for land in U.P., and since that time tenures of land have been treated as if they resulted from market transactions and existed in a market environment. In fact, neither assumption has been justified at any time despite the legal framework, and it is this gap between fact and assumption that has created the troubles in which land management has wallowed for over a century. Before Regulation VII the Company assumed an English land market, but fraud, ignorance, and disruption prevented anything approaching the proper functioning of a market. After Regulation VII conditions were close enough to those of a true market to complete the destruction of the Indian village economy, but far enough from those of a true market to prevent the emergence of a truly Western system.

Regulation VII, section 1, stated:

> whereas a moderate assessment being equally conducive to the true interests of Government . . . the efforts of the revenue officers should be chiefly directed, not to any general and extensive enhancement of the jumma [i.e., total revenue demand], but to the objects of equalizing the public burthens, and of ascertaining, settling, and recording the rights, interests, privileges, and properties of all persons and classes, owning, occupying, managing, or cultivating the land, or gathering or disposing of its produce, or collecting or appropriating the rent or revenue payable on account of land, or the produce of land, or paying or receiving any cesses, contributions, or perquisites to or from any persons resident in, or owning, occupying, or holding parcel of any village or mehaul [i.e., estate].[22]

This was the essence of Regulation VII: stabilizing the revenue, equalizing its burden among the estates and the cultivators, and, more important, accurately recording each and every holding and the rights of everyone having any claim in a holding. From this time on, the record of rights served as the basis for assessment and was regarded as prima facie evidence that the recorded owner was in fact the owner. Before Regulation VII whoever signed to pay the revenue became the owner. After Regulation VII degrees and types of ownership other than that of revenue payer were recognized and afforded the protection of law. The record of rights served as a title deed. By announcing a policy of stable and equitable assessments of revenue, the government in fact began to transfer the content of ownership to the recorded owner with whom the revenue was settled, for the government was no longer *de facto* owner by virtue of expropriating all the surplus that could be called rent. The "equalizing of public burthens" rather than the "general and extensive enhancement of the jumma" meant that henceforward the land revenue would be a tax, not a rental charge.

The rest of Regulation VII set forth the procedures for and conditions of the revenue settlements. The existing settlement with "Zamindars or persons acknowledged as proprietors or possessors of a permanent interest" in a mahal (an estate in land) was continued for five years on the ceded districts, and elsewhere on a year-to-year basis. On the expiry of five years the zamindars were to continue on the same terms unless the collector notified them of his intention to revise the settlement. Revenue-farming leases were limited to twelve years and preference was given to those possessing an interest in the land. The zamindar could refuse to engage if he did not like the terms, and his land would be farmed or held in khas (under the management of the collector), but the zamindar did not lose his interest in the land when he refused to sign. He received an allowance, called malikana, of 5 per cent of the amount he had offered to settle for, and could at a later settlement become a full landowner again by agreeing to the later settlement. In admitting any person for an engagement of the revenue the government did not intend "to compromise private rights or privileges, or to invest the *suddar malguzars* [persons representing the village] with any rights not previously possessed by them." Since it was "the anxious desire of Government, and the bounded duties of its officers, to secure everyone in possession of the rights and privileges which he may lawfully possess, or be entitled to possess," the officers were authorized to adjust the rights of suddar-malguzars and under-tenants. This provision meant that the internal arrangements of a mahal were open to interference on the part of the collector in order to assure that partial ownership rights were not expropriated by the head of the mahal. In making a settlement the officers were to investigate and record "the fullest possible information in regard to landed tenures, the rights, interests, and privileges of the various classes of the agricultural community." The record was to list everybody with a heritable or transferable interest, the internal relations of the coparceners, and the revenue rates per bigha of each description of land or kind of produce; any cesses or charges not listed in the record were illegal. It was further provided that pattas (written agreements) might be granted to mofussil (intermediate) zamindars and ryots.

Where several parties possessed separate heritable and transferable properties in land, the government might settle with one or more, "due provision being made for securing the rights of the remaining parties." Owners or occupiers with a heritable and transferable right under the suddar-malguzar and persons with a hereditary right of occupancy subject to the payment of a fixed rent could be made parties to a mofussil settlement recording the specific terms under which they held, and the terms were to be included in the patta of the suddar-malguzar. A joint property might be partitioned by the collector, with the sanction of the Board of Commissioners, according to the interests involved, and the separately owned and occupied lands settled separately.

The policy generally followed under Regulation VII was to settle with the joint body of village owners and to grant a malikana of 22.5 per cent of the revenue, later reduced to 10 per cent, to superior talukdari claimants. Where rajas, zamindars, and talukdars had acquired landlord status but a distinct village community survived beneath them, there was a mofussil settlement with the community clearly stating its rental obligations.[23]

If no proprietor, village body, or officeholder existed, a proprietor had to be found or created.[24] These ownerless villages were settled with farmers called mustajirs, who in time were recognized as proprietors. The reason for this policy seems to have been the administrative inconvenience of settling with, and collecting revenue from, many different people. Although the joint village was the prevalent type in northern India, it was not universal. Joint villages had grown up in groups among older villages of the ryotwari type, and had obtained ascendancy over them, but their complete disappearance in the North-Western Provinces was the result of the British settlement system.[25] A talukdari system which had existed in Agra virtually disappeared, while on the other hand a ryotwari system in Bundelkhand was replaced by the joint zamindari system.[26]

The revenue demand fixed under Regulation IX of 1833 (which altered the principle of assessment appreciably but had little effect on the legal position of ownership) was based on a high estimate of rents, and this caused many sales. By 1874, 12 per cent of the land in Aligarh district had been transferred by revenue sales and 72 per cent alienated otherwise, but doubtless a good deal "alienated otherwise" was parted with as a result of the revenue burden. When a money-lender foreclosed on a property which had been mortgaged in order to pay revenue in earlier years the proceedings were not called "revenue processes," but the true cause of the transfer was an earlier revenue payment. Half of all land had been permanently alienated and a third temporarily alienated through usufructuary mortgages.[27]

Before 1859 the most important change in landlord rights, other than the recognition of occupancy tenancies, was the gradual reduction in the government's claim to a share in the landlord's rents. The effect was to increase the value of real property, but it did not alter the principles. Originally the government demanded 90 per cent of the net rents as revenue, but in 1822 this was reduced to 83 per cent. Eleven years later the demand was brought down to two-thirds,[28] and in 1855 in the process of settling the district of Saharanpur it was decided to reduce the proportion to one-half.

The settlement of the North-Western Provinces has been called "the perfection of Indian management" on account of the security of tenure, the peace and prosperity in the countryside, and the high value of land. The picture is not accurate, for not only were the records often in error, but Rajput landowners borrowed easily, easily lost their land in consequence, and finally resented the British for placing and keeping "shopkeepers" over them. Further, the heirs of original headmen were frequently not so competent as their forebears and the land became subdivided under inefficient landlords, while it was later discovered that despite the efforts made in the direction of a complete record of rights, the position of the cultivating ryots had not been defined clearly enough.[a]

a. However, thought Campbell, the ease with which the new system permitted nonagriculturalists to acquire property, and the particular opportunity afforded to them by compulsory sales through the civil courts was not entirely

Regulation VII of 1822 was "wise and just in some of its principles" and "in many respects far in advance of the times,"[29] but the procedure enjoined upon the settlement officers was far too heavy a burden for the administrative machinery at their disposal. We may quote Baden-Powell's quiet summary of a noisy and chaotic period: "The existing land-tenures are, to a considerable extent, the product of changes which the later native misrule and our own revenue mistakes brought about."[30]

2. RENT

The rental market existed before 1859. It developed because the administration worked on the assumption that it existed and people became accustomed to the idea, but it did not have legal form until Bengal Act X of that year. When British rule was introduced, said Baden-Powell, it

> was considered an essentially just and wise policy to recognize or confer a proprietary right in the land, and consequently to hand over to the proprietors so recognized, the produce—or money-rates paid by the non-proprietary cultivators;—rates which would formerly have been directly taken by the King's agents. In return, our Government engaged with the proprietor that he should pay to the treasury a sum, fixed for a term of years, which was a moderate share of what it was estimated he could fairly make out of his estate. *The old customary revenue rates (with such local alterations as time and circumstances had brought about) thus became the rents which the proprietors get.*[31]

The rental market was implied in the British treatment of "produce- or money-rates."

A rental market can exist without money payments if potential tenants bid against each other in offering a share of the produce to the owner, but it is not easy to relate this market to other markets, since alternative crops bringing different prices would not affect the negotiations. Of course, the owner could receive bids in terms of shares of different crops and compare them with the

---

a bad thing. Many of the mercantile and capitalist classes were very enterprising and some of those who came into possession of proprietary rights in land did much to plant ryots on former waste land and to develop the resources of the provinces (Campbell, pp. 186–87).

prices of the crops, but in this case there would really be a monetarized rental market for land, disguised in a cumbersome way to
no purpose. Although elements were present, there was no rental
market in U.P. until the British arrived. There were payments to
the man whom the British recognized as owner, and these pay-
.ments were often in money. The British transformed these rudi-
ments into a market simply by believing that a market was there.

The Origins of Rent

Originally the raja or emperor took his share from the grain
heap at harvest time. As we have seen in Bennett's account of
Gonda, the share of each person—emperor, raja, official, priest,
cultivator, or servant—was determined by custom, the crop being
grown for the use of the villagers and not in response to price. In
the reign of the Mughal Akbar the share of the emperor was
converted into a money payment based on the average of ten years'
collections in kind and prevailing prices in the area. This change
applied only to the districts firmly under Akbar's control, and
even in this area it was not complete; elsewhere when grain payments were changed to money payments it was more common to
assess the revenue at so many rupees per plow. Assessment by plow
provided an entering wedge for profit motivation and competition
for land, since two farms of varying productivity might easily have
the same plow assessment.[32] Despite the opportunity, there does
not seem to have been much competitive behavior.

Three conditions seem to have led to the conversion of grain
shares to money rents. The increase in the number of cultivators
and the number of villages and estates made it increasingly difficult to collect the revenue in kind. At the same time, coined money
was becoming more plentiful, so there was less difficulty in effect-
ing the change. Thirdly, crops grown for export to Europe and
crops not easily divided or handled—sugar cane, spices, cotton,
and vegetables—were growing in importance. Land bearing such
produce was very early assessed to cash revenue, and always bore
a higher rate than land bearing foodgrains. Although these conditions made a change from grain to cash payments both more desirable and easier, the change did not result in market activity, nor
did the assessments become a tax upon the income derived from
cultivation. The cash rates of revenue soon took on the sanction
of custom and remained unchanged for long periods. They were

sometimes revised, and more frequently indirectly increased by levying other charges, but without reference to the principles upon which Akbar's minister Todar Mal originally fixed the cash rates.[33]

Another source of cash rates or rent was the custom of appraising the crop before it was harvested and fixing the raja's or landlord's share at so many maunds. This was done both before and during British rule. It was a short step to the practice of paying the share in cash at current prices instead of harvesting and paying the appraised share in kind. After a few years the landlord and tenant would agree to fix the rent at the average of the payments of the preceding few years;[b] and instead of leading to a rental market the introduction of cash rents resulted in the creation of a cash-rent tradition to replace the grain-share tradition.

Both Campbell and Baden-Powell are agreed that the sums extracted from the cultivator before the British came were very high, whether the exactions were in kind or in cash. Baden-Powell thought the rates taken "were quite as high as *could* be paid, and often represented the entire profits, leaving the cultivators only enough to live on."[34] Campbell says that the ruler's share or rate was "not unfrequently" driven beyond a "full rent" in that settled ryots who were attached to the soil by affection, habit, and a sense of property sometimes had to pay higher rates than were charged to temporary cultivators who had to be given favorable terms to attract them to take up the lands left vacant by wars and famines.[35]

In Gonda, Bennett found "that in the original form of the society money did not enter at all into the relations which subsisted between the purely agricultural classes, nor does it now in the north of the district, except in the case of such crops as sugar cane and poppy, whose division is effected with difficulty, and which occupy an infinitesimal portion of the whole area." Only in rich and old areas had money rents been common before the British. They had been introduced because of the "utter impossibility" of

b. Baden-Powell, 2, 75. A further source of cash payments for land is to be found in the *khiraj* levied by the Muslims upon conquered non-Muslims. The *mukassimah khiraj* was a percentage of the crop in kind, but the *wazifa khiraj* was a cash estimate based on average yield. It was also more like rent in that it was due whether or not the land was cultivated, and so differed from other revenue on the land in being a personal obligation. See Z.A.C. *Report*, p. 72. With the fall of Muslim power the *khiraj* merged with other revenue from the land.

any nazim supervising the division of grain in each of his villages. "The general result of their introduction was that the revenue ceased to bear a fixed proportion to the total produce." This meant that the revenue became more stable, but at the same time it permitted speculation since the grain share which the speculator could claim as a revenue farmer varied from the money revenue he had to pay. People did bid to hold villages. "The sums paid for them began to be essentially similar to the ordinary rent on a farm." Another reason for the change to cash rates in Gonda was the heavy burden of the rates. The share of the cultivator was at a minimum, so that as population increased and the subdivision of the land proceeded the percentage of the crop which went to the raja had to decline. But whereas the raja would not accept a reduction in his share he would accept the "equally efficient remedy of substituting cash payments," which was facilitated by the large increase in circulating silver which took place after 1800. But even when cash rates were introduced it did not occur to anyone to attach a separate rent to each field, and the idea was not fully grasped as late as Bennett's *Settlement Report* of 1875.

> The common plan was to assess the payment on the cultivator's plows, Rs. 16 to 24 per annum being taken for each four bullock plow employed in the cultivation, according to the yield of the soil. The most ordinary form which the conversion took was the direct one of calculating about the average annual value of the Raja's share of the gross produce of the farm, and fixing a lump payment in lieu of it, the area not entering into the calculation. Even now, when an enhancement is required, it is not usually calculated on the fields themselves, but on the lump payments. When the revised demands were lately declared, the landowners tried to meet them by asking a rise of so many annas in the rupee on the payments of cultivators throughout whole villages. These payments having been originally fixed many years ago, did not by any means correctly represent the present values of the farms for which they were made, but the idea of estimating the value of each plot of land separately, and securing a rise by the impositions of corresponding rents, is not one which I have seen acted on.[36]

In Gonda cash rents were adopted without the adoption of market behavior.

Money payments led "to the gradual effacement of the old lines
on which the rural society had been constructed." There could
have been no competition for land while the produce was divided
by shares, but with cash rents the value of lands paying the same
amount could diverge since rent by value of the product was "very
imperfectly understood." Outsiders could be tempted to bid for
a more valuable farm. "It is true that this kind of competition was
so opposed to the old fixity of tenure, which was the necessary result of payments in kind, that it was rarely to be seen in practice,
but it became for the first time possible, and has been very much
stimulated by recent legislation."[37]

Rents under Early British Rule

These cash payments to the raja or paramount claimant to the
land were the foundation upon which the British built their rental
market. The cash payments themselves did not start the market.
Baden-Powell points out that once zamindari and independent
rights over the land were recognized, it meant to the English that
all other cultivators were ryots or tenants and it therefore followed
that they were subject to enhancement of rent and ejectment. The
English intended to protect the tenants but they did not know
how: they prohibited extra cesses, and required the landlords to
grant pattas (leases), but the ryots could not read the amount
stated on the lease and in any case did not want to be bound in
a poor year. Some tenants perhaps did not want to admit their
inferior status.[38] Some control of the market did result from recording all the rights in the villages under Regulation VII, and
more particularly from the granting of occupancy rights under
Mr. Thomason's *Instructions to Revenue Officers* of 1844, but the
granting of rights did not overcome the difficulties that naturally
arose from the illiteracy of the ryots and ignorance both of the
new rental system and the new system of law under which they
could enforce their rights. Baden-Powell sums up the developments of the nineteenth century:

> Having, however, recognized proprietary right, we did
> not desire to withhold what were, at any rate from a Eu-
> ropean point of view, the natural and legal consequences
> of that proprietary right. Except where we stepped in with
> enactments to protect certain specified classes of "tenants,"
> we left the proprietors free to get more rent out of the land,

if it could be got by fair means dependent on competition and the increased value of the soil and its produce; and that very soon came to be the case. Waste land was eagerly taken up for cultivation: good government brought security and peace; roads, railways, and canals were made, and the value of land rose greatly; while population increased with it. Produce of all kinds also sold for a far higher price. The managers of estates no longer had to seek for tenants and to coax them to remain; people began to come and ask for fields to cultivate, and were willing to bid against each other for them. The rents could then no longer remain at the old rates; but what they really were and how they changed, it was not easy to ascertain.[39]

As competition for land arose it was found that despite the recording of rights the position of the ryots had not been sufficiently defined; rents rose, and ejectments were common.[40]

It would be wrong to suppose that the revolution in land tenures was wrought overnight. Right up to the end of the nineteenth century there were great imperfections in the rental market. The population was a long time in getting accustomed to the new ideas, and while the British administration at first did not appreciate that a totally different kind of organization could exist, it never tried to force the pace. For instance, in Muradabad, a district in Rohilkand, cash rents were unknown in 1818, and in 1840 rents were still paid in kind in some areas.[c] The results were anomalous. There was a rental market, and in response to the market rents rose as population and the prices of agricultural products increased, but there were many delays between the stimulus and

c. Baden-Powell, 2, 75. In 1, 242, he says that, as of 1892, "so tenaciously is old custom clung to in India, that in many native states the ruler still takes his revenue in kind." Bennett (pp. 62–63), writing of the 1870s, also comments on the slowness with which a monetarized market was accepted:

> Payments in kind for the village servants generally survived the introduction of cash payments to the raja, but they also are gradually falling into disuse. Instead of their contributions from the grain heaps, the patwari and chaukidar are now generally remunerated by fixed annual salaries or assignments of land free of rent. The assistance of day labourers at fixed wages is taking the place of the mutual co-operation of the different cultivators. The whole framework of the old society is passing away, and with the use of money the operation of the ordinary principles of supply and demand is becoming more prevalent. Their application is, however, as yet far from universal.

the reaction, and in many places there was an almost total indifference to market forces for long periods.

Baden-Powell considered this a marked feature of the rental
market in the North-Western Provinces:

> Rises and falls in *prices* do not by any means regularly
> affect rents, as they should in a pure system of competition
> rent. In a recent inquiry held regarding a proposal of the
> Government of India in 1882 to simplify all new (revision)
> Settlements, by raising the assessment on the solid ground
> of a rise in prices, the unanimous opinion of the North-
> Western Provinces was that, as the *rental* was the basis for
> calculating "assets" (50 per cent of which represents the
> Government revenue), the proposal was impossible, as mar-
> ket prices did not generally affect rents, except at long in-
> tervals, and only partially.
>
> Rents are still fixed at customary rates, to some extent
> derived from former assessment rates paid to Government.
> Rarely are they crop-rates—so much charged on a more val-
> uable, and so much on an inferior crop. Often they are
> soil-rates, oftener still lump-rents, agreed to on an internal
> feeling of suitability to the advantages of an individual
> field, or similarly to an entire holding or lot of a few acres,
> held by the tenant.[41]

Furthermore, questions that became very important later were
not in the forefront of the land problem in the earlier years.
Campbell says that in Bengal, the North-Western Provinces, and
the Punjab occupancy rights were not an issue between landlords
and tenants because there was no clear line between occupancy
tenants and tenants-at-will and because a distinction between revenue rates and rent rates was unknown. "It is certain that in the
whole course of litigation, from 1793 to 1859, there was no case
in which any ryot's rent had been raised by the agency of the
courts, on any other ground than that it was below the customary
rates of the neighborhood, and should be raised to that standard,"
although special provisions in contracts would override this general rule. Actually rents did rise as prices rose through the imposi-
tion of extra cesses and the compromising of claims between landlords and tenants. Once the body of ryots had accepted an increase,
individuals could be forced to accept it too, since courts would

then grant increases up to the prevailing rates, but the increase in rents did not keep pace with the rise in the value of land.[42]

The failure of the people to respond to the stimuli of the market is illustrated by Canning's inquiry into the rights of tenants in Oudh.

> It turned out that most of the ryots did not care to claim fixity of tenure. Even the grant of proprietary right under our system, accompanied by fixed burdens punctually paid, are scarcely ever appreciated in the earliest years of our rule; and perhaps, seeing how often the first possessors of such dangerous rights have been sold out and reduced far below their original position, the natives are not so far wrong as we suppose. It is, then, hardly surprising that most of the Oudh ryots, who had so long looked on the free right of rebelling and running away as their best safeguard, did not much like anything which seemed to bind them down, and wholly rejected the leases which it was sometimes attempted to thrust upon them. There was also no standard of law and right; and though the ryots said that a Talookdar ought not to turn them out, when asked whether he formerly had the power to do so, they said "of course he had—the man in power could do anything."[43]

Two points are outstanding about this inquiry, even though one may prefer to discount it, especially as we now know that answers to questionnaires may not mean what they seem to mean. First, the tenants' complete lack of comprehension, for so it must have been, of what was involved in the market mechanism is startling. They were simply throwing away their armor. Second, the realistic appraisal of the former position of the talukdars, which could have done them no good in persuading the British of their rights, throws a great deal of light on the question of who held what rights before the British came. As we saw, when examining conditions in Oudh in the first half of the nineteenth century, one cannot ignore the actual position of the parties. The statement of the Oudh tenants merely points to the difference that existed between what people thought ought to be the code governing their relationships and what was in fact the code.

Where the condition of the people was very bad, however, the system of customary rights broke down more easily. Speaking of

Saharanpur the *Gazetteer* said that "the right of occupancy was
unknown previous to the passing of Act X of 1859."[44] The lack of
occupancy rights was not due to the power of the landlords or the
actions of the settlement officers, "but to the fact that *all* village
cultivators were so much depressed that there was not any distinction."[45]

One would expect that in India any Western import would run
into difficulty upon meeting the caste system. Rents were largely
regulated by custom, and this meant that caste affected the rent
paid by a tenant. Rent rates in Oudh were much more affected by
the caste of the cultivator than in the North-Western Provinces.
In the district of Bareli the higher caste cultivators paid lower
rents. Sometimes the reduction was afforded because of the respect-
ability or sanctity of the higher caste tenants, and in other cases
the higher castes were required to pay less because they were not
such good agriculturalists "by nature."[46] The idea of the rental
market is to eliminate the poorer tenants by raising the rents above
what they can afford to pay, but paying lower rents because you
are a worse tenant is the antithesis of a proper rental market.

CHAPTER 5

The Quiet Years of Imperial Rule:
From the Mutiny to World War I

1. THE OUDH COMPROMISE

The Indian Mutiny, which ended the period of administration by the East India Company, divided the rulers from the ruled by a barrier of distrust and distaste, and led to half a century of peaceful but slow development of the subcontinent, had its proximate cause in the annexation of Oudh. The kingdom of Oudh was a large state, although reduced in size by the cessions of Banaras and the Ceded Districts. These cessions were the result of the total inability of the kingdom to manage its affairs. During the first half of the nineteenth century the management showed no appreciable improvement, and the Company decided to occupy the remainder of the kingdom in February 1856, in order to end the tyrannies and oppressions of the talukdars and to protect the people.[a]

Upon occupying the kingdom Lord Dalhousie ordered a three-year settlement with the parties in possession, talukdars having to prove their rights in court.[1] Since the purpose of the occupation was to end the oppression of the talukdars, it was "not surprising scant justice was done the Taluqdars and that settlement was ordered with the village communities."[2] Despite instructions to settle with the villages, the actual settlement was strongly taluk-dari. Of the 25,543 villages included in talukas in 1856, 13,640 or 62 per cent, paying just over half the revenue, were settled with talukdars. Post-Mutiny figures are not exactly comparable, but of 34,897 villages in Oudh, 66 per cent, paying 59 per cent of the revenue, were settled with talukdars. This gave rise to the remark of the chief commissioner just after the Mutiny that the pre-Mutiny settlement had been almost as much talukdari as the post-Mutiny one, although each was made under exactly opposite instructions.[3]

Despite the fact that the settlement had been favorable to them, the talukdars of Oudh felt deprived and threatened; the seizure of Oudh was a warning to other independent princes; and they joined in a war to oust the British. This last effort of the old order to protect itself occurred at a time when the troops of the Company were dissatisfied and ready to mutiny. The nationalist-aristocratic war and revolt combined with the sepoy mutiny to turn the North-Western Provinces and Oudh into a theater of war for over a year.

With the destruction of the center of Indian resistance by the capture of Delhi, the British turned to pacifying the outlying tracts, and conciliation was preferred to guerrilla warfare. When the British and Indians fell out the first settlement fell in. Lord Canning, the new governor-general, decided to re-establish relations with the talukdars by starting with a clean slate. The first move was his proclamation confiscating all the land so that he could "restore the great landowners and redress the injustice which he thought they had suffered, on condition of their full and complete allegiance."[4] The injustice was the conferring of rights upon the villages in 1856. The political objective was to make allies of the talukdars, who, it was thought, were the only

a. Campbell, p. 215. Campbell was a party to the decision.

people of influence in the area.[5] Many communities had "joined the taluqdar, their former liege lord; and as the people had thus shewn practically that they acknowledged the position of the taluqdars, it was determined to recognize the rights and status of the taluqdars as proprietors of land."[6]

Strachey argued that the Canning–Montgomery promises to the talukdars in order to end the Mutiny were in honor binding on the government, despite his dislike of the promises and their results and his desire to proceed with action to protect the tenantry.[7] He cited the case of Raja Harwent Singh, who lost 200 of his 322 villages in the settlement of 1856–57, yet gave refuge to British officers during the Mutiny. These officers "saw the men with whom the settlement had been made come in and tender their allegiance to the Raja. 'Without making any boast of it,' writes Colonel Barrow, 'he daily pointed out to me men who had been under him and his ancestors for generations, voluntarily retiring from the position in which we had placed them, and again ready to take engagements from him on his own terms. There can be no doubt that the mutual understanding between the parties was such that it should never have been disturbed by us.' "[b]

Whereas in Bengal the large zamindars were given their position partly for convenience in collecting the revenue and partly in the belief that they would seize the opportunity to enrich the country, the talukdars in Oudh were given their position partly, no doubt, from motives of justice,[c] but largely from motives of political expediency. Bengal might be characterized as an economic, Oudh as a political settlement. Neither settlement worked out well.[d]

b. *Gov.-Gen. Council, 6: 1867*, p. 286. Of course the Raja's men were also under pressure to find a protector when the British lost control of Oudh in the Mutiny.

c. See Strachey in *Gov.-Gen. Council, 6: 1867*, p. 283. The orders of Canning in 1858, "have placed the Taluqdars of Oudh in an altogether peculiar position. They hold their estates upon a tenure unknown in any other part of India, and rights have been created by the British Government which it is now necessary to protect by law."

d. Stack (p. 139) says that "from one-half to three-fourths of the revenue of the different districts of Oudh is paid by talukdars, holding for the most part, very large estates." Baden-Powell, 2, 334, cites the large talukdari estates of Rae Bareli where, of 1,735 villages, 1,719 were held by the Tilokchand Bais, a conquering Rajput clan. One hundred chiefs of this clan between them owned 1,198 villages and the largest eleven had 35,000 acres. It is clear that the settlement of Oudh was made largely with talukdars.

The first settlement of Oudh was conducted under the regulations laid down in the Record of Rights Circular of 1860. Subproprietary rights between talukdar and cultivator were to be revived as they existed in 1855, while all other cultivators were to be treated as tenants-at-will no matter whether they held at fixed rates or with occupancy rights. Some officers immediately pointed out that the anarchy preceding the annexation had cost many real proprietors their rights.[8] The question of who was entitled to a subsettlement and whether such rights should be entered in the grant to the talukdar gave rise to a running fight lasting until 1864. It was indeed a strange fight, and looks very much like a case of administrative sabotage on the part of the chief commissioner of Oudh, Sir Charles Wingfield. The governor-general, Canning, supported the rights of the underproprietors, while Wingfield held that only by giving everything to the talukdars could stability be achieved. Canning was in turn supported by the secretary of state for India, Lord Halifax, then Sir Charles Wood. When Lord Lawrence succeeded Canning the fight continued, Wingfield holding out for recognizing only those rights existing in 1855, while Lawrence insisted that since there had been so much misrule in the preceding two decades the period for qualifying for recognition of underproprietary rights should run back twelve to twenty years. The peculiarity of the fight between Wingfield and his superiors was not that he disagreed with them, which would have been fitting and proper although few then or now would sympathize with his arguments,[e] but that he deliberately disobeyed unequivocal orders to alter his policy. In the event the talukdars agreed to recognize, subordinate to their own, rights that had existed twelve years prior to May 1858. Wingfield was told to record these rights and endorse the talukdars' sanads or resign. He resigned.[f] Sir John Strachey succeeded Wingfield as chief commis-

e. The view was not unique. Maj. Gen. Sir H. M. Durand supported Wingfield as a "North-Western Provinces man" who "broke clear from the prejudices with which he started, and arrived at the conviction that justice was as due to a man with 800 villages as to a man with eight acres." *Gov.-Gen. Council, 5: 1866*, 337.

f. A full account of the correspondence between Wingfield and Canning and Lawrence is to be found in B. R. Misra, *Land Revenue Policy in the United Provinces under British Rule*, pp. 107–17, but for our purposes we need only know that those favoring complete surrender to the talukdars gave in, and that proprietary rights of a secondary nature were to be recorded. Baden-Powell (2, 213) takes a rather peculiar view of the matter, saying that it is

sioner with instructions to end the conflict and uncertainty. There was an outcry on the part of the press, with Lord Lawrence "protesting" that he had never had a thought of undermining the protalukdar policy of Canning.[9] Strachey managed to bring the dispute to a close. His solution, the Oudh Compromise, was a success if judged by the fact that it stopped the arguments, and a failure if judged by the conditions to which the cultivators were reduced. However, it was not in Strachey's province to alter the rules of the Record of Rights Circular, or to increase the rights of the cultivators, but only to establish the talukdars and underproprietors.

The Oudh Compromise was a division of the differences between the government and the talukdars. The British wanted to record and establish as many rights as possible for those holding or cultivating land underneath the persons who settled for the revenue. The talukdars wanted to obtain as many rights as they could lay hands on. In the compromise the talukdars agreed that they would make no objection to subsettlements with underproprietors if the government in return would permit no occupancy rights to accrue in the future. They feared the application of Bengal Act X of 1859 which created a right of occupancy for any tenant who had held the same land for twelve years, and it was to avoid the creation of new rights under the twelve-year rule that the talukdars accepted subsettlements. A subsettlement was a settlement with the government by the underproprietor, who acquired thereby a written guarantee of his terms of tenure.

The Oudh Compromise was formally embodied in two acts: Act XXVI of 1866 (The Oudh Sub-Settlement Act, 1866), and Act XIX of 1868 (The Oudh Rent Act, 1868). Act XXVI of 1866 gave the effect of law to the rules of subsettlement which had already been promulgated by the chief commissioner and then set them forth in the schedule of the act. To be entitled to a subsettlement the underproprietor had to have held under a contract and kept alive his claim for twelve years between 1836 and 1856 if the village was in the taluka before 1836, and for one half the period plus one

---

"not of the least importance . . . to go over the correspondence" since "this made no difference, as the government retained full power to legislate on the subject, and its intention . . . was never doubtful." Everyone else regarded the controversy as of some importance, and in view of the troubles that resulted from failure to make an early record in the North-Western Provinces it is easy to see why. On the other hand, it would equally be a mistake to emphasize the importance of Wingfield's attempt at sabotage, since he failed.

year that the village was in a taluka before 1856 if the village had
entered a taluka after 1836. This limited the number who could
claim a subsettlement.

Under Act XXVI the talukdar was responsible for the land
revenue, but the subsettlement with the underproprietor specified
the payments which the underproprietor had to make to the talukdar. If the underproprietor had held at a fixed rate, he continued at such rate, which was to be readjusted at the next settlement so as to keep "the respective shares of the profits . . . unal-
tered." If the underproprietor had paid land revenue plus dues,
he was to pay land revenue plus 10 per cent in lieu of dues. If he
had paid a proportion of the "profits or produce" he was to continue to pay the same proportion. In all other cases the underproprietor's payment was based on his previous payments but had to
be at least 10 per cent greater than the land revenue. In any case
where the share of the underproprietor would have been less than
12 per cent, there was no subsettlement. Instead, the claimant received a heritable and transferable right to at least 10 per cent of
the gross rentals.

The act was not passed without doubts. Mr. Riddell argued
that Regulation VII of 1822 already provided for subsettlements,
and that "the agreement with the Taluqdars in which the bill
originated was two-sided, and in return for their sub-settlements
the Taluqdars were to make certain concessions to their ryots. The
Bill . . . said nothing whatever as to . . . concessions." The replies
of the Governor-General and Mr. Muir were remarkable for their
naïveté. Muir was sure "the Courts would have no scruples in
carrying into effect to the letter the rules relating to non-proprie-
tary cultivators," despite the widely understood difficulty of ad-
ministering British justice in India. The Governor-General "believed that the Taluqdars would act in good faith toward the ryots.
. . . The ready assent . . . to the sub-settlement also justified the
expectation that they would carry out in its entirety the scheme
now proposed to be legalized."[10] It is hard to understand how any
one could believe that the talukdars would fight for legislated
privileges if they did not intend to use them.

Act XIX of 1868, the Oudh Rent Act, embodied the British
share of the Compromise. Section 5 provided that a tenant who
had lost all proprietary right in the lands he held or cultivated
should have a right of occupancy if he or some person from whom
he inherited had been in possession as a proprietor within the

thirty years before February 13, 1856, provided that neither he nor a co-sharer of his had underproprietary rights. The occupancy right was heritable but not transferable, and lapsed if the tenant was ejected under a decree for arrears of rent. However, the act did not substitute law for contract, for Section 5 provided that "Nothing contained in the former part of this section shall affect the terms of any agreement in writing hereafter entered into between a landlord and tenant." The rest of this act will be discussed when we take up rent, but the significance here is that Oudh was exempted from the twelve-year Rule of Bengal Act X of 1859, and so had very few occupancy tenants: only 1 per cent of the land was cultivated by occupancy tenants against 21 per cent by owners and 78 per cent by tenants-at-will. The Oudh Compromise gave greater rights to the talukdar of Oudh than was given to the zamindari landholders of the North-Western Provinces.[g]

The final measure enacted to establish land tenures in Oudh was the Oudh Estates Act of 1869. This act substituted a legislative definition of a talukdar for the complex of custom, grant, and *de facto* power upon which the talukdar had based his claim. Six lists were ordered to be drawn up, recording all talukdars—those whose estate by custom devolved to a single heir, those whose estates by the terms of their sanads devolved by primogeniture, those whose estates devolved by ordinary law of tribe and religion, grantees whose estates by the terms of their grants devolved by primogeniture, and grantees whose estates devolved by ordinary law of tribe and religion. Thereafter a talukdar was a person whose name was on one of the lists, or an heir of such a person. There were no other talukdars. The listed talukdars were those with whom a summary settlement was made between May 4, 1858, and October 10, 1859, or to whom a talukdari sanad had been granted before the passing of Act I of 1869.

g. Baden-Powell, *2*, 246. There is a wry element in the remarks of the Governor-General upon the passage of Act XIX: "I can only desire further to add that I trust the policy which, I hope, will this day receive the sanction of the Council, will be so worked by the Taluqdars and their descendants that we shall never have cause to regret that policy. It is in the hands of the Taluqdars themselves to make their privileges a blessing or a misfortune to their relatives, to the subordinate proprietors, and to the cultivators of the soil, and I trust that they and their descendants will so discharge the duties that are bound up with their rights that the British Government will be satisfied that the policy which is now being declared is sound." *Gov.-Gen. Council, 8: 1869*, pp. 31–32.

These talukdars "acquired a permanent, heritable, and transferable right in the estate comprising the villages and lands named in the list attached to the agreement or *kabuliyat* executed by such Taluqdar when such settlement was made, or which may have been or may be decreed to him by the Court of an officer engaged in making the first regular settlement of the province of Oudh,"[11] but most of these rights of ownership were not absolute. First, under Section XXX a talukdar could opt out of lists number 3 and number 5, which provided for primogeniture. Second, Section XXXII was a saving clause for creditors whose rights were specifically given priority over the provisions of the act. Third, the special qualities of talukdari status could not be transferred to a person who was not a talukdar or entitled to inherit the land, so that a third party could not acquire talukdari rights by buying an estate from a talukdar, but could purchase only those rights which he would have acquired had he bought other land from someone not a talukdar.[h] Lastly, the government retained complete freedom to protect tenants. The first schedule to the act reproduced two letters from C. Beadon, secretary to the government of India, to C. J. Wingfield, chief commissioner of Oudh, and gave legal sanction to the policies set forth in the letters. These letters clearly announced the policy of the government to protect inferior zamindars and village occupants, to uphold their rights in the soil, to allow their legitimate claims at the next settlement, to fix and record the amounts or proportions due from intermediate holders, and to "re-establish and maintain in subordination" to the talukdars "the former rights, as those existed in 1855, of other persons whose connection with the soil is in many cases more intimate and more ancient than theirs." Further, these letters recognized that to make such protection of inferior claimants effective the government had to define and record the inferior rights and limit the demands upon inferior holders for the duration of the settlement to the amount fixed by the government when computing its revenue demand.

Ownership in Oudh was by no means very different from own-

h. I of 1869, Sec. XV. Around 1890 some 62 per cent of villages in "Estates" (i.e., in talukas) were still held talukdari; see Baden-Powell, 2, 220–22, 227. On pp. 231–34 and 334–35 he gives figures for all districts except Bara Banki ("over 1,200" out of "over 2,000" talukdari), Hardoi (1,569 villages were "not talukdari"), and Kheri ("mostly talukdari"). Computing from the figures given for the other districts, 69.5 per cent of all villages were talukdari.

ership in the rest of U.P., but as a result of the growth of the talukdars before the annexation and as a result of the political power they made evident during the Mutiny, tenures in Oudh did acquire certain peculiarities. In the first place, the estates were much larger in Oudh than in the North-Western Provinces. Secondly, persons who, had they come under British rule during the first half of the nineteenth century, would have been given an allowance and removed from the land, were made into owners. In the third place, rights of a subordinate nature but having certain of the attributes of ownership were fewer. Fourth, among the owners recognized by the British in Oudh there was established a special group, the talukdars, who were singled out for special treatment in regard to succession, and later by Act XXIV of 1870 in regard to liability for the debts they incurred.

2. THE TRANSFER OF OWNERSHIP FROM LANDLORD TO TENANT

The British created owners of land in the North-Western Provinces by recognizing superior rights in the land—the right to engage to pay the revenue and to retain any surplus rents or profits —and making them freely salable on the market. The recognition of salable rights in land was often accorded to the wrong persons through ignorance, and for the same reason many secondary claimants who formerly had some rights in the produce of the land or some security of tenure lost their rights or security in consequence of the grant of sole ownership. In Oudh salable rights in land were accorded to a limited group of talukdars because of their political power. Many persons were deprived of customary or traditional rights in land as a result of the restricted recognition of subordinate rights, but it is an open question how many of these persons actually enjoyed these rights with any security in the half century before the British annexation.

There was also during this period a limited recognition of subordinate or inferior rights in land. In the North-Western Provinces Regulation VII and the settlements made thereunder recorded and secured the rights of co-sharers in village ownership, and did the same for other customary rights. In Oudh a great many of the inferior rights were purposely ignored, but the sub-settlements, the recording of underproprietary rights worth less than 12 per cent of the gross rents, and the recording of occupancy rights held before 1855 show that the British were aware that there was more than one party with justifiable claims to the land and that the British intended to secure these rights to inferior claimants in so far as they could.

Two trends in British land policy are distinguishable from 1859 onward.[i] One trend can be looked upon as an increase in the rights granted to tenants, but we shall look upon it first as a restriction upon the rights of owners and secondly as the transfer of rights of ownership from one group to another—from whole owners to tenants who thereby became in fact part owners. The other trend was a series of moves to protect the owners from the workings of the market mechanism, and under this trend we may subsume similar efforts to protect part-owner-part-tenants.

Occupancy Rights: The Tenant as Owner

Restrictions on the powers of owners and the transfer of rights from owners to those holding under them were accomplished through the Land Revenue and Rent Acts, which came along every two to three decades. The first of the acts giving general legal status to land tenure policy was Bengal Act X of 1859, which applied at the time to the North-Western Provinces. As we have seen, Section 6 provided that any tenant who had held the same land for twelve consecutive years was to acquire a right of occupancy in that land. This twelve-year rule was to apply to any land held for twelve years in the future as well as to land held before 1859. Occupancy rights were heritable but not transferable. The essence of the right was in the limitation on the enhancement of rent. There were only three grounds on which the landlord might raise the rent payable by an occupancy tenant: that the tenant paid less than the prevailing rent paid by other occupancy tenants in similar conditions, that the produce or productive powers of the holding had increased for reasons other than the tenant's own efforts, and that the area of the holding could be shown by measurement to have increased. Conversely, the tenant could claim a reduction in his rent on the grounds that he paid more than the prevailing rate, that the holding had decreased in

---

i. I have treated the Oudh Compromise before taking up the post-1859 period because, although it actually came after 1859, it was a peculiar exception to the trend easily explicable on political grounds, and from 1870 onward policy in Oudh followed policy in the North-Western Provinces in general outlook, even though it was limited by the existence of the Compromise.

productivity due to no fault of his own, and that his land could be shown by measurement to have decreased in size.[12] Occupancy rights were not new to the North-Western Provinces, for R. M. Bird in making the settlements during the 1830s and 1840s had adopted the same rule in recording and adjudicating occupancy rights. However, by promising that in the future occupancy rights would accrue, the government made a significant change, for the landlords now knew that if they left a cultivating tenant on the same plot for twelve years they would lose the right to raise the rent. In the long run the twelve-year rule did increase the number of occupancy tenants, but the immediate result was a large increase in evictions, for the landlords saw quite clearly that they could prevent the successful operation of the rule by evicting tenants during the eleventh year.[j] At the time it was reasoned that the twelve-year rule would simplify the problem of adjudicating traditional rights, since it would be sure to include all those with a claim based on custom, and in fact would undoubtedly include many who otherwise would have had no claim to occupancy rights.[13] So far as the future was concerned, there can be no doubt that the accrual of occupancy rights after 1859 was an innovation, for the claim was now legal and not traditional. On the other hand Campbell says that twelve years was the traditional Indian term of prescription.[14]

Occupancy rights introduced a measure of confusion into the market as the British had originally visualized it. They deprived the landlord of control over the land, except in extreme cases where the tenant grossly misused the land or used it contrary to the terms on which tenants held in the area, for in all other cases the landlord had to wait until the tenant defaulted on his rent before he could evict him. Occupancy rights divorced ownership from control, for so long as the tenant held on a year-to-year or at-will basis, the landlord was able to require him to grow a certain crop in a certain way. In fact landlords in U.P. did not as a rule pay much attention to the what and the how of their tenants' cultivation, but in principle they were free to do so, and the legal

---

j. Misra, p. 168, calls the rule "the most pernicious doctrine in the whole history of land legislation"; and says (p. 130) that the effect of the rule was to abolish the traditional occupancy claims of resident cultivators and to form an additional group whose claims had no connection with the customs of the area.

system was so constructed that responsibility for what happened rested ultimately upon the landlords.

The transfer of management functions does not necessarily impair the efficiency of the market system; America and Britain provide classic examples of the divorce of ownership from management control in very efficient industries. The limitations on rents gave a share of the fruits of ownership to the occupancy tenants, but this involved only a redistribution of wealth. What was important was that the occupancy right was not transferable.[k] Father could pass it on to son, but its value was never subject to the test of the market. The granting of occupancy rights was the antithesis of earlier policy. It happened as early as the 1830s, only three decades after the introduction of the Western concept of ownership and the law of sale. It was given a permanent legislative form in 1859, *yet there has been no recognition that for a century the British maintained a form of tenure that was not responsive to the market forces which were counted upon to direct resources and increase the well-being of the citizens of U.P.*

It must not be thought that Bengal Act X was a negation of market policy. Section 8 specifically left the rents of nonoccupancy tenants to agreement between landlord and tenant, and the body of the act was concerned with the procedure of rent collection, distraint, eviction, and the legal provisions necessary for a free market.

A permanent and full legal structure for land tenures was provided for the North-Western Provinces in 1873 and lasted throughout the period of British rule. The land system of Oudh was gradually modified to conform to the system established by the North-Western Provinces Rent Act XVIII of 1873 and the North-Western Provinces Land Revenue Act XIX of 1873. Act XVIII was

k. There were two other kinds of owner-tenant in the North-Western Provinces: permanent tenure-holders and fixed-rate tenants, found only in the permanently settled districts of Benares. The permanent tenure-holder is analogous to the subsettlement holder in Oudh, and since the revenue in Benares was fixed in perpetuity, so was his rent. He was usually an intermediate landholder and not a cultivator. Perhaps the best way to state his position in Western terminology is to say that he was a leaseholder rather than a freeholder, and that his leasehold never expired as long as he paid the ground rent. The fixed-rate tenant was the Benares equivalent of the occupancy tenant. Tenants who had cultivated land for 12 years before the Permanent Settlement in 1795 received the right to hold at the same rent forever, but unlike occupancy tenants they could sell their rights.

amended in 1879, 1881, 1886, repealed by Act II of 1901, which was repealed by Act III of 1926, which in turn was repealed by Act XVII of 1939; but, throughout, the enforcement and judicial procedures and the procedural protections to litigants remained basically the same. Act XIX was amended in 1886 and repealed by Act II of 1901, but again the underlying structure was not altered. The corresponding acts regulating tenures in Oudh had similar histories. Amendments and new acts redistributed the rights of ownership, limited the working of the market, enlarged the duties of settlement officers and collectors, and created a complex of different kinds of tenures. Each successive change took one or two steps interfering with the market mechanism, or altering the substantive content of rights; but all retained the idea that there was an owner who rented to a tenant, and the idea that there were contractural relationships between landlord and government and landlord and tenant which were enforceable in the courts. Furthermore, each act embodied the basic idea that the relationships were economic—a nexus of buying, selling, renting, and taxpaying —and that profits, rents, and sales would guide the use of resources and the disposal of products in a smooth and socially satisfactory way.

The unit of ownership was the mahal, the local area which had a separate record of right and for which there was a separate settlement of the land revenue.[15] The mahal might of course be owned by one person or by a group of co-sharers.

Sir land was the land on which no lesser rights could accrue under any conditions, and which became subject to an exproprietary tenancy if the owner lost his other rights. Sir land was land recorded as sir at the preceding settlement and so recorded since; land cultivated by the proprietor, his servants, or hired labor for twelve years continuously; and land recognized by village custom as the special holding of a co-sharer and so treated in the distribution of burdens and profits.[16] Substantially the same definition was included in the Oudh Rent Act XXII of 1886, with the modification that a proprietor had to have cultivated the land for only seven years before 1886, or had it treated as sir in the distribution of profits and charges for only seven years.

When several persons held a mahal jointly, the settlement officer had the power to settle with all co-sharers jointly, or with representatives "elected according to the custom of the mahal,"[17] but in either case the entire mahal and all the proprietors were jointly and separately responsible for the revenue.[1] The settlement of the revenue was tantamount to recognition of ownership.

The Land Revenue Act of 1873 continued the policy of establishing proprietary rights inferior to those of the primary claimant. Sections 54 and 55 permitted the settlement officer to make subsettlements under which the subproprietor paid the land revenue, plus a share of the profits, which the government paid over to the owner. If the inferior claimant refused the settlement he did not lose his rights, but received 5 to 15 per cent of the return to the owner with whom the settlement was made. Section 56 allowed the settlement officer to assign rights in a portion of the mahal if a co-sharer otherwise would have had a right to cash or produce payments from the tenants in that portion, or to "maintain enjoyment of present rights or their equivalent" in any other way he saw fit.

Under Sections 4–6 of the Rent Act of 1873, fixed-rate tenants included all who had held at the same rent since the permanent settlement in 1795; if anyone had held at the same rent for twenty years it was presumed that he was a fixed-rate tenant. This act gave another class of privileged tenant legal recognition for the first time—the exproprietary tenant. The courts recognized such a right in 1864, and mention of it can be found as early as 1832.[18] A proprietor or underproprietor who parted with his rights became an exproprietary tenant on the land that had formerly been his sir land, and he enjoyed the rights of an occupancy tenant.[19] The exproprietary tenant paid four annas in the rupee less than a tenant-at-will. Section 8 continued the twelve-year rule, and Section 9 permitted transfer of occupancy rights only between co-sharers by inheritance. However, the court interpreted this to mean that an occupancy tenant could sell his rights to his landlord,[20] and so in 1881 even these sales were barred.[21] Still another class of tenants was recognized by Section 20 of Act XII of 1881: tenants at revenue rates—those who had paid the same rate paid by co-sharers in the mahal to meet the revenue—could not be removed nor their rents enhanced except when the revenue was increased. They were similar to those cultivators before the British era who by custom held a position economically equal but politically inferior to the true co-sharers.

1. XIX of 1873, Sec. 46. In Oudh, a different situation obtained. The liability in a taluka extended to one village or part of one village only, and not to the whole taluka. See Baden-Powell, 2, 264.

The Oudh Land Revenue Act of 1876 created a similar exproprietary tenure, but the Oudh Laws Act XVIII of the same year
was interpreted to mean that exproprietary rights accrued only
if the mahal were attached in accordance with the Civil Procedure
Code and if the sir lands in question were cultivated by the proprietor at the time of the attachment order.[22] Not until Act IV
of 1901 (Section 2) could exproprietary rights accrue in Oudh
whether the alienation was voluntary or involuntary.

Since insecurity of tenure has always been a major charge levied
against the zamindari system, it is important to recognize that the
Oudh Rent Act of 1886 limited the power of the landlord to
raise rents or evict tenants. Under Sections 36 and 37 a tenant-at-
will became entitled to hold the land for seven years at the same
rent as that which he agreed to pay when entering upon the contract.

3. RESCUING THE DEBTOR

While the powers of owners were being restricted by transferring
rights to tenants, the legislation of the period also attempted to
protect owners from the effects of the exercise of their powers.
The starting point for mismanagement of landholdings was the
power to become indebted. As long as a landholder does not have
the right to sell his land, the wise lender will limit the advances he
makes. When the landholder gains the right to sell his land the
amount a lender will advance increases greatly, for now he has
means of recovering a large sum: he can force a sale. It is the existence of security, and power over that security, which induces the
money-lender to expand his operations. It is the possibility of
raising large sums by pledging his land that induces the landholder to borrow and spend on a previously unknown scale.

The market for land, the provision of monetary credit, and the
disruption of traditional landholding and land management pat-
terns were closely connected. Increased indebtedness was the cause
of increased land transfers and of the reduction in status of many
ryots from cultivating proprietors to tenants.

There are two economic reasons for pledging land as security
for a loan: to raise liquid capital for investment to increase the
productivity of the land, and to acquire land by purchase instead
of by rental. In the latter case the transaction is expected to save
money in the long run, and the money that would otherwise be

paid in rent is used to pay the interest and principal on the mortgage. In the former case, the return on the investment is supposed to provide the means for paying interest and repaying principal. In U.P., as elsewhere in India, the opportunity presented by the market was misused. Instead of using the power to pledge land as security in order to mobilize resources for increasing productivity, the borrower used the money he could raise for paying inflated prices[m] for land in order to acquire the prestige associated with land ownership, and for consumption expenditures—frequently for marriage or other ceremonial occasions. As the expenditure of the money raised did not provide means for its own repayment, repayment could come only from new savings for which borrowers did not make provision, and the result was a large volume of burdensome debt leading to foreclosure, forced sales, and reduction of the owner who borrowed to the status of a tenant. To argue that the owner who so misused his borrowing capacity deserved to lose his land, and that the country was better off without such foolish people controlling the land, ignores the fact that misuse of borrowing capacity was the rule rather than the exception, so that one man's fall from grace produced a successor who was himself very likely paying an inflated price for the land with no intention of using it economically; and that the purchaser of the rights in land was quite apt to be a money-lender, merchant, or member of a noncultivating caste, so that control of the land actually passed to less rather than more efficient management. A good deal of social tension was caused by the resulting subjugation of proud owners to merchants upon whom they had been accustomed to look down.

The British reaction to this problem was to try to protect the

---

m. It has been argued that the receiver of the inflated price must have liquid assets available for productive investment, and that the original saver must have released resources for productive use, but productive investments do not necessarily follow. It is true that someone was able to save—and this raises the question of whether any community is too poor to save—but his savings were used to buy land. The seller could use the proceeds for productive investment but in fact he usually did not. He sold for one of two motives: to increase his consumption or to repay debt. In the former case the original savings became consumption. In the latter case a money-lender received the money and lent to someone who used the loan to finance consumption or to buy more land, and so the circle went until the savings found their way into consumption. Demand for land therefore reflected the amount of new savings and credit available from money-lenders and not the productivity of the land.

indebted owner from the working of the link between the land
and money markets—or from his own folly. The idea of the pro-
tective legislation was to put indebted estates upon an economic
footing and to avoid as many foreclosures and forced sales as
possible.

The first of these "debtor protection" acts stemmed from the
post-Mutiny Oudh Compromise. The merits of the talukdars of
Oudh were limited to the knightly virtues of military prowess and
leadership. As administrators their regime had been chaotic; as
estate managers they were worse than Henry VIII. Their absolute
ownership of estates was confirmed in 1868 in order to prevent a
recurrence of rebellion, but it was soon apparent that they were
in danger of losing their position because of incompetent management. The Oudh Taluqdars' Relief Act XXIV of 1870 allowed
talukdars to turn over estates to managers appointed by the chief
commissioner. In exchange the talukdar was exempt from suit,
arrest, or attachment of property for private debt and received a
living allowance from the manager, who undertook to pay arrears
and revenue to the government and to repay the private debt.
Until the estate was again solvent the land could not be sold except by joint agreement between manager and talukdar.[23] The
act was the first explicit legislative admission by the British that
the maintenance of status and social stability might be more important than economic efficiency and the law of risk-taking. The
act was also a tacit denial of the principle that no one is as diligent
in looking after his own welfare as oneself.

Thirty years later, by the Oudh Settled Estates Act II of 1900
a debt-free talukdari estate could be registered as a "settled estate"
and thereafter could be alienated only for the period of the alien-
or's life plus seven years. A solvent talukdar could secure himself
against future risks, including his own incompetence or weakness
in the face of temptation.

At the turn of the century Rajput cultivating proprietors in
the Bundelkhand area were losing their lands to lower-caste money-lenders, and the social tension became dangerous. For much the
same reasons as led to the Oudh Compromise and subsequent acts
benefiting talukdars, the Bundelkhand Encumbered Estates Act I
of 1903 was passed. Upon application a special judge assessed the
private indebtedness, limiting debts including accrued interest
to twice the original debt after adjusting interest to a reasonable
level.[24] If the total debt was less than six times the annual earn-

ings of the land the government paid the debt and the proprietor repaid the government over fifteen years at 5 per cent. Larger debts were liquidated by combinations of partial sale, government management, and twenty-year usufructuary mortgages. Only in the last resort was all the land sold.[25]

To prevent a recurrence of the problem the Bundelkhand Alienation of Land Act II of 1903 prohibited the sale of land in the area except to a member of the same agricultural caste resident in the district. A stranger or a nonagriculturalist could acquire no interest other than a twenty-year usufructuary mortgage, which was deemed to repay any outstanding debt, or a lease for less than twenty years.[26]

The acts had four effects. The volume of debt became the lowest in U.P.; the acquisition of land by nonagriculturalists was stopped; the supply of credit also became restricted and interest rates rose; and a new group of money-lenders arose from among the cultivating castes which could acquire land.[27] There is irony as well as virtue in these results.

4. RESTRAINTS ON THE RENTAL MARKET

Bengal Act X of 1859 recognized the occupancy rights that had been granted and provided that such rights should accrue to any tenant holding land for twelve consecutive years. Every tenant was entitled to receive a patta, and the occupancy tenants were to receive pattas "at fair and equitable rates. . . . The rate previously paid by the *raiyat* shall be deemed fair and equitable, unless the contrary be shown."[28] The rent of an occupancy tenant could be enhanced if the rate were below the prevailing rates of other tenants of the same class on similar land, if the value of the produce or the productive powers of the land had increased otherwise than through the tenant's own efforts, or if the quantity of land became greater than that on which he had been paying rent. The tenant could sue for abatement on the latter two grounds, and after the passage of Act XIV of 1863 on the ground that his rent was above the prevailing rate.[29] If the tenant were in arrears on his rent at the end of the Bengal (agricultural) year the landlord could eject him.[30] At this time it was not intended to protect the tenant against himself. Section 7 permitted a written contract to overrule the provisions of the act if the contract contained any "express stipulation" contrary to the provisions of the act. The pattas of nonoccupancy tenants were to be granted at agreed rents;[31] that is, the market was absolutely free.

Before Act X, suits against occupancy tenants for the enhancement of rent were permitted, but in fact occupancy rents were invariable and the problem of eviction did not arise as long as rents were paid. Furthermore, enhancement based on increased productivity of the land was unknown in Bengal and "not practically operative in the North-Western Provinces."[n] The newer zamindars by purchase had little respect for tradition, so after Act X they pushed rents up to the "assumed" rent rates on which the settlement was based, and after each settlement the rents went up. "In the majority of cases the tenants began to be rack-rented." The zamindars in the North-Western Provinces tried to break the twelve-year rule by ejecting tenants before they had held a plot for that long. Year by year notices of ejectment increased, and between 1882–83 and 1897–98, the area under occupancy tenants fell from 63.92 per cent of the total area to 58.38 per cent.[32] The fall was not so great in absolute acreage since land under cultivation was increasing throughout the century, but in view of these figures one must discount the statement of the Zamindari Abolition Committee that fixed-rate tenants, permanent tenure-holders, and occupancy tenants together constituted but a small class and that occupancy rents could be increased for a number of reasons as frequently as desired.[33] Because of the evictions Act X was called a "Magna Charta for landlords."[34] Moreland says that it was common for the landholder to get a formal decree of arrears of rent in the eleventh year, serve an uncontested notice of ejectment, and then readmit the tenant at a slightly higher rent, usually after the tenant gave the landholder's agent a gift. The evils of ejectment were thus not as great as the statistics indicate,[35] but this sort of ejectment was certainly contrary to the purpose of the act. Provisions for enhancement and provisions for ejectment are interdependent. A prohibition of enhancement would be meaningless unless ejectments were also controlled, and to prevent arbitrary ejectment would be foolish if the landlord could enhance the rent as much as he wanted.[36]

The courts' interpretation of Act X was more generous to the

n. Campbell, pp. 186, 207. Misra says that occupancy rates were in some districts invariable and elsewhere traditionally only raised when revenue was raised, but that by laying down causes for enhancement rents could rise *"independently of any rise in the Government revenue"* (p. 131, italics in original).

tenants than the legislators had intended. The courts ruled that
an occupancy tenant could do anything with the land except destroy it.[37] This was explicitly changed by the Rent Act of 1873,
which required occupancy tenants to get the owners' permission
for most changes in the real capital of the holding. The courts
also held that if the heirs of occupancy tenants divided the land
they were still jointly responsible for the rent, and that whether
the occupancy right was salable was a matter of local custom.[o] The
courts also found that since occupancy rights had not been defined
they had to decide each case on the basis of local custom, and
since the customs varied they had a difficult job.[38]

The position of the occupancy tenants was immensely strengthened by the decision in the Great Rent Case.[39] The European
indigo planters in Bengal had placed themselves under the zamindars as subholders, and exerted their influence as landlords to
induce the tenants to grow indigo. Rents and prices were both
regulated by custom and did not rise as the value of the indigo
abroad and other land at home rose. The ryots discovered that the
indigo prices paid by the Europeans were unprofitable, and their
discontent became a sort of rebellion against the indigo planters.
A commission made an inquiry into the troubles and decided
that the indigo planter should pay his tenants the market price.
The planters accepted the decision and proceeded to charge the
ryots higher rents. They even went as far as to try to extract penal
rents in order to force the ryots to take lower prices for the indigo.
The chief justice of the High Court held that the ryots must pay
a fair rent; and that a fair rent was the highest rent obtainable on
the market. This was tantamount to saying that economic rent
should go to the owner—that is, the chief justice held that rack-
rents were the proper rents—and the landlords were granted full
claims. The ryots thereupon refused to grow any indigo on the
old terms or to pay the new rents. The case came before the full
court of fifteen judges, who reversed the decision of the chief justice. The full court held that as rents of occupancy tenants could
be enhanced only for specific reasons, the rents could be enhanced
only in proportion as that cause operated. If prices of agricultural
products rose 50 per cent, then rents could be raised 50 per cent,
but no more. The decision granted a proprietary right to the ten-

o. Campbell, p. 206, but the Rent Act of 1873 specifically made occupancy
rights nontransferable except by inheritance.

ants[40] and established the right of occupancy tenants to hold at a rate below the market rate.

On the other hand, the legislative granting and the judicial enforcement of occupancy rights did not mean that tenants who were entitled to the rights actually enjoyed them throughout the province. Although one-third of the tenants in Gorakhpur and one-fifth of those in Basti were entitled to rights of occupancy, it was found in 1869 that the tenants did not claim their rights. They submitted to abwab (illegal cesses), and to all sorts of fees and extortionate measures imposed by the landlords; the areas were so depressed that the tenants did not dare to object.[41]

In view of the tenderness with which the talukdars of Oudh were treated, it is not surprising that the rental market in land created by Act XIX of 1868 (The Oudh Rent Act) was much closer to the ideal market than that envisaged for the North-Western Provinces in Bengal Act X. As in the North-Western Provinces, every tenant had a right to a patta setting forth the terms of his tenure, and the landlord had a right to a counterpart from the tenant, but in all other respects the act was much harder on the tenants. The landlord could claim a higher rent if the rent of the occupancy tenant was more than 12½ per cent lower than the rents paid by tenants at will, and "Nothing contained in the previous part of this section shall affect the terms of any agreement in writing hereafter entered into between a landlord and tenant."[42] The tenant could sue for abatement of his rent only on the grounds of diluvion from changes in river beds or some specific cause stated in his lease.[43]

Under Section 9, "Tenants not having a right of occupancy are entitled to leases only on such terms as may be agreed on between them and the landlord." Further, Section 35 stated: "The Court shall in no case enquire into the propriety of the rate of rent payable by a tenant not having a right of occupancy. The rent payable by such a tenant for any land in his occupation shall be such amount as may be agreed upon between him and the landlord; or, if no such agreement has been made, such amount as was payable for the land in the last preceding year." These sections left the rent of nonoccupancy tenants strictly to the market, and are exactly what the ideal market requires in the way of a legal framework. It followed from these provisions that the tenant could contest his liability to ejectment on only three grounds: that he held under a lease or court decree; that he was an occupancy tenant; and that the notice of ejectment had been improperly served[44] (which ground would not protect him for long).

The tenant could not be ejected until he had been recompensed for any improvement other than maintenance made within thirty years, if the improvement increased the letting value of the land. However, in recompensing the tenant for improvements the landlord could give a beneficial lease instead of cash, *at the landlord's option*, and the court in awarding compensation had to take into account any help given by the landlord, including the existence of a favorable rate of rent.[45] If the tenant accepted the tender of a lease for a term of twenty years or more he could not claim any recompense for improvements he might have made in the holding. Whatever help these sections may have given the tenant was reduced by the provision (Section 4) that nothing in them should affect the terms of a written contract.

The object of tenancy legislation was to improve the tenant's condition, and two means were employed: removing a particular transaction or condition of tenure from the market, and transferring a portion of the proprietary rights to the tenant. The Oudh Rent Act did neither, for any rights it gave the tenant ceased when he signed a contract. Even the occupancy tenant kept his rights only by refusing to sign a contract. For tenants-at-will, which meant most cultivators in Oudh, the Oudh Rent Act provided no rights or protection. Having established a rigorous market system in Oudh, the British stuck by their decision until 1886. As was the case with the whole of the Oudh Compromise, the Oudh Rent Act was a step backward in the course the British were pursuing.

The North-Western Provinces Rent Act XVIII of 1873 was similar to the Oudh Rent Act but was more favorable to the tenants. The rent of a fixed-rate tenant could be changed only on grounds of alluvion or diluvion from changes in river beds. Exproprietary and occupancy rents could be enhanced by a registered written agreement or by a settlement officer or court on the same grounds as in Oudh. However, once enhanced or abated the rent could not be changed until ten years had elapsed or a new settlement was made. The exproprietary rents had to be 25 per cent below the rents of tenants-at-will. A tenant could have his rent reduced if the productive powers of the land had diminished or if the area had been reduced by diluvion,[46] but there was no provision for a reduction on the ground that the rent was above the prevailing rate for similar lands held by similar tenants. An effort was made to eliminate the effect of caste upon rents by Section 20, which forbade giving weight to caste in determining rents in any official proceeding until some caste differential could be proved to be the local custom. Again we find a section (22) stating that nothing "hereinbefore" shall be used as grounds to alter exproprietary or occupancy rents agreed to by the landlord and tenant until the term of the agreement has expired. In short, landlords could still deal with their exproprietary tenants and occupancy tenants outside the provisions of the act.

The provision that a tenant-at-will had to pay no more rent than he paid in the preceding year unless he and the landlord agreed on a higher rent and recorded it with the patwari or kanun-go[47] was ineffective since the landlord was free to eject a tenant-at-will at the end of the year, and was assured of receiving the market rate.

The problem of drought and famine was recognized. An officer so empowered by the provincial government might remit or suspend rent when crops were damaged or destroyed, wholly or partially, but if he did so he had to remit or suspend the revenue demand to the extent of one-half the rental remission or suspension, or such portion as the total land revenue bore to the gross rental.[p] Upon ejectment a tenant had to be compensated for any improvement he had made which increased the letting value of the land: tanks, wells, drainage, and protection against floods and erosion, reclamation, clearance, or enclosure of land for agriculture, and repair of any of these.[48] In 1881 it was provided that a non-occupancy tenant must first receive the permission of his landlord to make the improvements before he could claim compensation upon ejectment.[49] The compensation might be made in cash, by a rent on the land, by a beneficial lease, or by a combination of these methods, but the landlord could choose the method, and the collector was to settle the dispute.[50] When a case for the determination of the rent of an occupancy tenant came before a settlement officer as the result of an application for enhancement or abatement or a dispute as to what the rent was, the settlement officer might fix the rent by reference to the "standard rent-rate sanctioned" by the Board of Revenue, or by reference to the rates that

p. XVIII of 1873, Sec. 23. This section was amended by XII of 1881 so that remission or suspension of rent followed on the remission or suspension of revenue and did not precede it. This of course is different from the matter of basing the original assessment on existing rents.

tenants of the same class customarily paid, and such rent was binding for ten years.[51]

Act VIII of 1879, amending the Revenue Act of 1873, allowed
the settlement officer to interfere with the relations of landlords
and tenants by fixing the amounts and dates of payment of rents.[52]
Act XII of 1881 permitted a landlord to void a lease if the revenue
were increased and the tenant would not accept the change in
rent determined by the collector, and permitted the tenant to void
the lease if the landlord would not accept a lower rent when the
revenue demand went down.[53]

The rigorous insistence upon payment of revenue and rents on
the day fixed led to one bad result. Baden-Powell mentions that
the "sudden demand for large quantities of silver money on certain dates, causes prices to fall (because of the withdrawal of silver) while the rate of interest rises; grain has to be thrown into
a slackened market, and loans must be negotiated on usurious
terms."[54] This trouble cannot be blamed on the lack of foresight
of the cultivators, for a similar crisis occurs in every region with
an inelastic money supply. It is simply the result of poor credit
facilities.

We have seen that the Oudh Rent Act of 1868 left the landlord
free to rent his land as he chose. Baden-Powell says that there was
a question as to whether this was "altogether desirable" since it
abandoned the ordinary tenants "even though by their caste and
history it was clear they were voluntary or contract settlers on the
land."[55] For this reason and to encourage better farming through
greater security of tenure a "seven-year rule" was introduced in
the Oudh Rent Act XXII of 1886. The seven-year rule stated that
any nonoccupancy tenant who was not a subtenant might retain
the land held by him at the passing of the act for seven years from
the last change of rent, or area held, at the rent then payable.
Every such tenant admitted in the future was to hold the land at
the rent first agreed upon for seven years, and after any change in
the rent or area a new period of seven years at a fixed rent com-
menced.[56]

At the expiry of seven years the rent could not be enhanced by
more than one anna in the rupee (6.25 per cent), and to prevent
evasion a new tenant succeeding at the end of seven years was not
allowed to pay more than his predecessor paid plus 6.25 per cent.[57]
Land held by tenants protected by the seven-year rule did not return to an unrestricted market upon their death, for heirs could

fill out the seven-year term. But the heir was not entitled to a renewal with the 6¼ per cent limit, so the landlord was again free to let at competitive rents.q It was thought that the seven-year rule would induce landlords to grant long-term leases. The tenant holding under a lease of eight years or more was granted the same protection against enhancement as a tenant holding under the seven-year rule—that is, no more than 6¼ per cent increase for his next lease—but the landlord did not have to pay a court fee of one-half the annual rent charged for serving notice of ejectment at the end of seven years.[58] Since roughly one-half of the annual rent had to be paid to the government as land revenue, it meant that the landlord had to sacrifice his income from the holding for one year in order to eject a tenant. Since the landlord could lose one year's profit by letting to tenants under the seven-year rule, an eight-year lease would increase his returns by 14 per cent over eight years, almost 2 per cent a year.

Originally the plan had been to have the landlord pay the tenant compensation of one year's rent, but under the pressure of the talukdars this was reduced to half a year's rent. Moreland points out that although the talukdars agreed to the sacrifice of their profits for a year, they feared derogation in the eyes of the tenants and insisted that they pay the sum not to the cultivator as compensation but to the government as a court fee.[59]

The seven-year rule was not as successful as had been hoped. The limitation on the increase of rents was circumvented by charging nazrana—a lump sum bribe or concealed rental paid for the privilege of being admitted to a holding. It sometimes amounted to as much as Rs. 200 or Rs. 300.[60] Considering that rents ran somewhere around five rupees per acre it is clear that the real rent on a large holding of ten acres would be double the recorded rent. It is also clear that by this time the idea of the market was sufficiently understood to lead to efforts to evade the law when the law tried to achieve results different from those which market forces would effect.

With the Oudh Rent Act of 1886 it was no longer possible to contract out of the provisions of the law. Section 4 was explicit on the overriding force of the law:

q. XXII of 1886, Sec. 48. The other land on the free market was sir land, land of shifting cultivation, land cleared within fourteen years, and land from which a mortgagee or *thekadar* (a lessee of the management of an estate) had been ejected (Secs. 4, 49).

Nothing in any contract made between a landlord and a tenant before or after the passing of this Act shall entitle a landlord to eject a tenant or enhance his rent otherwise than in accordance with the provisions of this Act.

Nothing in any contract made between a landlord and a tenant after the passing of this Act shall take away or limit the right of a tenant, as provided by this Act, to make improvements and claim compensation for them.

In so far as tenants refused to pay nazrana and relied on the law, this section should have assured the intended regulation of the market.

The act also allowed a landlord to confer occupancy rights upon a tenant by registering a document to that effect. This meant that there could be a one-way market for occupancy rights—the landlord could sell them, although he could not buy them. This in itself should show that the occupancy right was really a form of partial ownership. There could also exist a sort of market for the sale of occupancy rights by the tenant to his landlord. The tenant could not alienate his occupancy right, but he could sign a lease in which he gave up the substance of these rights for the period of the lease in exchange for some benefit conferred by the landlord. It might be more accurate to say that the tenant could lease his partial ownership back to the landlord. He would not receive an annual sum called a rent, but he could receive some benefit whose capitalized value would be equal to the rental value of the rights sacrificed. There are no records of such transactions,[r] since they would not be revealed by the land records.

In regard to making improvements and granting compensation, there were provisions more helpful to the tenant in this act than in the Oudh Rent Act of 1868. The tenant had to get the permission of the landlord to make an improvement, but if the landlord refused permission, the tenant might apply to the deputy commissioner of the division, who could grant permission if the improvement were "suitable," not too costly, and if the landlord were unwilling to make the improvement himself. When such a disputed improvement was made, either party could have the cost of the improvement registered. No mathematical formula was given for computing compensation for improvements when the

r. There does not seem to be any advantage to the tenant over the advantage he had in exercising the rights conferred upon him by legislation.

tenant left the land, but the factors to be considered were "the amount by which the value, or the produce, of the holding, or the value of that produce, is increased by the improvement," the condition and cost of the improvement, the benefits the tenant had already received from the landlord, and where relevant the length of time the tenant had had the use of reclaimed land.[61] Of more importance to the tenant, the landlord no longer had the right to choose the method of compensation, which had to be in money unless both parties agreed to some other method.[s] The tenant could claim recompense for improvements even when he voluntarily vacated his holding.[62]

In practice the rental market at the end of the nineteenth century was not as free as it was in law. Enhancement of rents was in principle left to contracts between the landlords and their tenants, but under the "actual" rates system of assessment in use, the settlement officer told the villagers how much he thought the rents should be raised and exerted his influence to get the tenants to accept higher rents and the landlords to accept lower rents than they were demanding. The result was not exactly what the settlement officer suggested, but a little higher or lower depending upon the "bargaining positions" of the landlord and tenants.[63] This may be taken to mean that the settlement officer was not as strong as the forces determining the demand for and supply of land plus any noneconomic considerations of prestige, poverty, and ignorance.

The difference in policy in Oudh and in the North-Western Provinces is reflected in the great difference in the figures of land cultivated by owners and privileged tenants. Exact comparison is not possible because our figures for the North-Western Provinces are in terms of land area for 1892 and for Oudh in terms of proportion of cultivators for 1882. Nevertheless, the differences are great enough to be striking (Table 1).

One can state with confidence that most cultivators in Oudh were tenants-at-will, whereas over half the cultivators in the North-Western Provinces were proprietors or privileged tenants. The difference in the condition of the cultivators was also apparent to observation, for British officers thought the tenants-at-will in Oudh were "miserable" and the commissioner of Rae Bareli

s. XXII of 1886, Sec. 28. The landlord could make any improvement of the land of a tenant-at-will, but an occupancy tenant had the additional privilege of refusing the landlord permission to make the improvement (Sec. 29).

TABLE 1. *Types of Cultivating Tenures in the North-Western Provinces (1892) and Oudh (1882)*

Type of Cultivator	Percentage of cultivated land in N.-W.P.	Percentage of Cultivators in Oudh
1	*2*	*3*
Proprietors	24.0	7.5
Permanent tenure-holders and fixed-rate tenants	1.0	0.0
Occupancy tenants*	36.5	4.5
Tenants-at-will	38.5	88.0

*Including exproprietary tenants.

Source. Col. 2, Baden-Powell, 2, 191 for "current" figures; book published in 1892. Col. 3, Misra, p. 158, citing *Conditions of the Tenantry in Oudh*.

Note. Since proprietors and occupancy tenants have larger holdings than tenants-at-will, the true differences are not so great, but allowance for this fact would not change the general impression.

remarked that the condition of tenants-at-will had "been made more miserable by our own mistakes."[63a]

The major purposes of the North-Western Provinces Tenancy Act II of 1901 were to satisfy the landlords' objections to subleasing, to put an end to nominal ejectments for the purpose of preventing occupancy rights from accruing, and to introduce the seven-year rule already in effect in Oudh.[64] The landlords' complaint was met by Section 26, which forbade a sublease without the written consent of the landholder but required landlords to recognize a sublease if the intermediate tenant's interests were extinguished before the expiry of the sublease.[65]

The provisions to prevent nominal ejectment were exhaustive. A tenant was deemed to have held the same land for twelve years if: he had been wrongfully ejected and then reinstated or had otherwise regained possession; he had been ejected through no fault of his own and was readmitted to the land within one year; he had surrendered the land on a promise of other land, express or implied, and was admitted to land within a year; or he had lost possession of his land and was readmitted to other land as provided in Section 14.[66] That section stated that if the tenant had lost the land in any of the latter three ways, and if the landholder admitted him to any other land within a year, the new land or such portion of it as did not exceed the letting value of the land he had held originally was to be deemed the same land for purposes of acquiring occupancy rights. If there were a series of transfers from one holding to another, the area on which occupancy rights accrued was to be equal in letting value to the holding in the series with the lowest letting value.

The seven-year rule of Oudh was introduced into the North-Western Provinces in a modified form. Landlords were encouraged to grant leases of seven years or more by exempting land held under long leases from prescription under the twelve-year occupancy rule. However, if a landlord sued to eject a tenant on the expiry of his lease and the tenant proved that the purpose of the ejectment was to enhance the rent, the court was to determine a fair rent and the tenant could then hold at that rent for another seven years.[67] Seven-year leases never covered as much as a million acres, while occupancy rights were extended from 12,700,000 to 14,366,000 acres in the next twenty-five years.[68]

The rights of privileged tenants to make improvements in their land was extended. Permanent tenure-holders, fixed-rate tenants, exproprietary tenants, and occupancy tenants could make any improvement, except that the latter two classes had to have the landlord's written permission to plant trees. A nonoccupancy tenant had to have the landlord's written permission for any improvement except the construction of a well, which the landlord had the right to construct instead of allowing the tenant to do it.[69]

Two other provisions are of particular interest in a study of the rental market. Section 10 empowered the collector to fix the rent of exproprietary tenants at three-quarters of the rent of nonoccupancy tenants.[70] Prior to 1901 the rents of exproprietary tenants were supposed to be a quarter less than that of nonoccupancy tenants, but only the settlement officer, or courts in a legal dispute, could fix the exproprietary tenant's rent. Now the rent of this class of tenant was fixed by the collector, but exproprietary rents were related to market rents since the collector fixed the rents on the basis of nonoccupancy rents, which were market rents.

Section 52 was even broader, and much more significant in its implications. The provincial government in the "interests of public order" might empower the collector to settle all rents, reduce them if they were "unfair or inequitable," and commute grain or produce rents to money rents. The criterion was simply the collector's sense of what was right. Once the rents were fixed by the collector they could not be changed for ten years in the case of exproprietary and occupancy tenants, and for seven years in the case of nonoccupancy tenants.[71]

Twenty years later agrarian rioting and the demands of the Eka movement revealed the gap between the system of land tenures as it was supposed to work and as it did work. The law already conceded every demand of the movement, either explicitly— for it had been clear for a long time that the British regarded the recorded rent as the only rent payable, and the payment of nazrana or the doing of begar (forced labor) had been banned as early as the settlements under Regulation VII of 1822—or implicitly, for there was no objection to demanding receipts for rent paid, and certainly any ryot or group of ryots who insisted on receipts would have been backed up by the courts. That the Eka (unity) movement made these demands showed that the ryots were unable to force the landlords to recognize the rights which the law had already granted to them. A few examples will serve to illustrate the nature of the exactions or cesses as they were called. Common extras added to the stated rental were nazrana when the tenant built a house, planted trees, or dug a well. As long as the amounts were reasonable no one objected. Charges were levied on tenants who grew special crops such as sugar cane, but the amounts charged rose so that they became objectionable. Big zamindars were known to ask a maund of wheat whenever a wedding took place in their families and to demand one day's plowing of their sir land.

While the existence of illegal cesses shows that the rent laws were often broken and were not a guide to the rental income actually realized from the tenants, by the same token the cesses also show that the rental market was gathering in strength during the period of British rule. When the British first established a rental market it was a free one, yet the customs of the communities remained strong enough to prevent quick or accurate response to the stimuli of demand for land and the prices of its products. But as the British reversed their policy—slowly, incompletely, step by step, in an effort to limit the effect of the market upon the rents of the tenants—the rental market grew in strength, and breaches of the law occurred in an effort to maximize the gains from landed property. The more unsuccessful the administration's policy proved from the point of view of its legislative enactments, the more successful it proved from the point of view of the original conception.

CHAPTER 6

The Years of Turmoil:
World War I to Independence

1. OWNERSHIP

As the Mutiny had marked the end of Company rule and the establishment of the British Indian Empire, so the First World War marked the end of the nineteenth century in India as it did in Europe. From 1919 until 1948 Indian history is largely the history of the struggle of the Congress party for national independence. Struggling nonviolently, and occasionally fighting violently, the Congress party transformed itself under the leadership of Gandhi, Nehru, and Patel into a mass movement. In 1935 a measure of home rule was accorded the Indians, who elected provincial legislatures in 1937. Parliamentary ministries had responsibility for the revenue and tenure laws, so that toward the end of British rule it is the Indians themselves who must be praised or blamed for the legal structure governing relations on the land. Even in the twenties and the early thirties, before the Congress provincial government had jural power, the British administrators could no longer make policy with a free hand, for always there was the threat of violence in the background. After the Second World War broke out there was a hiatus in the debate over tenures, for non-cooperation with the war effort and then the troubles of partition absorbed the energies of Englishman and Indian alike, and it was not until the late forties that attention was again turned to the issues of land tenure.

The United Provinces was a center of agitation throughout the period. Trouble started in the autumn of 1920 with rioting in Partabgarh District. The Kisan Sabha (peasant movement) demanded changes in the law and the end of abuses of power by the talukdars. The rioting spread to Rae Bareli District, and then the movement collapsed as a result of poor leadership and involvement with the movement for political independence. It was shortly succeeded by the Eka (unity) movement which tried to persuade tenants to pay no more than the recorded rent, to insist on receipts for rent, and to refuse nazrana or to do begar. It too collapsed, lacking organization and leadership, but the riots growing out of the movements did induce action on the part of the government, although it should be noted that some changes in the tenancy laws had been in the official air for some time.[1]

Until the Congress-sponsored reforms of 1939 the legislative history of Agra (the name attached to the old North-Western Provinces after their incorporation in U.P.) and of Oudh remained separate in form but throughout the last three decades of Imperial rule the laws were essentially the same in purpose and in wording. The obligation to abide by the concessions made to the talukdars in the Oudh Compromise had been weakened by the failure of the talukdars to live up to the spirit of the agreement, by the continuing poverty of the province, and by the time that had elapsed, for no government feels the same obligation to the grandchildren of a special group as it did toward the grandparents with whom it made an agreement.

In Oudh the tenants-at-will, who had in 1886 been given security of seven years' tenure at a constant rent after each change in the rent, became "statutory tenants" and were granted life tenure by Act IV of 1921. The provisions of this act were extended to

Agra by Sections 19 and 20 of Act III of 1926. The terms of tenancy could be altered every ten years, but only by a special officer and not by negotiation between landlord and tenant. Every tenant who did not already have occupancy rights became a statutory tenant, with the exception of nonoccupancy tenants holding on special tenures: permanent tenure holders; tenants on sir land, groveland, pasture, land covered with water growing singhara, land acquired for public works and public utilities; tenants in tea gardens and river beds; and subtenants. The heir of the statutory tenant inherited the holding and held it for five years on the same terms as the deceased had held, but at the end of that term the land again became the unfettered property of the landlord, who was free to rent it on the best terms he could get.[a]

It was evident that by 1926 the law had almost completely divorced the owner of land from control of his land, except for his sir, his khudkasht (land he cultivated himself), the small amount that became available five years after a statutory tenant died, and, in relatively rare cases, land of an exproprietary or occupancy tenant who died without heirs. These restrictions on landlords' powers were designed to protect the tenants from the exactions of landlords, but the divorce of ownership from control can and does take place without doing fatal damage to a market for land. It is only when the land is withdrawn from the market that the market system can no longer direct resources. By making exproprietary, occupancy, and statutory rights inalienable and transferable only between co-sharers in occupancy rights and between tenants and the government, a large step was taken toward ending the market for the sale of land. By 1926 the rights of tenants encompassed many rights we should expect to find in the possession of the owner, and these rights, with the income they brought to the holder of the rights, were inalienable. However, what was done to restrict the sale market was balanced by two other factors. First, collectors, settlement officers, and special officers tried to fix appropriate, fair, or equitable rents. They tried to reach the results that one would expect of a market, using the small amounts of land still left wholly to the owner as a guide. Secondly, tenants could sublet. Although the freedom of tenants to sublet on their

a. There was another peculiar tenure in U.P. It was always recognized, both before and after the British conquest, that the groveholder could not be evicted as long as the trees stood. Since he owned the trees, eviction would have robbed him of his trees. Cf. *Rái Bareli Report,* MacAndrew's Appendix.

own initiative was severely limited, they had unlimited rights of subletting with the owner's permission. Control over land had been divided between owner and tenant, and in fact ownership itself had been divided between landlord and tenant, but if the two chose to cooperate they could pool their rights and together let the land freely. Although the rights of ownership had been redistributed and the relationships between the possessors of the various rights had been altered, the sum of the rights which go to make up an owner of land remained and could be exercised on the market.

In one respect the legislation of the 1920s strengthened the position of the proprietor. Section 5 of the Oudh Rent (Amendment) Act IV of 1921 liberalized the provisions regulating the accrual of sir rights so that any land cultivated and recorded as khudkasht in 1920–21 and any land the proprietor cultivated in the future for ten consecutive years became sir. Sir was, however, limited to 10 per cent of the proprietor's interest in the mahal. The Agra Tenancy Act III of 1926 introduced the same liberalizing principles to the rest of U.P. Section 4 recognized existing sir plus all khudkasht of twelve years' standing in 1902 and all khudkasht of 1925–26, and fixed limits to the amount of sir a proprietor could hold. If the mahal was smaller than 30 acres, one-half could be sir; if between 30 and 600 acres, 15 acres plus 15 per cent of the area over 15 acres; and if greater than 600 acres, 100.5 acres plus 10 per cent of the area over 600 acres.

Relief for the Debtor

The Oudh Talukdars Relief Act had been passed as part of the Oudh Compromise; the Bundelkhand Settled Estates Act was designed to forestall violence on the part of a militant group which resented losing land to noncultivating money-lenders; but both acts originated in the heavy burden of indebtedness which the talukdars and the Rajputs had taken upon themselves and in the capacity of these groups to destroy conditions of law and order. In the 1930s the whole Province suffered from indebtedness and presented the same danger. The fall in agricultural prices threatened the holdings of all cultivators and the Congress Nationalist and "No-Rent" campaigns had made clear the Province's capacity to resist or to riot. The advantages of the Bundelkhand Encumbered Estates Act were made available to all proprietors in U.P.

by the U.P. Encumbered Estates Act XXV of 1934. After the special judge had raised what funds he could from property other than land and buildings, new mortgages and usufructuary mortgages were employed, but where the special judge felt that the estate could repay the debt at 4.25 per cent the government paid the creditor in bonds bearing 3.25 per cent and undertook to collect the debt over twenty years at 4.25 per cent. Where the special judge felt that the debts were too large to be repayable land was transferred to the creditor *at a valuation based on pre-Depression prices.*[2] The same principle—that creditors could claim land only at pre-Depression prices[b]—was also applied to civil and court decrees.[3]

In the same year two acts regulated the extension of credit to agriculturalists. The Usurious Loans (U.P. Amendment) Act XXIII of 1934 declared interest above 12 per cent on a first mortgage and 24 per cent on any loan excessive, while a court was allowed to adjudge excessive mortgage rates on secured loans above 7 per cent and on unsecured loans above 9 per cent.[4] The U.P. Agriculturalists' Relief Act XXVII of 1934 limited interest on debts arising from court decrees to the lower of 4.5 per cent or the rate paid by local authorities for Government of India loans;[5] and set forth a schedule of interest rate maxima for all future loans based on Government of India loan rates, the amount of the loan, and the security involved. The new maxima on unsecured loans varied around 15 per cent and on mortgages around 5 per cent.[6] There were also provisions requiring money-lenders to keep records.[7]

The Tenancy Act of 1939

The Tenancy Act (XVII) of 1939 deserves special attention for three reasons: it was enacted by an elected legislature whereas all previous tenancy and land revenue laws had been imposed by the British; it took a long step toward the abolition of a rental market for land; and it reversed the previous policy of encouraging the

---

b. The method of computing pre-Depression values was complex. The land was valued at a multiple of the value of "annual profits" derived from free market sales of land. Special judges arrived at multiples varying from 13 to 85, and this range was then reduced from 20 to 37. (Z.A.C. *Report*, p. 211.) The system was not consistent—"inaccurate methods" leading "to obviously wrong results," and "unreliable" according to the Committee (Ibid.)—but the Board of Revenue regarded the act as successful (Misra, pp. 247–48).

creation of sir land over which the proprietor exercised all rights of ownership.

Before 1939 one could assert that any bad results of tenurial legislation were the responsibility of the British, but beginning with the 1939 act responsibility lay with an Indian legislature. *The notable characteristic of Act XVII was that it did not differ significantly from earlier legislation.* Although there were new provisions in the act, *they were in the spirit of the legislation introduced over the years before,* and after reading the laws governing land tenure as they developed from 1850 onward one feels that if an Indian legislature had not enacted the Tenancy Act of 1939, the British would have passed a similar law.

New limitations on subletting illustrated the growing distaste for a rental market and presaged the very strict provisions of the postwar act abolishing the zamindars. The right to rent was restricted both in regard to who could rent and how often the same plot could be let or sublet. There was to be no further subletting by a subtenant and no more subletting by a tenant on sir land.[8] Occupancy, exproprietary, and hereditary tenants[c] could not sublet for more than five years, nor could they sublet within three years of the expiration of the preceding lease. Other tenants could not sublet for more than one year nor within a year of the expiration of a sublease.[d] It was now no longer possible for owners and tenants to agree to pool their rights and jointly to let to subtenants in a free rental market, but an interrupted market could continue to function. This provision would have assured that all privileged tenants actually cultivated their land, since the land could not be let all the time, were it not that the definition of cultivation allowed a tenant to hire labor to do the field work, which is what Brahmins and Rajputs, often exproprietary tenants, did. When land was freed of tenants by the absence of heirs or by eviction, the owner could let the land at any rent. According to Section 92, "a tenant on being admitted to the occupation of land is liable to pay such rent as may be agreed upon between him and

c. Tenants who had been statutory tenants, or who could qualify for the classification, became hereditary tenants whose rights passed on from generation to generation instead of ceasing five years after the tenant's death. XVII of 1939, Sec. 29.

d. XVII of 1939, Sec. 40. Sec. 41 exempted the usual grouping of blind persons, invalids, females, lunatics, idiots, minors, and servicemen from these restrictions.

his landholder." This provided a means whereby over a period of time the rents and uses of land would tend to reflect the requirements of the market and also provided a guide to officers in their rent-fixing duties. The freedom to let to a new tenant did not extend beyond the first agreement, for thereafter the rent was fixed for ten years or until the next settlement, when it would be revised by the rent or settlement officer.[9] All these restrictions upon the joint and separate rights of owners and tenants did not abolish the rental market for land. The provisions of the Tenancy Act of 1939 continued the previous policy of maintaining the market but interfering with it whenever and wherever it seemed to be bearing oppressively upon the cultivator.

Whereas up to this time there had been an increase in the amount of land classified as sir, partly as a sop to owners who were losing rights over their other land and partly because it was felt that land to which no one other than the owner had a customary claim should be kept as much like freehold as possible, it was now no longer possible to increase the area of sir and in fact the area of sir was decreased by the act. The reasoning underlying the reduction of sir to a minimum and the prohibition against subletting of sir was that small zamindars derived most of their income from their sir lands and frequently cultivated them, whereas the larger zamindars acquired sir to let it and did not depend upon it for a very large portion of their incomes.[10] It should also be noted that the purpose of this act, like that of all the other tenancy acts, was to increase the security of tenure of tenants and slow down the rise in rents which the unrestricted market allowed. It was therefore only reasonable to limit sir land, which was originally meant for the personal cultivation of the owner and was not supposed to be the attractive rental investment it had become. Sir land consisted of all land already recognized as sir, unless the proprietor was assessed to a local rate of more than Rs. 25 or possessed more than fifty acres of sir. If the proprietor was assessed more than Rs. 25 in local rates, the sir acquired by virtue of the Oudh Rent (Amendment) Act of 1921 or the Agra Tenancy Act of 1926 ceased to be sir. If the proprietor possessed more than fifty acres of sir and some of it was let, then the sir ceased to be sir provided that fifty acres remained classified as sir. The act provided no way in which a proprietor could turn land into sir. Furthermore, there was a reversal of policy in regard to the substantive content of the right in sir. No longer was it to be similar to freehold, but rather it could not be sold and was transferable only by gift or by exchange of land. Tenants on any of the land which ceased to be sir became hereditary tenants.[e]

The other provisions of the act followed the trend of previous legislation. An owner losing his rights became an exproprietary tenant on his sir and on his khudkasht of three years' standing. There was no way in which he could surrender his exproprietary rights, and exproprietary tenants continued to pay a rent two annas in the rupee lower than occupancy tenants cultivating similar land with similar advantages.[11] The provisions in the acts of 1921 and 1926 allowing a landlord to evict tenants in order to make any one of a number of improvements in the use of the land were dropped, except that hereditary tenants might be evicted if the owner desired to build or to plant a grove up to a maximum of five acres.[f]

Proprietary interests of tenants were extremely difficult to extinguish. These interests were extinguished when the tenant died without an heir, when the interests were sold for arrears of rent or the tenant was evicted for arrears of rent, when the tenant voluntarily surrendered or abandoned his land, when the land was publicly acquired, and when the tenant's rights merged into the proprietary right by virtue of the tenant inheriting the proprietary right. If a tenant exchanged one plot of land with his landholder for another plot he retained all his old rights in the new plot. The occupancy tenant continued to pay two annas in the rupee less than the hereditary tenant, and occupancy tenants in Oudh were permitted to make any improvement in the land with the permission of the owner, who had to reimburse them upon ejectment for the improvements which they had made. In Agra occupancy and exproprietary tenants could make any improvement except the construction of buildings or tanks without the owner's permission, and throughout U.P. hereditary tenants had the same rights in this matter as the occupancy tenants in Agra.[12] Up to this time the owner's permission was needed to plant trees because the groveholder was virtual owner so long as the trees stood, but under Section 80 any protected tenant might plant trees with the proviso that he did not thereby become a groveholder unless he were a

e. XVII of 1939, Secs. 6, 9, 16. Sir rights were lost over land held as khudkasht in Oudh in 1920 or in Agra in 1926 and cultivated by the proprietor.

f. XVII of 1939, Sec. 54. These grounds for ejectment were abolished by the U.P. Tenancy (Amendment) Act X of 1947, Sec. 10.

hereditary tenant. The justification of this provision was that the rights of tenants had so increased that there was not very much difference between a groveholder and a tenant with perpetual tenure so long as he paid his rent and did not abuse the land. The only significant difference between a privileged tenant and a groveholder was that the groveholder's rights were transferable. In fact, the holders of inferior rights were approaching the status of an owner of leasehold under English law, with the exception of the right to sell. Instead of being personally liable for the rent, the tenant was now liable only to the extent of the value of his rights in his holding, for all arrears were extinguished upon eject-ment. When a tenant was in arrears on his rent he could only be ejected if the owner paid him any excess of the value of the im-provements over the arrears.[13]

The right of co-sharers in a mahal to pre-empt had long been recognized in forced sales for arrears of revenue and sales where the recorded custom of the community granted the right. The right of pre-emption carries with it an implication of an owner's interest in the land, and certainly in U.P. this was the understand-ing. It was therefore significant that the right of pre-emption was extended by the Tenancy Act of 1939 to tenants as well as to own-ers. The interest of a protected tenant might be sold in execution of a decree for arrears of rent as if he were an owner. All parties to the land, and the definition was wide, had a priority in the order of pre-emption. First option went to a subtenant at the price bid, second to the owner if he were willing to pay 5 per cent more than the highest bid, third to a resident village laborer or servant, fourth to a resident cultivator who was not a proprietor, fifth to the landholder, and sixth to any proprietor or underproprietor, with the provision that among two claimants of the same class the higher priority would go to the one with less land.[14] This scheme of pre-emption was a return to the idea that all members of a village community had an interest of a proprietary nature in all the land of the village, and in market terms was a tacit legislative admission that all these persons were part-owners.

Finally, the position of tenant was so close to that of owner that a usufructuary mortgage-lease was designed. If a court thought that arrears of rent could be paid in this way it might, instead of selling the tenant's interests, lease the land to a third person for no more than six years on condition that the third person would pay the arrears, one year's rent in advance, and the rest of the rent as it

came due. At the end of the term of the lease the tenant who was
in arrears recovered the land.[15] There was a very close analogy
between these leases and the twenty-year usufructuary mortgages
developed in the Settled Estates Acts.

During the decade following the Tenancy Act of 1939 the provincial government moved further away from the free market and
further restricted the powers of landlords. Small landowners paying a revenue of less than Rs. 25 could have their land declared
"protected," after which the land could be alienated only with the
permission of the collector.[16] Collectors were empowered to require a landlord to cultivate unused land on penalty of settling
hereditary tenants on the land[17] and fifty thousand acres were
brought under the plow.[18] Agricultural incomes above Rs. 2000
were subjected to a progressive agricultural income tax, and the
government began to consider raising the revenue demand, which
had fallen to Rs. 6.5 crores[19]—an interesting reflection on the
common charge of a burdensome revenue demand.

2. RENT

The 1920s

Much of the substance of the laws governing rents can be deduced from the rights of ownership conferred upon tenants by
the acts of the 1920s and 1930s. There are, however, a number of
provisions that apply more strictly to the position of the tenant as
a lessee, and some comment is needed to explain the structure of
the rental market as it developed up to the time of the passage of
the postindependence reforms.

With the Rent (Amending) Act of 1921 the proprietor in Oudh
could no longer give up his exproprietary rights upon selling his
property, unless he managed to do so six months before or after
the sale of his property.[20] The old standard for fixing the rents of
exproprietary and occupancy tenants was changed from the "rate
generally payable by non-occupancy tenants for land of similar
quality and with similar advantages in the neighborhood"[21] to
the "fair and equitable rate payable by statutory tenants for land
of the same class or classes of soil," and these tenants were to have
their rent fixed every tenth year by a rent officer.[22] It had finally
been decided to bring most rents under administrative control.
There is no reason to believe, however, that the rents were to be
entirely different from market rents. The British seemed still to

be struggling toward a system that would result in the rents which intelligent and far-seeing landlords would negotiate. On first being admitted to the land the tenant and landlord agreed upon a rent.ᵍ If no rent were agreed upon the landlord could sue the tenant and have the sanctioned rents of the rent officer imposed,[23] but since the sanctioned rent was in the nature of a ceiling it is hard to conceive of the landlord having recourse to the courts. A concomitant of having an official fix the rents was the granting of power to the collector to collect arrears of rent, rates, or cesses as if they were arrears of revenue—that is, without civil litigation.[24] The government evidently felt that if it were to fix the rents it had to see that the owner received the rents.

The ryots' complaint that they did not receive receipts for the rent they paid was met by requiring a landlord to give a written receipt setting forth a full description of the transaction and permitting the tenant to choose to which installment of the rent he wished the payment credited.ʰ However, the tenants still did not avail themselves of the law's privileges, for it was found that the obligation to grant receipts was often evaded and the tenants did not feel themselves in a position to go to court against the far wealthier and more influential landowners.[25] The same difficulty arose in regard to the declaration that premiums paid for admission to land or to avoid ejection were illegal.[26]

The acts of 1921 and 1926 brought the problems of rent determination and security of tenure together in a more consistent whole. The rent of an occupancy tenant in Oudh could not be enhanced unless it was less than seven-eighths of the rent of statutory tenants on similar land. The statutory tenant in Oudh with life tenure was guaranteed ten years at the same rent, and could contest a notice of enhancement on the expiry of the statutory period on the ground that the proposed enhancement was not "fair or equitable";[27] while in Agra the rents of exproprietary, occupancy, and statutory tenants could be enhanced on the grounds "that there had been a rise in the average local prices of staple food crops during the currency of the present rent," and the tenants could claim abatement on the grounds that the prices had fallen. The period during which rents were fixed was put at twenty years in Agra.[28] Both acts created "roster years": in Oudh every tenth

g. IV of 1921, Sec. 15. The same provision is found in III of 1926, Sec. 43.
h. IV of 1921, Sec. 7. The same provisions were included in the Agra Tenancy Act III of 1926, Secs. 107–09.

year and in Agra every twentieth year. If possible the roster years
in each district were to be so arranged as to coincide with the last
year of the revenue settlement.[29] In the roster year a rent officer
with the rank of settlement officer was to propose "fair and equitable" rates of rent for statutory tenants based on assessment areas,
called circles, and the various types of soil. The standard from
which he was to work was the "stable rent payable by substantial
tenants who depend for their livelihood on the produce of the
soil, due regard being had to the movements in prices and the letting value of land." The rent officer was also to record specifically
the extent to which caste was taken into account and the extent
of any class of tenants holding at favorable rates of rent.[30]

Three things are noteworthy about these sections. First, the
task of determining rents was transferred from the market to an
officer specifically appointed to determine rents. Second, this officer was to try to do what the market should have done—determine
rents in accordance with what the land would bear, since "substantial tenants" implies some degree of independence in bargaining on the part of the tenant and "prices and the letting value of
land" could only mean that the officer was to guess at the market
relationships which would have existed if the market had worked
as it should. There would have been no problem if he were meant
to take the "letting value" as he found it. The whole purpose of
appointing the officer was to reach a different letting value—a rent
that would encourage the cultivator to improve the land—and to
remove anomalies resulting from previous rent laws (such as the
limit of 6¼ per cent on enhancement under the seven-year tenancies in Oudh) and from the creeping rise of rents in the form of
exactions. Third, the administration still had to recognize the
force of caste and custom in the determination of rents, despite
its dislike for such concessions: lower rents for reasons of caste reduced the revenue based on rents and shifted a portion of the public burden on to other tenants.

A new cause for eviction was introduced by the act of 1921. At
the end of the statutory period of ten years a landlord could evict
a tenant who did not reside in the village in order to admit to the
holding a cultivator who did.[i] As was always the case when the
government tried to increase the tenants' security of tenure, the
gaps in the law gave the landlord extra incentive to evict when he

i. IV of 1921, Sec. 43. The law in regard to compensation upon ejectment was
not changed (IV of 1921, Sec. 13; III of 1926, Secs. 109–17).

could, and to try to rent the land anew to a tenant who had no established rights. Thus the provision that the heir of a statutory tenant did not become a statutory tenant unless he received a lease from his landlord or was allowed to remain beyond the period of five years granted by law[31] gave the landlord every reason to eject the heir at the end of the five years of grace. Once during each generation rents of land could be freely negotiated, and with the pressure of population on the land there was a rush for the twentieth of the land that became available each year.[32]

The tenancy acts of 1921 and 1926 did not have a peaceful life, but there is some evidence that they might have been moderately successful if the turbulent thirties had not overwhelmed them. Ejectment suits in Oudh of the kinds barred by the act of 1921 fell from 37,844 in 1921 to zero four years later.[33]

The Great Depression

The rent-fixing procedures were thrown into turmoil by the fall in prices following 1930. Over the next few years the administrative machinery of rent and revenue control was involved in reducing rent and revenue charges to keep pace with the decline in prices. In 1930–31 revenue of Rs. 10.9 millions and rent of Rs. 41.1 million were remitted. A Rent and Revenue Committee appointed in the summer of 1931 recommended reducing rents to the 1901 level, since prices had fallen to the 1901 level. Because rents of different classes of tenants had risen by differing amounts in the three decades since 1901, the tenants in each village were divided into classes, and rents were reduced in proportion to the amount they had increased, but not below the 1901 level. The revenue demand was also reduced by one-half of the difference between the 1930 demand and 40 per cent of the new rent roll.[j] The rent remission for 1931–32 was Rs. 41.1 millions and the revenue remission Rs. 11.3 millions. These figures are very close to the *ad hoc* reductions of 1930–31 and raise the question of whether the 1930–31 reductions were a brilliant stroke or the 1931–32 reductions "arranged" to get the same results.

j. Misra, pp. 214, 220–23. The revenue reduction formula was a compromise between a reduction of revenue to the 1901 level, which would have given rebates only to zamindars whose revenue had been assessed after 1901, and a reduction proportional to the fall in rents, which would have disproportionately benefited zamindars whose revenue was assessed at the low levels of 1901.

Two other acts were passed to help tenants. The Assistance of Tenants Act of 1932 granted remission of rent up to 25 per cent where the nonpayment of rent for 1930–31 and 1931–32 was in good faith, the landlord to receive remission of revenue *pari passu* up to 40 per cent. If the remainder of the unpaid rent was more than one-third of a year's rent it could be paid in noninterest-bearing installments over two years.[34] The other act was the U.P. Temporary Regulation of Execution Act. A cultivator paying rent, or a local rate of less than Re. 1, might apply for a stay of execution of a decree by paying 25 per cent of the sum due. The court was then to fix not more than five annual installments in which the cultivator was to pay 40 per cent of the decreed amount if the rate of interest on the debt had been more than 24 per cent, or 50 per cent if the rate of interest on the debt had been less than 24 per cent. The installments were interest-free. Furthermore, if the cultivator paid his rent and 20 times the local rate in any year, he was deemed to have paid the installment.[35]

Although the effect of these acts was to abrogate contracts, and the sanctity of contract is essential to markets, they did not reflect a trend unique to U.P. Acts of similar import were passed in many places in the world in reaction to the catastrophic drop in prices in the thirties. The U.P. acts, like the others, were indicative of the general failure of the market mechanism to cope with the Great Depression throughout the world, even in countries where the market had worked well before.

The problem of carrying out the programs of rent and revenue remission absorbed the energies of the revenue and rent officials. The sudden decline in prices prevented a smooth transition to the rent officer system. Consequently, no body of precedent, principles, or methods grew and we cannot tell how the system of fixing rents would have worked.

In addition to the inherent administrative problems, the government had to face a situation of great social unrest marked by riots, civil disobedience, and "No-Rent" and "No-Revenue" campaigns. The "No-Rent" campaign of early 1931 was managed by the Congress and spread rapidly. Violent clashes occurred between landlords and tenants. "No-Revenue" was added to "No-Rent" in the Congress campaign in late 1931, and the arrest of Gandhi and Nehru did not make compromise easier.

In 1935 the Government of India Act turned the tenancy problem over to the provincial legislatures and there was an inter-

regnum until the legislature was elected in 1937 and set to work
on its own tenancy act. The acts creating statutory tenancies and
rent officers lasted eighteen and thirteen years, but only during
the first few years were economic and political conditions stable
enough to test the acts. It is therefore difficult to evaluate the
legislation of the 1920s.

The Tenancy Act of 1939

We have noticed that in 1939 the statutory tenant became an
hereditary tenant and that subleases were severely limited. By
and large the tenancy act of that year made no major changes in
the rental market in addition to those mentioned earlier. The
system of fixing rents was regularized and the laws of the two parts
of U.P. were unified. The bases of rent-fixing were the "sanctioned
rates." At any time a rent officer might be appointed to fix the
rents of occupancy and hereditary tenants, and thereafter there
could be no change in the rents for twenty years unless there were
a large change in prices. If the prices of agricultural products
did not change appreciably, the twenty years might be extended.
The rent officer had the powers of a court in rent cases.[36]

Before fixing rents the rent officer was to classify the assessment
circles and the soils. Then he was to propose rent rates for hereditary tenants which "shall be such as will result in rents payable
without hardship over a series of years by cultivating hereditary
tenants with substantial holdings and shall be based on genuine
and stable rents paid by such tenants." To find the rents payable
without hardship he was to consider:

(a) the level of rents paid by tenants admitted at different
    times and in particular to rents agreed to on admittance
    in the period 1901 to 1905;
(b) the prices of agricultural products at such times;
(c) the changes in the crops grown and the amount of prod-
    uce;
(d) the value of the produce, so that the rental valuation did
    not exceed 20 per cent of that value;
(e) "the expenses of cultivation, and the cost to the cultivator
    of maintaining himself and his family";
(f) the rates of hereditary and occupancy tenants, old and
    new.

The officer had to state whether peculiar or unusual conditions in a village required modifications of the general rates proposed for validation by the Board of Revenue.[37]

Several comments may be made in regard to this procedure. First, it assumed that there were rents which could be paid without hardship. In the poverty-stricken state of U.P. it is doubtful whether hardship was avoidable at zero rents. If rents were eliminated they could not be a cause of hardship, and the hardships of poverty would continue. Thus the officer had an impossible job. He could always lower rents because there was hardship, but since he was not supposed to eliminate rents he could do no more than employ some personal idea of excessive hardship in terms of general conditions in the area and reduce a few particular rents. After considering criteria (a) through (f) the officer had existing rents and market factors, and still had no usable criterion of hardship and still no way to fix rents which could be paid easily by an impoverished peasantry.

Second, the holdings in the United Provinces were very small. If the officer picked genuinely substantial holdings they would not be typical of the great mass of holdings, which were not substantial. If he picked more typical holdings on which to base his rent rates the results would have been more realistic, but the tenants on these holdings would certainly have been suffering hardship. Thus the holdings used as standards for fixing rents must have been too large to be typical or too small to permit the holder to pay any rent without hardship.

Third, the guides the officer was told to follow were still the factors determining rents on a free market, and it is to be noted that he was not required to discount market factors even though they were among the factors which led to the situation the act was designed to remedy. The only exception was the cost of maintaining the cultivator and his family. This must, of course, be highly subjective, but it was a definite break with market criteria, and was virtually the only one in the whole body of land tenure legislation. The cost of maintenance had nothing to do with the productivity of the land or the productivity of the cultivator. It was an assertion that every man had a right to a livelihood. The rent officers had a good deal of trouble in determining costs of cultivation when so many of the costs—especially the main one, labor—were implicit.

The rents of occupancy tenants were to be fixed two annas in the rupee below the rents of hereditary tenants, and the rents of exproprietary tenants two annas in the rupee below occupancy rents. Subtenants and tenants of sir when suing for abatement of rent were deemed to have sanctioned rates one-third higher than the rents of hereditary tenants.[38] This one-third we may take as a rough minimum measure of the degree to which proprietary rights had been transferred from the owners to the tenants. Exproprietary tenants had retained about half of the returns to ownership.[k]

Rents and revenues could be reduced if there were a major natural calamity. If "owing to some extraordinary cause there had been a sudden and substantial" rise in prices, an officer might be appointed, with the consent of the legislature, to raise rents and make consequential changes in the revenue demand before the date on which rents and revenue would normally come up for revision,[39] but such changes were not made during the wartime and postwar inflation.

Rents could be enhanced if the tenant paid substantially less than the standard rate; if the productive powers of the land were increased by fluvial action or by the effort or at the expense of the landlord; or if the area of the tenants' holding were increased by fluvial action. Rents were liable to abatement for the converse of these causes, and for specific grounds contained in the lease. But if the rent was enhanced, the increase was limited to 25 per cent provided the new rent was at least three-quarters of the standard rate.[40]

Ejectment, the best weapon the landlord had for forcing an increase in rents, was very difficult. The only grounds were illegal transfer or subletting of land, and the breach of a condition in a lease or an act detrimental to the land, except that tenants on sir land could be ejected by notice on the grounds that they were tenants from year to year or that their leases had expired. These ejectments were limited by granting tenants on sir five years from the date of the act or from their admission to the land, whichever was later, at the same rate of rent.[l]

---

k. ($\frac{7}{8}$) divided by ($\frac{4}{3}$) gives a rental for the exproprietary tenant of something over one-half the rental for subtenants, but we may assume the subtenants acquired a certain amount of "ownership" if their rents were legally limited too.

l. XVII of 1939, Secs. 20, 171–72, 177. In 1947 Sec. 5 of Act X prohibited ejectments of tenants of sir until 1952.

Section 90 faced the problem of attempts to evade the intent of the law:

> No landholder shall take a premium for the admission of a tenant to a holding, and it shall not be a condition of any tenancy that the tenant shall render any service to or do any work for the landholder, whether for wages or not.

and the next section prohibited *all* cesses except those sanctioned by the provincial government for bazaars and fairs.

CHAPTER 7

The Revenue Officers and Assessment:
Unrecognized Socialism

To understand the history and significance of the market for
land in U.P., one must comprehend the peculiar position of the
revenue officers in that history. In principle the government took
a share of the income from the land, and the duty of its officers
was to fix that share and to oversee its collection. In practice the
revenue officers decided how large the income from the land was,
how it was to be distributed, and substituted themselves for the
market mechanism in the fixing of rents and the establishment of
rights over land.

The revenue hierarchy was headed by the Board of Revenue,
which was responsible to the provincial government and, through
it, to the Governor-General-in-Council. Under the Board of Revenue were the commissioners of the nine divisions, and beneath

them the forty-odd collectors of districts,[a] who were assisted by assistant collectors of the first and second classes. Their Indian assistants were the tahsildars appointed by the Board of Revenue,[b] the hereditary kanungoes, and the patwaris appointed on the basis of heredity, local custom, or the nomination of the revenue payers. The day-to-day administration of revenue policy was in the hands of these officers, but special officers were appointed to assess the revenue. These were the settlement officers, appointed one to a district every thirty years, and in virtual command of the economy of the district for several years while they made their investigations, assessed the revenue, and settled with the landholders. After the Oudh Rent (Amendment) Act of 1921 and the Agra Tenancy Act of 1926 another officer was added, the rent officer, to fix standard rents for statutory tenants every ten or twenty years and to settle rent disputes arising during the rent-fixing operations. Whenever the government took upon itself a new duty in regard to the regulation of the market and the distribution of ownership rights, it fell to these officers to give effect to the new policy.

While the specific duties of the revenue officers grew and changed with the growth and changes in administrative policy, their kinds of duties and powers were firmly established by the end of the nineteenth century. The legislation of the 1870s, which provided a complete legal framework for the tenurial system, also set forth the officers' duties and powers as they had developed, and more or less as they have remained to the present day.

As early as Regulation VII of 1822, the collectors were empowered to act as civil courts for summary trials of suits for rent, against excessive demands or undue exactions or rent, for adjustment of accounts between landholders and "under-tenants of whatever description," and all suits in regard to matters connected with rents or the assessment of land revenue.[1] In other words the collector combined the Anglo-American judicial functions of judge and jury. Sections 23 through 25 of Bengal Act X gave the collector all the powers of a civil court, while Act XIV of 1863, amending the Bengal Rent Act, invested settlement officers with

---

a. The number of districts varied from time to time as the province underwent minor reorganizations, but was usually 47 or 48.

b. XIX of 1873, Secs. 43–45. Until 1891 the North-Western Provinces and Oudh had separate Boards of Revenue which were amalgamated in that year under Act XX of 1890.

all the powers of a collector and of a civil court for land causes.[2] The power to act as a civil judge in land disputes meant that the settlement officer could make his record practically perfect[3] ("perfect" in British Indian terminology means 'not subject to revision' and does not mean "ideal"). The central position of the revenue officer is illustrated by the list of his secondary duties: he was in charge of such matters as excise, stamps, and registration of documents, all matters connected with the collection of revenue, recovery of arrears, suspension or remission of revenue, the settling of boundaries, all facets of land revenue law, disputes between landlord and tenant such as enhancement, ejectment, and improvements, the registration of changes in proprietary interests, the partition of estates, the management of estates whose settlement was declined by the owner, or which were in default, the management of all estates under the Court of Wards, special settlements of alluvial areas, the reduction of land revenue resulting from diluvion, the assessment of revenue-free holdings, the acquisition of land for public purposes, loans for agricultural improvements and to aid cultivators, and the cesses for roads, schools, and famine relief; he watched over the effect of the settlement to see if it bore too heavily, and he noted the condition of the people, the frequency of mortgages and sales, and the degree of indebtedness in his district. Questions of irrigation and water rights, the construction of water channels and canals, colonization and the location of new villages, were all referred to the collector. He was charged with the relief of the hopelessly indebted under the Encumbered Estates Acts and other relief measures.[4] To this list we may add the fixing of rent on exproprietary holdings upon temporary or permanent alienation, commuting of rents in kind to money rents,[5] and all those functions which the state undertook to carry out in the rent and tenancy acts of the last three-quarters of a century—fixing of rents, enhancement, abatement, the enforcement of tenant rights, and the demarcation of sir under the Tenancy Act of 1939.[c]

All matters of land tenure and eventually most market processes passed through the hands of a revenue official. Since most rural income was derived from the land, the collector or settlement offi-

c. XVII of 1939, Sec. 15. The demarcation of sir under the provisions of the act was entrusted to assistant collectors, but even so the job was not done by the time the Zamindari Abolition Committee reported in 1948.

cer had a power over the economy such as few officials anywhere have had.

The injustices of the early settlements made before 1822 have been mentioned in Chapter 4, and we need only allude to the system here. The officer estimated the gross assets, that is to say, the total rents and profits derived from the land, deducted 10 per cent for the support of the proprietor and 5 per cent for the payment of the patwari and other village expenses, and required the proprietor to engage to pay the rest to the government. The officer depended on a tahsildar who was paid a percentage of the amount realized, with the result that the estimate was a guess and frequently wrong. Adjustments were often immediately necessary, and ignorance and the inelasticity of the revenue demand resulted in the forced transfers and sales which altered the original structure of ownership.[6] With a margin of 10 per cent allowed to the proprietor, it is easy to see that a small error in the assessing officer's guess would leave the proprietor with a negative net income, if he could not find a way to squeeze more out of his tenants.

The purpose of Regulation VII of 1822 was to record the rights of all interested in the land so that future assessments of revenue might be based on knowledge and equity. A settlement might be revised during its currency in order to determine the correct jumma (total assessment) and to record as fully as possible all rights in the land, but the revised settlement was not to alter the sum payable to the government unless "there was material error or concealment of lands," or an alteration was necessary to enforce orders regarding the rights of different classes or persons.[7]

As Section 1 was the heart of the resolution in regard to ownership, so Section 7 was the heart in regard to the assessment of the government's share: "The assessment to be demanded on account of the years subsequent to the year 1234 Fussily (1827), to which leases renewed as above may extend, shall be fixed with reference to the produce and capabilities of the land, as ascertained at the time when the revision of the settlement shall be made, unless under special circumstances justifying a prospective enhancement of the Government demand." This apparently reasonable sentence contained a great deal of dynamite. It was interpreted to mean that the assessment should be levied on the net produce, in turn defined as the produce left after the costs of cultivation had been defrayed—that is, after deducting wages and the profits of capital.[8] Quite clearly this meant that the government revenue de-

mand was to be levied upon Ricardian economic rent.[d] Perhaps
the interpretation put upon the clause is the most revealing indication of the implicit market assumptions lying behind British
policy, for other administrations might have interpreted "with
reference to the produce and capabilities of the land" completely
differently. The operation implied was vast: "It was (not unnatur-
ally) at first supposed that, in order to ascertain the revenue which
represented the Government share of the produce of land, the
true produce of every field must be ascertained; so that, after deducting the costs of cultivation, the wages of labour, and the
profits of capital, the 'net produce' might be known, and the
share of the Government (a fraction of the net produce) determined."[9] The local machinery and staff was insufficient, and ten
years later it was calculated that sixty more years would be required to complete the work in some districts.[10] Aside from the
administrative difficulties in the way of the system, a consideration
of its assumptions will show that it was an impossible job from
the very beginning. The costs of cultivation is a reasonable concept if there is a price upon the inputs, but there was no such
price in the early days of British rule. If seeds and implements
had been bought upon the market, if wages had been paid to those
working on the land, and if the capital employed had been found
upon a capital market, the computation of costs of production
would have been an accounting procedure which, ignoring illiteracy and the burden of checking the returns, was possible. But
all these costs were implicit. Seed for next year's crop was taken
from this year's grain heap; labor was supplied by the cultivator
and his family; there was no capital market; costs of implements
and repairs were embedded in the shares of the village artisans in
the grain heap. The computations required a market mechanism
that did not exist.[11]

Regulation IX of 1833 was designed to end the impossible job
set the collectors by Regulation VII. "So much of Regulation VII
of 1822 as prescribes, or has been understood to prescribe, that
the amount of *jumma* to be demanded from any mehaul shall be

---

d. I confess that upon first learning that Regulation VII had required such
a computation I was put to some difficulty in discovering what clause in the
Regulation actually contained the requirement, but this clause was certainly
the one, for Regulation VII was interpreted in this way, and Regulation IX
of 1833, which was designed to reverse the interpretation put upon Regulation
VII, deleted this paragraph.

calculated on an ascertainment of the quantity and value of actual produce, or on a comparison between the costs of production and value of the produce, is hereby rescinded."[12] This provision allowed the operation of a new system proposed by R. M. Bird. Since cash rents were becoming common in the North-Western Provinces, he proposed that the settlement be deduced from the cash rents of an area and then distributed over the holdings. Baden-Powell says that the new system did not alter the principle but merely simplified the method,[13] but he is in error here. There was a change of principle, for the rents used to determine the revenue demand were no longer economic rents based on the differential productivity of land but were the historical rents actually negotiated in the past.

Although the change in method was in fact a change of principle, it was not meant to be. The object was to find a workable approximation to an assessment on economic rent, and in view of the difficulties—the customary rents, the frauds, the lack of costing markets, the existence of rents in kind—the method suggested by Bird was not a bad one.

Since it was impossible to compute costs of production, or even to compute the value of gross output,[14] the actual rents could not have been the economic rents. The method of 1822 was "rational economic accounting"; that of 1833 was "historical pricing," and the difference in principle is great. The British had here sacrificed their ideal of the market in the face of the Indian social structure.

The first method of assessment used under Regulation IX was called the "aggregate to detail method." The "aggregate to detail method" could be used for the rapidly growing cash rents, but could not depend upon them because they were not universal. The settlement officer took the last revenue on the whole of an area, circle, or pargana, and adjusted it in the light of statistics on changes in price, produce, and area cultivated. This new sum, a tentative revenue demand for the whole area, was divided among the villages to see what their shares might be. If the village shares seemed fair, the settlement officer divided the levy on each village among the holdings, and examined the burden on each holding to see if it were fair. If at any point it seemed to him that the revenue to be demanded from a village or holding was too heavy or too light, he was free to alter the figure. When he had finished adjusting the shares he summed them to see if his final total demand for the area was suitable. Whenever he was dissatisfied with the results, the settlement officer could work back and forth from the assessments on the holdings—through the village totals to the pargana total and from the pargana total through the village totals to the individual assessments—until he had individual assessments and pargana totals which he thought were fair both to the government and to the proprietors.[15] This method was formalized in *Thomason's Directions to Settlement Officers* in 1844.

The settlement officer's ideas of what was fair or light or heavy were of utmost importance in arriving at an assessment. According to the *Directions* the assessment was not to be calculated by any fixed or arithmetical process, or by any rule that a certain portion of the gross or net produce should go to the government, because "net produce could not be satisfactorily ascertained," and because, even if it could be ascertained, it would not provide a reliable guide for the future. The officer was to use "judgment and sound discretion" in considering the field map and village register, past experience with settlements, litigation, prices paid for the sale, lease, or mortgage of a village, the gross rental of the village compared with the gross rental of other villages, the character of the people and of the market, the capacity of the village for improvement, and the opinions of officials and neighboring zamindars in the pargana. "Too much importance was not to be attached to the maintenance of equal averages, whether over a general area, or on different qualities of soil."[16]

It would not be correct to say that assessments were left completely to the settlement officer, for he did have objective data in the form of past assessments, some idea of rents actually charged, in so far as the recorded rents were accurate, and a knowledge of the economic condition and progress of the district, but this data went through a process that could not help but be highly personal.

Under Regulation IX the government's share was reduced to two-thirds. Thomason's *Directions for Settlement Officers* and *Directions for Collectors* remained the standard official references until C. A. Elliott's "theoretical rent-rate" system was adopted in 1875. Meanwhile there were three modifications: the reduction of the government share to one-half; the substitution of plane table for rough chain surveys introduced by the Saharanpur Rules of 1855; and a general instruction to the settlement officers to ascer-

tain the average rental of each estate and to fix the assessment
with reference to it—the basis of assessment was to be the *"real
rental value of every property."*[17]

Elliott developed his "theoretical rent-rate" system during settlement operations in the district of Farrukhabad. The government share was a portion of the "net assets," which were the total
of rents paid, the rental value of land cultivated by the proprietor
or held from him rent-free, and sayar (the profits from the jungles,
orchards, fisheries, and pasture). The main component was the
rental income, "and the question was:—since we have no longer
rents fixed by custom to deal with, but something like real rent-
rates dependent upon competition, and yet the true facts are
mostly concealed from our knowledge; how are we to get at the
proper rents which should be the basis of our calculations?" Elliott's method was the answer to this question. The reason that the
true facts were hidden from the settlement officers was that the
land records were defective. Some land was let for very low rates
as a charity or in payment for services; there was no rent on sir
or khudkasht; some rents were excessively high, others excessively
low; and some rents were just fraudulently understated. Since
the village papers were defective, the settlement officer had to
look for other information and indirect evidence in order to estimate the probable rental value of a village. This led the settlement officer into detailed studies of rents paid on different classes
of soil and under different market conditions in an effort to eliminate unduly high and unduly low rents and to arrive at a best guess
as to the real rental capacity of the village.[18] Bennett cites an
illustration of the kind of reasoning from indirect evidence. In
districts where the change to cash rents had not been completed,
it was generally the case that the best lands were rented for cash
before the poorer lands changed from grain rents. The settlement
officer therefore expected to find high cash rents in areas where
much of the land still paid grain rents, and this expectation was a
guide to him in judging the accuracy on the rent-rolls. In Utraula,
for instance, the rent-roll was regarded as "obviously wrong," for
only 10 per cent of the land was paying cash rents while the recorded rents were at about the level an officer would expect to
find if 80 per cent of the land paid cash rents.[19] Elliott's contribution was to rationalize this sort of detective work to the *n*th degree.

The simplest method was to divide the sum of all cash rents, the value of all rents in kind, and the cash rental value of unlet or rent-free land by the total area, and then modify this average rent according to soil or other classifications. Averages over large areas were compared one with another and with specific local rents, and if the officer was satisfied, he computed the jumma by multiplying the average fair rent by the cultivated area. This total could be modified again by general considerations such as price trends, or prospective increases in rents, or area under cultivation.[20] Elliott refined the system by dividing the tahsils into circles each of which was relatively homogeneous in regard to the type of soil and market conditions, eliminating villages he considered unrepresentative. Then he divided the land in each village into hars, or homogeneous areas. The land was marked off as homestead, middle, and outer land, and the outer land divided into soil types: clay, loam, or sand. Since land close to the village was intensively farmed and received the greatest manuring, the soil, whatever its original state, tended to be homogeneous. All fields and their rents were listed according to the har in which they fell. Elliott then eliminated the abnormal rents, summed those left, divided the rent by the area, and so came out with the "prevailing rates." The prevailing rents were thus the average of normal rents in normal villages for different classes of holdings. He adjusted the prevailing rents in the light of other information or ideas of fairness he thought relevant. As a rule the standard rates were higher than the prevailing rates, as he took account of prospective enhancements of rent, but on occasion the standard rates were lower. The standard rent-rates, the proposed assessment, his methods, and the justification for any alterations in the prevailing rates to arrive at the standard rates were submitted to the Board of Revenue. When approved, Elliott applied the rates to the hars, making adjustments where needed for particular holdings, added the sayar profits, divided the figure by two to get the revenue demand, and announced the result at tahsil headquarters where proprietors could come to agree to the new settlement. This system was accepted by the Board of Revenue and served as the basis of the rules they promulgated in 1875 under the Land Revenue Act XIX of 1873.[21] The theoretical rent-rate system was adopted because it was so difficult to ascertain what the actual rents really were. As the recording procedure became more accurate and as rents came increasingly under the control of the Collectors, the problem of discovering the true rents became easier, and the rules embodying the theoretical rent-rate system emphasized the principle that recorded rents should be accepted wherever it was reasonably possible to do so. Rule 1 said:

> .The assessment of the revenue in each village is to be based as far as possible on the actual rentals recorded in the village rent-rolls, corrected where necessary—
> (1) for land held as sir or khudkasht . . . and rented at nominal rates;
> (2) for rent held on grain-rents, or land recorded as rent free or held at manifestly inadequate rates;
> (3) for fraudulent concealment of assets.
> The Settlement Officer is not at liberty to add to these rent-rolls any estimate on account of prospective rise in rents or prospective increase in cultivation.[22]

Not only was the officer to alter the recorded rents as little as possible in arriving at standard rents, but he was not to engage in guessing how much the returns from the land would increase in the future. Early practice had been to assume that waste lands would soon come into cultivation, but experience had taught the administration that there was no sure way of telling what lands would be brought under the plow. In addition, a high assessment based on prospective enhancement provided a legal cause for enhancement of rent to the standard rates announced by the settlement officer, and by this time the government was engaged in the process of controlling rents and trying to limit their increase.

Various methods were open to the settlement officers to correct the village rent-rolls. They could apply the average full rents of the village to sir, khudkasht, and grain-rented land; they could apply rents paid by neighboring tenants on similar land; they could apply rents from neighboring villages when the village in question had little cash-rented land; but in every case of grain-rent land they were to make sure that the land was not so let because the crop was precarious and could not pay any given rent over the years.[23]

In using his judgment, the settlement officer was instructed to stick closely to the village rent-rolls. Rule 6 required him to select a standard rent-rate for each class of soil in a village "which should correspond as closely as possible with the rents recorded as actually paid by cash-paying tenants in the villages which form the circle." Rule 9 stated that the settlement officer was to accept the corrected rent-rolls if they agreed "fairly" with the standard rent-rates he had computed. Rule 10 required the officer to accept the rent-roll even when it differed from the standard rate appreciably, if there were peculiar local conditions or if the rent-roll was low as a result of easy management, so long as the roll gave a "reasonable" increase. Even in cases of fraud, the actual rents in nearby villages were to be preferred to the standard rates. If the corrected rent-roll materially exceeded the standard rate, which would be the case most advantageous to the government, Rule 13 cautioned the settlement officer to make sure that the recorded rents "can be realized without undue pressure on the proprietor or tenants." Rule 15, too, was an act of self-denial on the part of the government, for it stated that "large and sudden enhancements of the revenue are to be avoided, even when the corrected rent-rolls would seem to justify them," and the settlement officer "should consider whether it would not be advisable to realize the enhanced demand by progressive rises spread over a limited number of years." Having used Elliott's system as modified by these strictures, the settlement officer fixed the assessment at one-half the assets (net income) of the estate, but he might use his judgment to the extent of taking a higher or lower percentage for "any special reasons," with the limitation that for percentages above 55 and below 45 he must have the specific sanction of the Board of Revenue.[24]

Two clear threads run through the assessment system as it had developed by 1875. First, the calculation of the assessment was left very much to the judgment of the settlement officer. Second, the settlement officer was enjoined to use the actual recorded data as much as possible. In Chapters 4 and 5 we saw how settlement officers, collectors, and rent officers were told to use recorded rents, but never to trust them—rather to adjust them toward some proper value that was really the value which would have occurred on a properly functioning market open to inspection. In assessing the land revenue, the settlement officer was given similar instructions. He was to use the recorded rents, which were an approximation of the market rents, but was not to rely on them fully. He was rather to compute a set of standard rates, based on the recorded rates but adjusted in the light of considerations one would expect to influence a market, and use these standard rates as a check upon the recorded rents which the administration was not willing to accept as representing the true market rents.

In Oudh the instructions to the settlement officers were much the same as those just described for the North-Western Provinces in 1875. By the time of the annexation and settlements of Oudh, the British had arrived at a well established system, and it was introduced into Oudh with greater purity than existed in the North-Western Provinces, which had been developing the system step by step. The "aggregate to detail" method was never employed, and the "theoretical rent-rate" system was not really used. Instead, the settlements in Oudh were based on the recorded rents to a much larger extent than in the North-Western Provinces, and each village was treated on its merits and not as part of an assessment circle. Standard rent-rates were computed, but not so much for the use of the settlement officer as for the information of the Board of Revenue, and eventually for suits for enhancement or abatement. Only if the recorded rents were unreliable or non-existent, as was the case in areas where grain rents were still common, were the standard rent-rates used in assessing the revenue.[25] The reasons the Oudh settlements could be made "almost exclusively" upon the basis of the recorded rents were "the prevalence of taluqdari tenures, and the fact that the great mass of cultivation was in the hands of tenants-at-will. . . . In the best cultivated parts of the province, the rents imposed by the taluqdars represented with sufficient accuracy what the land could fairly bear . . . the rent-rolls were well-kept and trustworthy documents on the whole."[26]

The system used in Oudh, which Baden-Powell called the "actual rent-rate system," became the system used throughout the United Provinces after 1888, and was written into the Land Revenue Acts of 1901 and 1929, which provided that the rents recorded in the village land records should be accepted for computing the total assets of the estates but that the recorded rents should first be corrected for land held under proprietary cultivation or at especially low or high rents, and after adding sayar income. With the almost universal adoption of cash rents, with the improvement in recording procedure, and with the control exercised over the rental market by the collectors and rent officers, the "theoretical rent-rate system" lost its justification and the "actual rent-rate system" became universal.

An article in the periodical *Pioneer* expressed the late nine-teenth-century English view of the methods of assessment: "Each then of these three settlements rested on a different basis—the first on the produce and its value; the second on gross rents assumed for large areas; the last on special rents paid for individual fields; and each successive stage was an approximation to the true theory of our present land revenue, namely, that instead of dealing with the cultivator we deal with the proprietor, and instead of taking a share of the produce we take a share of the natural rent."[27] The "true theory" of land revenue had actually been the same through-out—a share of the natural or economic rent. But throughout, the difficulty had been finding out what the economic rent was. Each "successive . . . approximation to the true theory" was another attempt to discover the economic rent. The original conception was plain: find out the value of the produce and deduct the shares owing to the other factors of production and the remainder would be the share owing to land. Under the circumstances it was both conceptually and administratively impossible. The second stage was an ingenious effort to use the data available while recognizing its limitations. The third stage was a development of the second, following on the improvement in the data available to the settle-ment officer. The significant thing about all the methods was that they were evidence of the failure of the land market to function properly. By 1833 the British had recognized that the structure and functioning of the economy would not provide them with the in-formation they needed in order to tax rent. The problem occurred not only in the North-Western Provinces and Oudh. To the west in the Punjab there was no method of finding out the rates which dispensed with "personal opinion and sense of fitness," while in the Central Provinces "the law had so limited the rights of the proprietors of villages as regards the old tenants, that it was also necessary by law to provide that the Settlement Officers should formally and legally determine fair rents."[28]

What happened is clear. Without markets to evaluate outputs and costs there can be no market rents. Without market rents one cannot levy a tax on economic rents. In order to approximate such rents the settlement officers were ordered to revise the rents they found recorded. As the revision was extremely complex[29] and re-lied upon the judgment of the settlement officer it was decided to base the assessment on the actual, recorded rents as much as pos-sible, but in the later years these rents were themselves fixed by rent and settlement officers. The "unrecognized socialism" of the assessment system of the United Provinces was the effort by the government to substitute the judgment of its officers for the mechanism of the market.

LAND TENURE UNDER THE BRITISH

We may now look rapidly at the rise and course of ownership in U.P. from the advent of the British to the Second World War. The British found an economic system based upon the division of the harvest among all the parties to economic, political, and social life, from the raja to the lowest menial. None was sole owner, each was a part owner; but to speak of ownership is misleading since there was no question of sale or of management other than the joint and customary management of the villagers. This system was disrupted during the eighteenth century by Marathas, officials of the Kingdom of Oudh, old rajas, new revenue farmers, and powerful local persons competing for political power and for control over larger or smaller areas. At first the British assumed that there was a single owner for each plot and treated the person whom they recognized as owner as if he were entitled to all the rights and privileges of an English owner. The results were that much land was given to the wrong persons altogether; that when land was given to the right person he received greater powers than he had had before; and that under the law of sale for arrears of revenue—and with the possibility of buying land and thus acquiring the prestige of land ownership—much of the land changed hands, so that by the early 1820s the owners of the land were different people with more rights than the claimants to the produce of the land a quarter of a century earlier.

When the British realized about 1820 that the cultivators had justifiable claims to a special position upon the land, the officers of the East India Company set about recording customary rights so that they might be enforced. In the process of settling the North-Western Provinces, in the 1830s, Thomason granted occupancy rights to cultivators of twelve years' standing, and so began the gradual encroachment of tenancy rights upon the rights of owners. This process received a setback between 1858 and 1869 in Oudh. As a result of the Mutiny, the subsequent need to keep Oudh pacified, and their strong *de facto* position, the talukdars were granted full rights of ownership, but policy reverted to its pre-Mutiny trend in the land revenue and rent acts of the 1870s and '80s. These acts transferred some of the powers and some of the profits of ownership to the tenants. The policy was continually strengthened: in 1886 and 1901 by closing loopholes and guaranteeing seven years tenure at the same rent; in 1921 and 1926 by creating statutory tenants whose tenures were secure for their lifetime and whose rent, after first being freely agreed to, was controlled by the collectors, settlement officers, and rent officers; and in 1939 by stopping increases in sir land and reducing the area of sir, and by preventing landlord and tenant from combining to let land continuously as competitive rents.

The acts to relieve debtors of the burdens of their debts were not so early, so frequent, nor so thorough as the acts to guarantee security of tenure. It is noteworthy that until the Depression of the thirties "debtor-protection" legislation was enacted only when a locally powerful, if not aristocratic, group was threatening trouble: only the talukdars of Oudh and the Rajputs of Bundelkhand benefited. Perhaps, as many Indians feel, this is evidence that the British favored the landowners. But the evidence is not clear, for zamindars in the North-Western Provinces did not receive these privileges, while the rent and tenancy legislation applied to the whole of U.P. The infrequency and lateness of the acts indicate a great reluctance to change the terms of a contract, a reluctance finally overcome before the Indians took over direction of their own affairs.

Looking back over the history of the rental market in U.P., we notice a conflict between the trend in legislation and the trend in actual adaption to the institution of the market. As legislation interfered with the market, people began to react to market stimuli in a more rational fashion. Following the complete introduction of a rental market in the first two decades of the nineteenth century, the British slowly began to regulate the market and to transfer its functions to the various revenue officers. The transfer of the functions of the rental market went hand in hand with the transfer of the attributes of ownership from landlords to tenants. But while the market was progressively limited by the creation of occupancy rights, of exproprietary rights, of statutory periods at fixed rents, of life tenancies, and finally of hereditary tenancies, the officers entrusted with the functions of the market worked under principles and instructions which amounted to a general direction to imitate the market—not the rental market which they saw before them, for there would have been no point in asking them to do what would happen anyway, but the market as it was originally intended to function, as it functioned back in England, as anyone defending the market would describe the functioning of the market.

While the market was being subjected to increasing regulation, it grew stronger. Whereas at first the state of Indian society forced the British to recognize customary rights and anomalous rental structures, at the end the British and the provincial government had to force the people to recognize equally anomalous legislative rules interfering with the working of the market. While the market failed to achieve the results expected when it was introduced, it did gather sufficient strength to undermine the tenant rights that were created when it had become apparent that the market as constituted was failing to fulfill its functions.

Despite the limitations on the owners' powers and the transfer of some of those powers to the tenants, the major characteristic of land tenure was individual ownership exercised in the context of market forces. Until 1939 the owner, treating the term broadly as the combination of the powers of landlord and tenant, could sell or let his land for what it would bring in the market. If he chose to let or use his land wisely he should have made as good a living as was possible, and if he chose to let or use his land foolishly he would eventually lose his land, either to a creditor or through a sale for arrears of revenue. Although the system was much criticized because of the poverty of the people, and although it was frequently pointed out that the owners did not do their best to employ the land economically or to invest in the land and so increase its productivity, the basic idea—that a market could be expected to induce the most productive use of land—was never challenged except on the ground that the particular person owning the land was not the sort who would react properly to the market stimulus, or on the socialist ground that no market could achieve the results it was supposed to. The Tenancy Act of 1939 did not introduce any revolutionary principles, so that until the postindependence land reforms the land tenure system of U.P. remained a system of private ownership where decisions were made by individuals whose main guides were supposed to be the prices of their products. The system was different from the traditional Indian one in which many persons took customary shares of a product grown for the use of the village and in response to local desire and tradition. A market system for land did work in the west, for the wealth and well-being of that area show that the market mechanism does not prevent, if it does not help, the process of economic growth. But the market system did not work in U.P., where poverty, recurrent agrarian crises, and periodic famines show that the people have not enjoyed a rapidly rising standard of living.

PART III

CHAPTER 8

The State of Agriculture

1. OUTPUT

The British policy of establishing a market for land in U.P. did not live up to expectations and was a failure. It was expected that the land market in India would work as well as it did in the West, and it was thought that under the stimulus of market forces the income of the country and the prosperity of the peasantry would increase appreciably. How great a change occurred in the income and well being of India under British rule remains an open question, the statistics and the emotions of the witnesses being what they are, but there was no large and steady increase in the material welfare of the population such as marked the nineteenth and twentieth centuries in Europe and America. The failure was the destruction of the old society, its working system and its values, without replacing it with another and perhaps better system. England lost its rural society but gained a highly productive industrial one. U.P. lost its village society but found nothing to make up for that loss.

The poverty of India is proverbial. The prospect of food shortage is *the* chronic problem of India today. Eighty years ago India exported some five million tons of food, while at the end of British rule its deficit ran to ten million tons. Daily food consumption fell from 1.5 to 1 pound per person and a third of the population suffers from chronic malnutrition and undernutrition.[a]

The productivity of Indian agriculture is low. Yields per acre of wheat, corn, barley, rice, and cotton compare unfavorably with those of most other nations; and where India is not at the bottom of the list its product per acre exceeds only that of very lightly populated economies where one would naturally expect low yield, extensive agriculture. A more striking example is the comparison, or contrast, of India's 30 gallons of milk per head of cattle to Denmark's 387.[1] We need not pursue the point.

Between the wars India became the eighth industrial nation of the world, but the ranking is misleading. Its population was the second largest in the world, and the third largest country in terms of population had but half its numbers. Furthermore, India's density of population is relatively high, so that one would expect a fairly large industrial product. Relative to its size and population density, India was not industrialized. The burden of its complaint is that eighty years ago industry supported over 12 per cent of its population, while at independence the figure was 9 per cent, and that over the years from 1870 the proportion of its population dependent on agriculture rose from 56 to 73 per cent.[2] The comparability of various censuses is controversial, but again accuracy in detail is unnecessary.

Before taking up the causes of poverty in rural U.P. and the relationship of land tenure and the market to that poverty, it would be best to ask what the condition of agriculture in the United Provinces was during the British era. There is strong feeling among Indians that, far from development having been too slow, agricultural conditions actually deteriorated under British rule. The Zamindari Abolition Committee says that while "the

a. Z.A.C. *Report,* p. 33. Quoting Sir Manilal Nanavati's address to the Indian Society of Agricultural Economics in 1945. Balance of payments figures would indicate a food deficit of some 5 and not 10 million tons, but with recurrent famine the issue is not important.

net area sown has remained practically steady . . . total production has diminished. . . . Thanks to the British policy of retarding
India's industrial development, agriculture stagnated and deteriorated, its yield steadily declined."[b] The Provincial Congress Committee in 1932 noted that the population of the United Provinces
had declined after 1900, "obviously due to [a] lower standard of
life and lack of capacity to resist disease."[3]

The history of agriculture in the United Provinces appears to
have two periods: one of growth during the nineteenth century,
and one of stagnation if not decline in the twentieth. In Muzaffarnagar District the proportion of irrigable cultivated land increased
from 18 to 60 per cent, or by 233 per cent, and the proportion
double-cropped from 4 per cent to 23 per cent, or by 475 per cent,
between the periods 1827–40 and 1897–1921.[4] The same comparison shows the value of the outturn per acre increasing by 1,000
per cent, from Rs. 8.1 to Rs. 81. Table 2 shows the outturn per
acre rising by substantial if not surprising amounts. The figures indicate an increase of three-quarters in physical product per acre.
When to these figures are added a consideration of the chaotic and
underpopulated state of the Province when the British first entered
and the steady rise in rents and revenues and prices, it is clear that
the nineteenth century was a time of increasing prosperity if still
a time of absolute poverty.

By the twentieth century, the cultivated area reached a peak
and increased no farther. The net cropped area fluctuated around
35 million acres within a margin of plus or minus 5 per cent,
while during the twenties and thirties the double-cropped area
fluctuated between 7 and 9 million acres. This condition was to
be expected in a thickly populated province, for sooner or later a
point must have been reached where all the land was cultivated, or
at least as much as could be brought under cultivation with peasant techniques. The same considerations would lead us to expect
some maximum for the area subject to double-cropping. However,
the stimulus of the war and the Grow More Food Campaigns led
to some increase in the area under cultivation, to a shade over 36.5
million acres, although the double-cropped area was still just under 9 million acres. The irrigated area continued to increase. In
the twenties there were some 8 million acres irrigated, but beginning in 1929 the figure jumped to 10 million, and again in 1938

b. Z.A.C. *Report*, p. 26. Throughout the *Report* the assumption is that the
economy deteriorated under British rule.

TABLE 2. *Agricultural Development in Muzaffarnagar District*

Outturn per acre in pounds

	Rice	Jowar	Bajra	Gram
Average 1827 to 1840	530	420	350	460
Average 1897 to 1921	900	640	450	810
Percentage increase from 1827–40 to 1897–1921	70%	52%	29%	76%

	Wheat irrigated	Wheat unirrigated	Wheat average
Average 1827 to 1840	1,000	620	650
Average 1897 to 1921	1,280	840	1,100
Percentage increase from 1827–40 to 1897–1921	28%	35%	83%

	Barley irrigated	Barley unirrigated	Barley average
Average 1827 to 1840	770	600	610
Average 1897 to 1921	1,500	1,000	1,120
Percentage increase from 1827–40 to 1897–1921	95%	67%	84%

Source. *Report on Agriculture in the United Provinces,* prepared under the orders of the Government of the United Provinces for the Royal Commission on Indian Agriculture, 1926, p. 117. Figures for 1897–1921 are from the Agriculture Department. Figures for 1827–40 are from Edward Thornton, based on the zamindars' records for 400,000 acres. The records were considered reliable because the settlement of 1841 was the first scientific settlement and the zamindars could not have falsified for the preceding 17 years; and because rents were in kind on estimated yield, and both zamindar and tenant had to agree, while there was frequent resort to sample crop-cutting. While the argument in Chapter 10 reduces the persuasiveness of this reasoning, nevertheless the data are as good as one is likely to find and more weighty than unsupported assertions about the province as a whole.

there was a jump to between 11 and 12 million acres, where the figure remained.[5]

The Zamindari Abolition Committee may be correct in its claim that gross produce fell despite the maintenance of acreage and the increase in irrigated area. Table 3 shows no evidence of any increase in the outturn of crops, although anything in the way of a definite decrease is not apparent either. It is difficult to interpret these figures because local reports were expressed as proportions of a "normal" crop of 16 annas. A crop three-quarters of "normal" would be reported as "12 annas." However, crops apparently

TABLE 3. *Outturn as a Percentage of Normal**

Year (ending June 30)	Rice (early)	Rice (late)	Wheat	Gram	Sugar
1923	73	80	86	125	102
1924	68	71	94	111	123
1925	77	81	80	96	76
1926	74	82	75	99	106
1927	80	86	78	84	121
1928	74	78	81	73	106
1929	43	40	77	52	84
1930	58	61	104	63	85
1931	54	69	88	67	87
1932	76	70	82	84	117
1933	54	45	86	75	123
1934	57	76	86	69	103
1935	70	83	83	82	110
1936	66	74	86	90	130
1937	72	90	87	102	150
1938	78	93	93	88	127
1939	76	91	88	77	87
1940	93	106	103	88	128
1946	73	100	76	97	119
1947	67	103	79	81	129

*"Normal" not given for earlier years. For 1936–37 on, "normal" was (the supposed) average of 1901–02 through 1930–31.

Source. *Seasonal Crop Reports, 1924–40, and 1947,* Statistical Appendix Statement V.

were never better than "normal,"[c] for one does not find reports of "18-anna" or "20-anna" crops. This system therefore effectively suppressed reports of increased yield and over the years undoubtedly had the effect of depressing yield statistics. This tendency to understate[d] output probably also affects the data in other tables.

The twentieth century was generally a period of agricultural development. In the United States, Italy, Spain, and Japan rice yields rose, while they remained constant in Burma and Egypt; in India they fell (Table 4). While wheat yields remained constant in the United States and Australia and rose in Argentina, Russia, and Europe, they fell by 12 per cent in India between 1909–13 and 1924–31, dropping from 724 pounds per acre to 636.[6] It is true that during the same period wheat yields in Canada declined

c. *Agrarian Distress in the U.P.* (p. 4) states that outturn was usually below normal.

d. It would also have been good nationalist politics in the 1920s and 1930s to understate output and thus reflect badly on the Imperial administration.

TABLE 4. *Average Yields of Rice in India (pounds per acre)*

1914–19	1926–31	1931–36	1936–39
982 ℔s.	851 ℔s.	829 ℔s.	805 ℔s.

Source. Z.A.C. *Report*, p. 32, citing W. Burns, "Technological Possibilities of Agricultural Development in India," p. 55.

by 18 per cent, but they were still 972 pounds per acre and Canadian agriculture is extensive rather than intensive. On the page that it cites the figures in Table 4, the Zamindari Abolition Committee gives a figure for Indian rice yields of thirteen 60-pound bushels, or 780 pounds. The year is not given, but from the context one gathers it is a recent year, and this appears to contradict the other figures. Another measure may be derived from Dr. Tiwari's book (Table 5). While the value figures indicate the crisis caused

TABLE 5. *Output of Principal Food Crops*

Year	Tons (millions)	Index (1921–22 = 100)	Value (Rs. millions)	Index (1921–22 = 100)
1921–22	1,229	100	3,091	100
1931–32	1,167	95	1,206	39
1938–39	1,078	88	1,284	42

Source. Shri Gopal Tiwari, *The Economic Prosperity of the United Provinces*, Table 32, p. 90, and Table 35, p. 94.

by the Great Depression, the output figures again indicate a definite fall in the physical product, and a fairly steep one as well. The Index of Indian Agricultural Production compiled by the *Eastern Economist*, using the years 1936–37 to 1938–39 as a base, also indicates further falls. Despite the emphasis on agricultural production and the small increases in area achieved by the Grow More Food Campaign, the Index shows no postwar year with production above the base, and only two of six years as high as the base year.[7]

We also have the results of studies, made by George Blyn, of the trends in agricultural output for all of India since 1893 and for British India since 1891.[e] While his estimates do not provide

e. Some of his results are reproduced in Daniel Thorner, "Long-Term Trends in Output in India," Chap. 4 of Simon Kuznets, Wilbert E. Moore and Joseph J. Spengler, *Economic Growth: Brazil, India, Japan*, pp. 103–28; and are hereafter cited as Blyn (from Thorner) with page from the above book. Other refigures for U.P. alone, they are not inconsistent with the information available about U.P. Blyn estimates average annual production of all food crops in India at 73.9 million tons in 1893–96, 74.0 million tons in the decade ending in 1916, and then at 69.6 and 69.3 million tons in the decades to 1936 and to 1946. Taking the data for 1893–96 as 100, the indices for food production in the decades ending in 1936 and 1946 were 94 and 93; for commercial crops they were 171 and 185; and for all crops they were 108 and 110. The per capita indices show a marked decline in the standard of living: using the same base period, per capita output of food crops fell to 68 during the last decade of British rule, of all crops to 80, while over the fifty-year period of Blyn's survey the outturn of food crops fell from 587 pounds per head to 399 pounds.[8]

Using 11-year "reference decades" from 1891–1901 to 1931–41, Blyn found that of 77 "crop-decades" 29 showed falls in output, 42 showed falls or rates of increase less than the rate of increase of the population, and, over the 51-year span, 7 out of 20 crops experienced declines in output. In the cases of foodgrain crops, the situation was worse. The rate of change in outturn for 11 of 25 "crop-decades" was negative, and for another 9, although positive, it was less than the rate of population growth. Of the 7 foodgrain crops, 4 showed declines over the whole period and only wheat grew faster than population. During the 51-year period, output of foodgrains declined at an annual rate of 0.15 per cent, while output of all food crops rose at an annual rate of 0.13 per cent. The figures for non-foodgrain crops and all crops were +1.60 per cent and +0.46 per cent.

The data show a definite break between the "reference decades" 1901–11 and 1911–21. Prior to 1911 both food and non-food crops increased, the former in step with population and the latter more rapidly than population. After 1911 output of food declined and the rate of increase of non-food crops fell by a fifth.[9]

Blyn's rates of change should be regarded with caution because the "errors of observation" in the collection of the raw data are probably large. The largest average annual rate of change in a

sults are from two privately circulated papers by Blyn: "Crop Production Trends in India" and "A Comparison of the Crop Output Trend in India with Trends in the Underlying Determinants of Yield: 1893–1946" (a more recent, but incomplete, study) hereafter cited as Blyn, "Crop Production Trends in India," or Blyn, "A Comparison . . ."

decade was —2.9 per cent for barley in 1921–31, but the rates
for rice varied from 0.0 per cent to —1.4 per cent and for wheat
from +2.1 per cent to —0.8 per cent. All these rates are well within the probable margin of error of the crop estimates.[f] Furthermore, Blyn believes that his estimates for the earlier years have an
upward bias.[10]

The only firm conclusion which can be drawn from available
information is that there have been no large changes in total
agricultural output during the twentieth century, although there
has been a definite increase in the outturn of non-food or commercial crops. Daniel Thorner completed his examination of the data
on Indian national product with the conclusion that a small rise
in the standard of living, a constant standard of living, and a
small fall in the standard of living were all consistent with the
information we have.[11]

The evidence leads to the conclusion that agricultural production increased up to the First World War, but since then has fallen
or at least has not risen appreciably in the face of a rising population. Interestingly enough, the decline in agriculture set in with
the extension of tenants' rights, and the fall in the proportion of
the population engaged in nonagricultural pursuits dates from the
early tenancy legislation. This *post hoc ergo propter hoc* argument is undoubtedly wrong, but it certainly casts some doubt on
the rightness of the belief that the extension of tenancy rights
must be beneficial to agriculture. Actually, the causes both of the
increase and the decline probably lie elsewhere: in the pressure of
population and the man–capital ratio, and in the structure of
village social relationships.

2. DEFECTS

Technological Defects

The technological defects of agriculture in U.P. are similar to
those throughout India, and are commonly listed:[12]

1. lack of irrigation
2. lack of manure
3. lack of good seeds

f. See my "The Limitations of Indian Village Survey Data" for a discussion
of the probable margins of error of observations, which may well run over 20
per cent.

4. crop pests and diseases
5. light weight of plows
6. weak draft cattle
7. lack of crop planning
8. waste in threshing and in storage
9. lack of both general and agricultural education
10. lack of facilities for canning, preservation, and transportation of perishable goods
11. lack of safeguards against drought and excessive rains

The Zamindari Abolition Committee believed that the correction of these defects required province-wide planning, research, education, and the provision of means, but that such improvements would be effective only after the social and economic impediments had been removed. The Committee was determined to justify a reform of the tenure system and invariably found that no improvement could succeed until reform was adopted. However, each of these defects can be corrected *only* by greater investment of capital resources, and properly employed investment would go far toward removing them *under any system of land tenure* including the zamindari system.

A brief picture of farm operations will point up the conditions generally referred to as "primitive techniques" and the absence of equipment. The plow is a large lump of wood roughly sharpened at one end, a handle stuck in the other end, and a rough hewn branch for a shaft. The improved or modern plow has a steel share bolted to a 2" x 4". The cultivator makes his own handle. The harrow is a board on which the cultivator stands. The seed drill is more complex: a bowl is mounted above a beam and feeds through four tubes of bamboo or brass to holes drilled in the beam behind four heavy wooden pegs which extend downward. The cultivator mounts the contraption forward of the beam and bowl so that he can add his weight while driving the bullocks. A woman or child feeds the seed into the bowl. In large expanses of U.P. it is common to sow broadcast, and to mix sorghum, rice, and wheat so that one or another crop will do well depending on the character of the season. Clumps of sugar cane are often found in these plots. To harvest a grain crop the cultivator takes a handful of stalks, cuts them with a sickle, and lays them on the ground. The squatting position used in this operation is comfortable in a chairless society, but the yield per swish of the sickle is minute.

To thresh and winnow, the bullocks trample and the women pour the grain from shallow baskets. Where there are government canals the water is tapped through channels of banked earth to the fields. In other areas there are Persian wheels—cups on a continuous chain which empty into run-off troughs, the chains being geared to circling bullocks—or simple leather buckets on a pulley, bullocks again providing the power.[g] But irrigation is not common.

Given the existing conditions, the peasants' adaptation is frequently efficient or well designed to minimize risk, but at every point in this process additional capital would lighten labor or increase output. India is not using the agricultural technique of a century ago in the West, but the techniques of the medieval world.

Organizational Defects

In its report the Zamindari Abolition Committee gave pride of place among all the defects of Indian agriculture to:

1. a semi-feudal land system and the existence of classes, both attributed to the British
2. the insecurity of the cultivator
3. the unproductive employment of agricultural wealth to support a parasite class ·
4. the lack of incentive resulting from the first three defects.[13]

It is not clear whether items (1) and (3) are technical, economic, or moral defects,[h] but as items (1), (2), and (3) are deterrents to agricultural production, they are important in so far as they have prevented, discouraged, or failed to stimulate savings and investment. The Committee felt that misuse of capital as a result of the zamindari system of tenure and the lack of incentive resulting from that system were of primary importance in delaying the development of agriculture. In the next chapter we shall undertake to show that the character of the typical U.P. zamindar certainly acted as a brake upon development,[i] but this character is at least as much

g. In the past decade some wealthier cultivators have bought diesel or kerosine powered pumps, but these are rare, and there were virtually none before independence.

h. How can the home of caste attribute class to the British?

i.' See Daniel Thorner, *The Agrarian Prospect for India*, for this argument *in extenso* and his concept of a "built-in depressor."

connected with Indian social structure as it is with the existence of landlords. Since the origins and results of the zamindari system are the subject of this book, we only need remark here that these "defects" in organization are defects only to the extent that they are the cause of other troubles.

Other defects in organization listed by the Committee were:[14]

1. lack of rural finance
2. concentration of rural finance in the hands of zamindars and mahajans (merchants) along with the "negligible" importance of cooperatives
3. high rates of interest
4. poor organization of rural marketing
5. misuse of available resources
6. inequitable allotment of burdens in the agricultural sector
7. absence of proper land management and the consequent hampering of state projects by existing rights in land
8. fluctuations in the prices of agricultural products.

Lack of rural finance is a symptom of lack of capital, and thus of the poverty of the countryside, but it also reflects the fact that control of finance is in the hands of people who do not employ it to increase productivity. Of themselves the other items are not evidence of a capital shortage. The "poor organization" of rural marketing indicates a failure of the market to penetrate the rural economy and stems largely from the household–subsistence orientation of the peasant. But by and large the defects are curable only if more capital—including capital expenditure on education and information—is employed, or they tend to prevent the needed accumulation of capital, as in the case of fluctuating prices. In conditions of poverty, rising prices lead to higher rural consumption, while falling prices lead to increased indebtedness rather than reduced rural consumption, and have the effect, which they have everywhere in the world, of increasing the risk of investment in agriculture and so of reducing the incentive to invest.

Uneconomic Size of Holdings

Holdings below the size that fully utilizes labor and equipment waste them. Indian agriculture, and especially agriculture in U.P., has a high proportion of such uneconomic holdings with disguised unemployment, waste of potential bullock power, and waste of agricultural equipment resulting. Most causes of low productivity on small and fragmented holdings can be classified as shortage of capital and inefficient organization of productive effort, but there is no measure of the loss due to smallness or fragmentation alone. It must be recognized that very small holdings used as allotment gardens are likely to be more productive per acre than larger holdings managed as farms, but where agriculture is the sole, or even main, support of a family, small holdings mean low incomes.j

The problem of small holdings is worse in U.P. than elsewhere in British India, as Table 6 shows.

TABLE 6. *Percentage of Families with Different Sizes of Holdings in Bombay, Madras, and U.P.*

Province	Under 2 acres (%)	2 to 5 acres (%)	5 to 10 acres (%)	10 or more acres (%)
Bombay*				
Gujarat	27.5	25.7	22.3	24.5
Deccan	19.8	16.7	18.8	44.7
Carnatic	12.2	19.2	21.7	46.9
Madras†	51.0	31.0	7.0	11.0
Uttar Pradesh	55.8	25.4	12.8	6.0

*Bombay had the fewest small holdings in British India.
†Next to U.P., Madras had the largest number of small holdings in British India.

Source. United Nations, *Land Reform: Defects in Agrarian Structure as Obstacles to Economic Development*, p. 8, citing "Report of the Congress Agrarian Reform Committee."

Overly small holdings are not a new problem in U.P. A Major Erskine found that by 1880 the average holding in Oudh was less than 5 acres, and in Gonda, Bennett found that the sir lands had been so subdivided as to leave no "surplus."[15] In the Punjab, which in this case he does not feel to be very different from U.P., Baden-Powell found that two of the most important causes of poverty and stagnation were the waste of money in litigation and

j. Recently six government-sponsored cost accounting surveys have shown that whereas "profit" per acre is directly correlated with size of holding, output per acre is inversely correlated. See Amartya Kuman Sen, "An Aspect of Indian Agriculture," *The Economic Weekly* (Annual Number, February 1962), pp. 243–46.

the excessive subdivision of land, both resulting from "bitter family quarrels and local enmities."[16] By the thirties of the twentieth century, the average size of holding in U.P. was 5.5 acres, ranging from the large average of 12 acres in Bundelkhand to as low as 3.5 acres in the eastern districts.[17]

The problem continues to get worse. The Indian Famine Commission (1946) found that average production per holding was about two tons of foodgrains in Madras, Bengal, and U.P., and about three tons in the Punjab, but that the proportion of holdings producing less than one ton was 74 per cent in Madras and 50 per cent in Bengal and Bombay; in U.P. it found that 50 per cent of the holdings produced less than 1.5 tons.[18] The Zamindari Abolition Committee decided that 10 acres was the minimum size for an economic holding, but gave favorable reference to the possibility that 6.25 acres might be the minimum. If the minimum were set at 10 acres, 94 per cent of the cultivators with 65 per cent of the land would be classified as farming uneconomic holdings. If the limit were set at 6.25 acres, 85 per cent of the cultivators with 45 per cent of the land would have uneconomic holdings. Six per cent of the land was held by the 37 per cent of the cultivators having less than one acre each.[19] In 1926 the hilly southern area had an average holding of over 10 acres, while the south-central and eastern tracts, where the bulk of the population lives, had average acreages of less than 6.25 acres. Of forty-five districts only seven had an average size of holding greater than 10 acres, and only thirteen fell into the range 6.3 to 9.9 acres.[20] By the mid-thirties the provincial average was 5.5 acres, and it had fallen to 3.5 acres by the late forties.

While it is true, as market gardening would lead us to expect, that gross output per acre is highest on the smallest holdings, net output per acre is higher on holdings of appreciable size. Direct comparisons between two countries are never conclusive, or necessarily roughly indicative, but the difference between the size of Indian holdings and the optimum size of holdings in other countries is so large that there can be little doubt that Indian holdings are far too small. Net output per acre in Denmark is highest on farms of 75 to 100 acres, in Switzerland on farms of 25 to 37.5 acres, in England on farms of 117 acres, and in the United States on farms of over 150 acres. Average holdings point to the same conclusion. In Europe, excluding Russia, the average size of farm is 19 acres; in eastern Europe, excluding Hungary and Poland, the average is 12 acres, and here the peasantry is very poor. Livestock farming is not suited to large-scale organization, yet Holland and Denmark find that successful farms vary from 50 to 150 acres, and that the best are at least 75 acres.[21] The Zamindari Abolition Committee's estimate that 10 acres are necessary to achieve an economic holding is certainly not large.

Fragmentation of Holdings

Not only are the holdings very small, they are divided into a number of fields widely scattered over the village lands, and upon occasion a man will have plots in different nearby villages. This presents an organizational rather than a technological problem. Perhaps 3 per cent of the cultivated area is unproductive because of the need for boundaries between so many plots. To this 3 per cent we should add some further allowance for headland (turning room) for the bullocks during plowing. There is the added inefficiency of moving from field to field in the process of cultivation; and this inefficiency undoubtedly results in lower output, since the time for plowing and sowing is limited and there are insufficient bullocks in good condition to plow all the lands of the village during the most suitable days.

Although the weight of opinion is strongly critical of fragmentation, the process is not without benefits, however meager. Witnesses before the Royal Commission on Indian Agriculture were sometimes inclined to minimize the evils of fragmentation by mentioning security resulting from the variety of crops a cultivator could grow on different plots.[22] But the U.P. Banking Enquiry Committee pointed out that a single good crop should keep the cultivator fed, and cited a case where consolidation resulted in almost all the land being planted to rice while the tenantry was "remarkably well-to-do." Similarly, it felt that although fragmentation provided some protection against the random incidence of hail, the preventive "was worse than the disease." The Committee thought that there was "much force" to the argument that consolidation would require separate homesteads and thus separate drinking wells and separate threshing floors, and would involve increased risk of dacoity and burglary,[23] but it is a little hard to see why, for villages and their fields together average about a square mile, so there could not be any overriding reason to break up the village site.

Agriculture in U.P. has been and is in a poor state. One expects that, whatever the effect upon the social system or upon values or upon the good life, the market so organizes and directs resources that they are used most economically, and that production is as high as technology and considerations of cost permit. Although economic growth and the development of resources is not implicit in market organization, Western experience of markets leads to the expectation that the well being of the citizens of U.P. would have increased over the years. There are many instances where the market does not achieve perfect results because social costs are inaccurately represented by money costs, or because monopolies or other organizational imperfections of the market prevent complete adaptation to market forces, but these are usually thought of as barriers to the optimum, not as explanations of continuous movement from bad to worse. Before we can evaluate the land reform measures of the past few years we must have a clear idea why the market failed to achieve the results that the British expected it to achieve, and that anyone might have expected it to achieve.

CHAPTER 9

Why the Market Failed:
The Wrong Reasons

Over the past half-century a number of reasons have been advanced to account for the stagnant level of welfare in U.P. Analysis of most of these explanations shows that they do not get to the core of the problem: the incomplete meshing of markets, the lack of capital to provide alternative means of employment, and the persistence of an Indian social code totally at odds with the requirements of a market mechanism. Of the traditional explanations, only the complaint that "the law of the book was not the law of the land" stands.

INEQUITY OF THE LAW

One of the traditional suggestions is that the land and tenancy legislation was unfair, or that it contained procedural matters that defeated its substantive purposes. The issue of fairness can be broken into three subsidiary questions: whether the administrators of the law subverted its intents; whether the administrators were effective in carrying out the intent of the law; and whether the law provided the legal means to safeguard the rights it purported to confer.

The answers to the first two questions are that the administration of the law was not in fact equitable, but that the inequities did not arise from bias or unfairness on the part of the commissioners, collectors, and judges. No one can read settlement reports or memoirs by officers of the administration without being impressed by the sincerity of their efforts to carry out the spirit of the land revenue and tenancy acts. The difficulty is to be found elsewhere, in the structure of Indian society and the code of ethics by which the villagers lived, a problem discussed in the next chapter.

Charges of abuse of police power are to be found in the U.P. Provincial Congress Committee's pamphlet on *Agrarian Distress in the United Provinces,* in which a long appendix reproduces the reports of specific investigations and a number of documents showing a devious and often brutal attitude on the part of a number of officials.[1] It is not necessary to recount the incidents, which upon occasion went so far as to involve the condoning of rape as a means of collecting arrears of rent. Suffice it to say that the reports are as convincing as one could ask, short of being an eyewitness, and the documented attitude of the government leaves little doubt that the accusations leveled were true. However, there are two points to be noted. First, established cases were few. For instance, there were two villages in Gonda subjected to first-class brutality, but only two in the whole district.[2] If we consider the figures for the seventies of the last century, we find that in Oudh from none to 150 persons were confined in jail on rent and revenue charges each year,[3] not a huge number by any means. Second, the excesses were committed in 1930–31 at the height of Congress agitation, and the behavior of officials was directed more against the Congress than against the tenants. It was not because the officials loved the landlords, nor because they wanted to trample on tenants, that they permitted instances of brutality in the collection of rents, but because Congress had allied itself with the tenants against the landlords, and the land tenure problem merged with the national movement.

It is hard to find documentary substantiation of the abuse of police power because such abuse was extra-legal and contrary to public policy. As will become apparent in the next chapter, fraud and brutality were common features of police administration, but the evidence for this is a long and often specific oral tradition which occasionally finds expression in memoirs. However, there is a great difference between the charge that the law was bad or that public policy was marked by favoritism and the charge that neither law nor public administration was able to achieve its ends.

The legislation was not unfair or trickily legalistic in the layman's sense. The procedure was straightforward and allowed sufficient time and alternative methods of enforcement to permit the potential "victim" to escape its harsher clauses.[a] To point out that the legislative protections and the judicial processes open to tenants were, by the standards of the West, full and clear does not mean that they were clear to Indian villagers or that the villagers had the means or the courage to use them. In legal procedures as in police administration, the principles of the higher authorities could not be made effective at the lower levels of society, but this failure of effectiveness cannot be regarded as a "bad" legal framework of tenure unless it can be shown that another law—not another and better administration—would have worked better. The failure, it will be argued in the next chapter, was a consequence of social structure, not of the law as enacted or of the law as the legislators hoped it would be enforced. A listing of the legal safeguards should show that the law itself was not to blame.

From the early days, the landlord was required to obey certain injunctions in order to exercise his rights. He could not sue or eject a tenant or distrain his goods unless he allowed every person concerned to inspect the village records properly made out.[4] By the middle of the nineteenth century the rules were becoming stricter. A tenant could collect double damages from a landlord who failed to give a receipt for rent. The period of limitation for suits for arrears of rent was three years, not a long time in view of the need to recognize the existence of bad harvests; and if the

a. There were anomalies. Baden-Powell mentions the case of three adjacent villages, one of which sold its rice after the rainy season, another its sugar in January, and the third its cereals in the spring, yet all of which had to meet the land revenue payments on the same date (Baden-Powell, *1*, 708). But by and large the legislation did its best to prevent fraud, chicanery, or quibbling as means of evasion.

suit was for an enhanced rent unconfirmed by the courts, it had to be brought within three months. A decree for ejectment was not final for fifteen days and was dropped if the tenant paid rent, interest, and costs to the court. The landlord could distrain unsecured crops only for the arrears due on the past year and could not distrain crops which had already been stored. On the other hand, movable property could be seized and sold, and if the sale of an undertenure raised insufficient money, the ex-undertenure-holder had to give up both immovable and movable property. The threat of jail was used. A debtor could be arrested to prevent him from absconding, but if the arrest were shown to be without reasonable cause, the debtor was indemnified up to Rs. 100.[5] If a judgment-debtor was able to pay but refused, he could be sent to jail.[6] It is to be noted that this provision bore just as heavily upon the landlord as upon the tenant. In 1863 execution was restricted to person or property, but not both simultaneously.[7]

The Oudh Rent Law of 1868 provided penalty damages of Rs. 200 for the collection of excess rent or the illegal collection of rent legally due. The same law went on to require execution against movables and then immovable property before underproprietary rights could be sold. Co-sharers had the option of purchasing a share sold for arrears if they paid the highest amount bid by the end of the day on which the sale took place.[8] The tenant was given a right to growing crops or the ungathered produce of the land unless their price was tendered by the landlord. Double damages were granted for the extraction of excessive rent in the North-Western Provinces Rent Act, and the penalty of Rs. 200 was carried over from the Oudh Rent Act. While standing crops could be distrained, the tenant was allowed to harvest them, and in the case of perishable crops, the distraint had to take place twenty days before harvesting. If the distress was groundless or vexatious the collector was empowered to award damages.[9] When movable property was seized, no implements of husbandry, no cattle employed in agriculture, and no artisans' tools might be seized,[10] and clothes were added to this list in 1881, as were the materials of a building occupied by an agriculturalist debtor.[11] Movable property could not be sold until ten days after seizure. If a whole mahal was to be sold, the collector could delay the sale in order to allow the debtor an opportunity to raise the money through a private sale, lease, or mortgage. Instead of selling, the collector could hand over the land to the creditor or to a third party if he thought the debt could be paid out of profits within fifteen years. If the collector could not raise the money by these methods, he recommended to the Board of Revenue that the mahal be sold, but the Board might try to recover the arrears through a fifteen-year lease. Only after making these efforts was the Board to order a sale.[12]

Similar rules were applied in the Land Revenue Act of 1873. An arrear of land revenue was recoverable first through the service of a writ of demand; then by arrest or detention if necessary; next by distress and sale of movables; then by the attachment of a share, patti, or mahal and its transfer to a solvent co-sharer; next the collector could annul the settlement, attach and manage the property directly or through an agent, and return it to the owner when the arrears were paid. Only after such efforts was the land to be sold outright. When the land was sold, the collector had to give thirty days' notice, and payment of arrears within that period ended the matter.[13]

The rules promulgated under Section 39 of Act XIX of 1873 exempted from settlement computations any increase in the rents which were due to the landlord's expenditure on irrigation or reclamation of waste, so there was no disincentive to investment on the part of the landlord—in fact quite the opposite.[14] Acts XVIII and XIX of 1873, which were the models for procedural acts to follow in both parts of U.P., set up an arbitration procedure for the settling of disputes. The arbitration panel consisted of a chairman, appointed by the collector or settlement officer, and equal numbers of arbitrators appointed by the parties to the dispute. The award of the arbitrators was binding if accepted by the officer ordering the arbitration.[15]

The "sundown" law of Bengal, which was originally applied in the North-Western Provinces, has received a good deal of attention. This rule required the payment of revenue by sundown on the day due, and failure to comply met with the immediate sale of the property. The rule had been a cause of much misery, but the days of the "sundown" law had passed by the middle of the nineteenth century. The rules of the later rent and revenue acts were more indicative of the conditions under which the land market operated. Clearly, the procedures set forth in the legislation provided ample opportunity to meet with the substantive requirements of the law. It is true that illiterate peasants were not in a position to take advantage of the law's provisions, that a wealthy man could use the law and litigation to make difficulties for the tenants, and that the zamindars did exercise great extra-legal powers, but such faults are attributable to the society—the caste, prestige, and social power of the zamindars—and not to the laws themselves, which did not take away by guile the rights they granted.

A few figures will serve to substantiate the claim that it was not the law that deprived men of their rights. In 1877–78, a famine year, there were only seven outright sales of property for arrears in the North-Western Provinces, and only two in Oudh. While *orders* of distraint of personal property ran at two to three thousand in a normal year in the North-Western Provinces, and under a thousand in Oudh, and were over eleven thousand for the whole of U.P. in 1877–78, the actual number of *sales* of personal property seldom rose to four hundred. Similarly, annulments of settlements ran under thirty a year, while attachments or transfers averaged around 250 a year.[16] These figures, for a region larger than Britain in size and population, do not seem excessive.

Success in evading the restrictions on the rights of owners was outside and not within the legal process. The landlord retained almost absolute power over his sir land, so that he could defeat the law if he increased the area held as sir. This was certainly done by the trick of ejecting a tenant from one field and readmitting him to another, but after 1886 in Agra and 1901 in Oudh such action was illegal. During the twenties and thirties, when agriculture was at its lowest ebb and the incentive to evade the law was greatest, the landlord's success in removing his tenants was insufficient to explain the widespread poverty and stagnation. The area of khudkasht in Agra increased by a good deal, from 300,000 to 1,300,000 acres, but the area of sir remained constant. In Oudh, where the talukdars, being larger holders, were not themselves so interested in cultivating, the area of khudkasht increased from over 300,000 to over 400,000 acres and then fell back to 360,000 while the area held as sir rose by 50 per cent, though

TABLE 7. *Nonoccupancy Tenants as a Percentage of All Tenants*

	1899–1900	1926–27	1935–36	1945–46
Oudh	82.2	10.5	11.9	5.1
Agra	41.9	4.0	6.2	2.7

Source. Z.A.C. *Report, 2: Statistics,* Statement 22(ii), pp. 90–91.

only to some 600,000 acres.[17] As against these landlord successes,
Table 7 presents ample evidence of the success of the tenancy laws
in achieving security of tenure. In Oudh the percentage of land
held as sir and khudkasht was 11 to 12 per cent, while in Agra it
was 21 to 22 per cent, mostly khudkasht.[18] As far as the record
goes, tenancy legislation secured to the tenant the tenure it was
designed to secure him.

LEVEL OF REVENUE DEMAND

A complaint of long standing has been that the assessment of
revenue was too high; that it caused famines, or at least prevented
the population from meeting the emergency; and that it stifled investment. The Zamindari Abolition Committee summed up this
attitude toward the level of revenue demand by saying that everyone suffered from the high revenue demand, but that the poor
suffered most since their rents could be raised.[19]

That revenue administration presented difficulties for the successful management of the economy cannot be doubted. At several
points Baden-Powell mentions the troubles caused by fixing the
demand for long periods. He says that:

> unless we adopt variable or fluctuating rates, *any* fixed as-
> sessment can hardly work. If it is very low, it will sacrifice
> revenue needlessly in good years; and in bad years, even
> then it will not be easily, if at all paid. . . . It will be seen
> that [the native governments'] system was always to keep
> up the assessment pretty high, but allow of an immediately-
> acting and thoroughly elastic system of easing off in bad
> years. Our system, it is true, tends to make the land-revenue
> partake somewhat of the nature of a *tax;* and rigidity and
> certainty are the necessary features of a proper tax-admin-
> istration; they have their advantage in compelling thrift
> and habits of forethought. But land-revenue is not wholly
> a tax, and cannot be effectively treated wholly on the prin-
> ciples of one.[20]

At another point he quotes with approval the Kheri Settlement
Report:

> In Bundelkhand, cycles of magnificent harvests, during
> which even heavy revenues are easily paid, are succeeded by
> periods of depression and scarcity, during which the *light-*

est demand, if rigidly collected, would cause distress. The true policy seems to me to be *not to impose very light* "jama's," which involve too great a loss of public revenue in good years, and which cannot be fully collected in bad years without hardship; but to fix a full demand which should be collected with discrimination; suspension, and (where necessary) remission, being liberally granted on account of failure of crops.[21]

As the British saw it at the end of the last century, the trouble was not that the revenue was too high, but that annual collection was too rigid for the conditions of Indian agriculture, which had productive years when the weather was favorable and poor years when the monsoon failed, came too early or too late, or when the rains were too heavy. The income out of which the land revenue had to be paid varied greatly, while the payments due were based on long-term averages.[b]

Under severe criticism from R. C. Dutt, the Governor-General proposed in 1902 a resolution largely devoted to a refutation of the charge that the level of revenue was the cause of famine. The resolution boils down to the statements that no change in revenue can prevent famines because they are caused by natural conditions, and that there is no reason to believe, on principle or on the basis of experience, that any increase in retained incomes would go into a famine reserve.[22] This is still the case, for inflation reduced the real burden of revenue by 75 per cent from 1938 to 1948, and yet there were famines and food shortages aplenty.

There is a general argument that high taxes prevent development, and it contains the implied assumption that savings from the tax collector would be used for improving the economy, but one is inclined to believe that if savings from the tax collector would not be used as a famine reserve, they would not be used for investment. Even if one concedes the argument for a reduction in tax burdens, it does not follow that land revenue is the tax that should be reduced; in this connection the Zamindari Abolition Committee believed that the tax system had been weighted against

b. To the argument that the cultivators should have saved in good years to meet the bad, the answer that the foresight needed was not there, and that had the foresight been greater poverty would not have permitted the cultivators to sacrifice the few chances they got to enjoy life, should be sufficient for anyone.

industry and in favor of agriculture. The Committee cited the Floud Commission in support of its contention that the exemption of agricultural income from the income tax had weighted the tax structure against the nonagricultural professions and classes and thus led to an overcapitalization of rent-receiving without helping agriculture, while at the same time retarding the development of industry.[23] This situation argues for heavier rather than lighter taxation on agriculture. Furthermore, the redistribution of the tax burden in order to lessen its incidence upon the smaller cultivator would not increase the amount invested, for the small cultivator is the man with the strongest reasons for increasing his consumption.[24]

It has been asserted that the revenue demand, fixed for long periods, does not take into account fluctuations in prices. This criticism would be valid only if the demand were fixed in times of high prices, which has not generally been the case. The problem of falling prices became acute only with the Great Depression. Before that time the criticism was not strongly voiced, for the reason that the trend of prices for agricultural output in U.P. had been rising until the 1920s, and except for a few years at the turn of the century did not fall until the '30s.[c] The lag in tax assessment

TABLE 8. *Burden of Rent and Revenue in Muzaffarnagar District*

	1840	1924	Percentage change 1840 to 1924
Value of outturn per acre (Rs.)	8.1	81	+ 900
Rent per cultivated acre (Rs.)	2.6	10.8	+ 315
Rent as a percentage of outturn	32	13	− 59
Revenue per cultivated acre (Rs.)	1.6	2.6	+ 63
Revenue as a percentage of outturn	20	3	− 85
Population per cultivated acre	0.89*	1.31*	+ 47
Estimated size of an average holding (acres)	17.0	11.5	− 22
Value productivity per person, i.e. value per acre divided by population per acre† (Rs.)	9.1	61.0	+ 580

*From Mansel's *Settlement Report on Agra, 1841.*

†Assuming the same ratio of cultivators to total population in 1840 as existed in 1924.

Source. *Report on Agriculture in the United Provinces,* p. 117.

c. See the discussion of prices below, p. 172 ff. Baden-Powell (*1*, 242) says that there was a "steady rise in the value of grain" during the nineteenth century.

caused by the long settlement periods was probably more of a help than a hindrance to the cultivators.

Table 8 compares the outturn, level of revenue, and level of rents in Muzaffarnagar district in the early nineteenth and early twentieth centuries. A drop in the proportion of revenue to outturn from 20 per cent to 3 per cent indicates that if the revenue demand was too high, its deleterious influence was declining and must have been much less during the period of stagnation than it was during the earlier period of development.

LEVEL OF RENTAL DEMAND

If the level of revenue demand was not to blame for the conditions of agriculture, it is still possible that the level of rents was to blame, and the charge of excessively high rents is made not only in U.P. but also throughout India and all of South and Southeast Asia. It may therefore seem somewhat unusual to deny that the high level of rents was the cause of agrarian distress, but it would appear that it was an effect of population pressure and the paucity of capital rather than the cause of poverty. Table 8 points to a drop in rents from 32 per cent to 13 per cent of outturn, i.e. 59 per cent, in Muzaffarnagar, and leads to the same conclusion in regard to rents as to revenue. If the rents were too high, then their ill effects must have been strongest during the period when development rather than stagnation was the rule. The table also shows that the productivity per person on the land in Muzaffarnagar increased by the surprising amount of 580 per cent. Agriculture was developing during the period, and the burden of rent was falling.

The Provincial Congress Committee, however, felt very strongly that rents were excessive. The Committee argued that the pitch of rents was not sustainable even before the Depression, and cited an admission to that effect in the report of the Court of Wards for 1929–30. The cultivators had been crippled by successive crop failures before the fall in prices. Further to support its claim, the Provincial Congress Committee pointed out that the rate at which rents were increasing had fallen, and that the landlords could not collect their full rental demand. Rent increases in the period 1901–15 bore to rent increases in the period 1916–30 the ratio of 31 to 17, and 4 to 1 in Oudh alone. In 1924–25 landlords collected only 83 per cent of total rental demand, in 1925–26 only 77 per cent, when prices were at their apex, and in 1928–29 only 63 per cent.[25] The Committee concludes from these figures that rents had risen so high that landlords were encountering difficulty in forcing them up further, and that even where they could extract an agreement to pay high rents, they could not collect the rents.

The United Nations investigation found that:

> Owing to the pressure of population on the land, the landlord is in a strong bargaining position in relation to the cultivators and can extract his own terms. The conception of a "fair rent," which is current in more advanced countries, has little relevance in agriculturally overpopulated countries, since the level of rents which exists is accepted as normal, even though it may be regarded as exorbitant in countries where the income derived from land occupied is far higher.

The investigators believed that the difficulties encountered in legislating lower rents or greater security of tenure were a result of these conditions.[26] In U.P. there is certainly a concept of a fair rent, at least among the administrators, and it is equally certain that rents were regarded as exorbitant. In fact, the legislation we have discussed was aimed at achieving "fair rents."

The trouble was not that rents were too high: the productivity of labor was too low. It is probable that the marginal productivity of labor in rural U.P. was, and is, zero. With actual holdings far below the minimum economic size, with a large population, and with small capital development, a low productivity of labor is only to be expected. The market prices of factors of production tend to measure the productivity of the factors; and so it should occasion no surprise that interest rates and rents were high and the returns to labor low. This argument of course implies that there was "underemployment" or "disguised unemployment" in the agricultural sector.[27] To these assertions two objections are frequently raised: that village labor is fully employed during the peak agricultural seasons, and that in fact hired labor is paid a wage higher than zero. Neither objection disproves a hypothesis of zero marginal productivity, for these apparent inconsistencies of observation and analysis can be explained both in Marshallian and in social terms.

It is argued that labor cannot leave the land without a fall in output under the given technical conditions, and that therefore the marginal product of labor is positive; but one must ask what is meant by the given technology, whether it refers to current practices or to the current state of knowledge. Instead of asking whether output would fall if fifty laborers left the village and there were no change in organization, one can ask if the village is capable of maintaining output by readjusting to the departure of the villagers without new investment. The fact that the villager has found a way of living with his current circumstances does not mean that he is incapable of adjusting to changes—enough changes have taken place in India to indicate the opposite—nor that he does not have the knowledge, wit, or imagination to reorganize his productive system in response to a decrease in the supply of labor. There is thus a sense in which marginal productivity may be zero, but this does not mean that one should expect the villagers to expel fifty "surplus," resident laborers because until labor leaves there may be no impetus to change current practices despite the fact that the peasants know how to adjust if they have to.

Marginalism visualizes in fact, although it is not logically necessary, a continuous process rather than a seasonal one. Nurkse points out that seasonal full employment must imply seasonal "disguised unemployment,"[28] so that it is possible to have a positive marginal product at some times during the year and a zero product the rest of the year. If during the harvest seasons (October–November and March–April) labor is productive, it is quite possible to find wages of Re. 1 per day which reflect a marginal value product of that amount. But this value productivity occurs only for a limited time during the year, so that a daily wage of Re. 1 is consistent with an annual wage, or productivity, of Rs. 30 or Rs. 40. It is even possible that the total annual productivity of labor is less if at any times during the year the marginal product of labor or its marginal value product is less than zero, a difficult proposition to establish. One need not show zero wages to establish the proposition that annual productivity of labor is so close to zero as to make it unimportant whether or not there is, during a limited period, a small return to the use of additional labor.

Analysis of the firm and the demand for inputs usually starts with the assumption that firms are homogeneous, and as the economic analyst of the business firm then moves on to adapt to the more realistic cases, so should we. Variation in size among cultivators' holdings and variation in size among cultivators' families means that there are farms on which the marginal productivity of labor is positive while there are other farms on which it is actually zero. In the village there are larger and more efficient holdings with a year-round demand for labor. The marginal productivity of labor is always greater than zero, and these farms hire permanent servants, usually for a share of the produce or a fixed payment in kind but sometimes for a cash wage. There are other holdings where additional labor will add to the produce of the farm during specific, limited periods but at other times will contribute nothing. These are the farms that hire transient labor, local labor seasonally, or recall relatives from the city for the harvest season. This situation arises because the farm is a little too large for the cultivator and his co-resident relatives at peak demand, either because the family is small, the holding is large, or the number of relatives who have found city residence is large. The third group of holdings are the very small ones, where the marginal productivity of labor is always zero or less than zero. The peasants on these farms do not hire labor, and furthermore, were two or three of these peasant families somehow to combine, one could disappear and the total product would not fall. Since these people are not impelled to move, the productivity of labor remains low.

All three such types of holdings exist in U.P., with the result that the marginal productivity of rural labor is close to zero and there are opportunities to earn wages on farms. There remains the question of whether the "disguised unemployment" on small holdings is greater than the peak demand for agricultural labor on the larger farms. The argument that all the people in the village are employed during the peak season—if accepted as an accurate observation, although this writer doubts that it is—implies that the more efficient, larger holdings require the services of cultivators from the smaller holdings. What appears to be more likely, especially when the large number of very small holdings is considered, is that the underemployment is indeed disguised; that jobs are provided for the landless and the transient, and the small holder does not use his time or equipment fully.

A final way in which apparent full employment combined with zero marginal productivity can exist is by shifting the burden onto the worker. This occurs when the worker is employed at piece rates.[29] The same total product could be gathered by a smaller work force in the same number of days, but the employing landholder permits as many as wish to gather the harvest, thus spreading the marginal zero return among the whole number of casual laborers.

To account in social terms for the existence of remunerative rural labor when productivity approaches zero is not difficult. The village system outlined in Chapter 2 continues to operate, albeit in modified and disappearing form, and it obligates the cultivators to provide support for the landless laborers in the village. Until the end of the thirties and the inflation of wartime, the ties that bound the client laboring families to the landholding leaders of the village retained sufficient vitality to assure a living to people who in a completely business-minded economy would have found themselves unemployed. Variations are found in different parts of the province, the rule being that the nearer to a town or the more effectively connected by road or rail with urban centers the more completely has the older village system disappeared. However, even in those cases in which the village has been largely changed by the proximity of a town, one still finds elements of the older village system.[30] The ties of mutual obligation and support take several forms, the strongest of which is kinship. Less strong are the patron-client relationships, often but mistakenly called "feudal." In addition, there is the unity of mutual self-interest and enmity toward others which characterizes factions within the village. The superior feels that he must support those who are loyal to him, whether as family head, patron, or faction leader. If he must provide for those under him, then he has no incentive to rationalize his economic operations. In effect, the followers must be paid in any case; to spread the load makes life easier and appears equitable.[d]

There is evidence to confirm the economist's reasoning. "A sort of survey" conducted by the Provincial Congress Committee in 1931 convinced the Committee that agricultural production could not even meet the costs of production.[31] The Committee attempted a computation of total costs of production and gross income for a typical cultivator, shown in Table 9. Before rents are admitted to the picture, expenses exceed cost of cultivation. The inclusion in expenses of food, clothing, and housing to represent labor costs shows that the cultivator earns less than enough to keep himself and his family alive for the full period of human life. In

d. For a more detailed discussion of intra-village relationships, see Chap. 10, Sec. 3, below.

TABLE 9. *Value of Outturn and Cost of Production*
on an Average Holding

Division	Value of produce (Rs.)	Cultivators' expenses (Rs.)	Surplus available (+) for rent and irrigation charges or deficit (−) before meeting such charges (Rs.)
Meerut	163.8	139.1	+ 24.7
Jhansi	59.5	127.8	− 68.3
Gorakhpur	86.8	141.6	− 54.8
Lucknow	63.3	130.1	− 66.8

Source. *Agrarian Distress in the U.P.*, p. 35.

some cases and in some districts, the marginal productivity of labor may not be zero, but as the above figures are averages, the marginal productivity of labor must be lower. The Zamindari Abolition Committee said that "according to available information, if the wages of labour at prevailing rates were included in the cost of production, the cost would in many cases exceed the value of the product."[32] Since the returns to a factor tend to equal that factor's marginal revenue product, the returns to rural labor in U.P. tend toward zero. Rents are not too high—returns to labor are too low. As long as the rural population increases as fast as or faster than the supply of the cooperating factors of land and capital, the population of rural U.P. will remain in distressed conditions.

Evidence in the *Report on Agriculture in the U.P.* presented to the Royal Commission on Indian Agriculture strongly supports this view. Table 10 shows four ways in which the prosperity or material welfare of the cultivators might be increased: a rise in price, an increase in outturn, an increase in the size of the holding, and a decrease in rent. As with many figures found in Indian sources, it is difficult to tell just what these figures represent. They are not figures of physical productivity, nor are they figures of gross income. They are figures of "surplus" left to the cultivator after the payment of his necessary expenses, and the basis of the necessary expenses includes not only such objectively computable figures as cost of seeds or irrigation, but such subjective elements as minimum clothing for the family.

Two characteristics of the figures are outstanding. First, a small fall in rents would have very little beneficial effect for the culti-

TABLE 10. *Possible Increases in Cultivators' Prosperity (in percentages)*

	Due to a 5 per cent increase in price received by cultivator (e.g. due to cooperative marketing)			Due to a 5 per cent increase in outturn (e.g. from improved seeds)		
		Increase in net surplus of an:			Increase in net surplus of an:	
	Increase in surplus	Occupancy tenant	Nonoccupancy tenant	Increase in surplus	Occupancy tenant	Nonoccupancy tenant
Meerut	7	8	10	10	12	15
Jhansi	9	13	14	17	24	25
Gorakhpur	12	17	18	30	44	46
Lucknow	8	—	12	16	—	24

	Due to a 5 per cent increase in the size of a holding				Due to a 5 per cent decrease in rent	
			Increase in net surplus of an:		Decrease in net surplus of an:	
	Increase in surplus per holding	Increase in surplus per acre	Occupancy tenant	Nonoccupancy tenant	Occupancy tenant	Nonoccupancy tenant
Meerut	10	5	11	12	1	2
Jhansi	17	11	21	23	3	3
Gorakhpur	30	24	41	44	2	3
Lucknow	16	10	—	21	—	2

Source. *Report on Agriculture in U.P.*, p. 119. For an explanation of the meaning of these figures see the accompanying text.

Note. The *Report* says that it is possible that outturn per acre could not be maintained in Muzaffarnagar with holdings of 17 acres, but in the above cases, especially Gorakhpur with an average of 4.2 acres, the holdings are below the economic level.

vator; compared with other changes, the benefits can be described as negligible. Second, the benefits to the cultivator of a given percentage increase in the size of his holding or in the capital at his disposal would be much larger than an equal percentage change in the price of his outturn. The cultivator stands to gain far more from increasing the factors of production cooperating with labor than he does from any financial or legislative improvement in his situation. And this brings us back to the original thesis that the problem is one of the capital-labor ratio and not of social injustice or unfair exploitation by the zamindar.

Table 10 lends support to our thesis in one more way. Gorakhpur in the east is the most heavily populated of the divisions, and it would benefit the most from an improvement in the land-and-capital-to-man ratio, while the low returns from a reduction in rents indicate that the overpopulation problem is physical, not financial.

FLUCTUATIONS IN PRICES

If we cannot attribute the vicissitudes of U.P. to the high level of rents, there remains one other possibility: fluctuations in prices. Instability of prices is perhaps the best of the unsatisfactory explanations. We shall examine here the classic case of the Great Depression of the early 1930s. The effect of the sharp and sudden fall in prices beginning in 1930 was very painful, but that disaster hit the cultivator after a long period of development, during which much tenancy legislation was passed to alleviate the cultivator's burdens and after agriculture had already started upon its period of stagnation and decline. In short, the explanation seizes upon an event that came too late to be the cause of chronic agricultural distress.

There is an important contrast between the Great Depression in the West and in India. In the West the Great Depression coincided with the breakdown of a functioning market system and with the growth of rigidities in the markets. In India the market had never functioned properly, and there were few signs of market rigidities or "stickiness." Had there been industrial and commercial alternatives in India there is reason to believe that the market would have worked successfully throughout the Depression, and an examination of rural and urban incomes and the productivity of capital indicates that industrial progress was quite possible in India during this period. In the West the Depression brought suffering to the farmer because it lowered the prices of his output and prevented him from finding alternative employment in the industrial centers since it had already created unemployment in these centers. In U.P. the cultivator suffered because the market system had never provided him with alternatives.

This contrast in the market positions of the West and India may also account for the differing effects of the Depression and the differing reactions to it. In the West the effect was widespread unemployment in industry and distress in rural areas, and the reaction was a modified form of planning and the employment of Keynesian fiscal policies. In India the effect was not appreciable in industry, and the rural areas reverted to production for subsistence and maintained living standards by borrowing.[33] While it is also true that the Western economies had developed sufficiently to bear the burden of the Depression and India had not, India was not required to bear the same kind of burden, nor, relative to its pre-Depression prosperity, so large a burden.

The effect of the Depression on agricultural incomes may be seen in Table 11. Between 1921–22 and 1931–32 the value of agricultural produce fell by almost two-thirds and had not recovered very much seven years later. Almost all farm produce in the province was either food or fodder. In some countries a fall in agricultural prices can be misleading because the farmer lives upon the actual produce and not upon the price of the produce, but there is danger in adopting this argument in U.P. There is a good deal of truth in it, but in order to pay their rents and debt charges the cultivators had to market part of their produce at harvest time and buy it back later at higher prices to feed themselves and to acquire seeds for the next planting. As a result, prices at harvest time were depressed. Since all prices declined in the Depression to a new level, the fact remains that, being close to a subsistence level, the real incomes of the cultivators did not decline by nearly so much as two-thirds. As Table 12 shows, rural incomes in real terms dropped by only 15 per cent from 1921 to 1939, while agricultural income proper had dropped less than a fifth by 1932, and fell further in the next few years to a quarter below its pre-Depression level by 1939. The latter drop, however, took place during a period of partial revival from the depths of the Depression, and must therefore be regarded as an indication of agricultural decline and not as an effect of the Depression.

TABLE 11. *Provincial Income* and Its Distribution among Various Occupations*

Occupation and Year	Number of earners including earner-equivalents of working dependents and of subsidiary workers (in thousands)	Estimated income (Rs. millions)	Estimated income as a percentage of total income (%)	Estimated income at 1921–22 prices† (Rs. millions)	Income per earner (Rs.)	Income per earner at 1921–22 prices (Rs.)	Index of real income per earner (1921–22 = 100)	Percentage of earners engaged in each classification (%)
1	2	3	4	5	6	7	8	9
1921–22								
Agriculture, pasture, hunting and fishing	15,660	3,122	64.3	3,122	199.4	199.4	100.0	78.7
Industry	2,540	619	12.7	619	243.8	243.8	100.0	12.8
Services, including trade, transport, government, professions, and domestic service	1,680	903	18.6	903	537.5	537.5	100.0	8.4
Total or average	19,880	4,644	95.6	4,644	244.3	244.3	100.0	99.9
1931–32								
Agriculture, etc.	15,850	1,219	49.9	2,595	76.9	163.6	82.0	74.7
Industry	3,140	376	15.4	801	119.8	254.9	104.5	14.8
Services, etc.	2,250	567	23.2	1,205	251.8	535.7	99.7	10.6
Total or average	21,240	2,162	88.5	4,601	115.2	245.1	100.3	100.1
1938–39								
Agriculture, etc.	17,220	1,302	43.8	2,553	75.6	148.2	74.3	75.1
Industry	3,180	465	15.6	913	146.4	287.1	117.8	13.9
Services, etc.	2,510	813	27.3	1,594	324.0	635.3	118.2	11.0
Total or average	22,920	2,581	86.7	5,060	129.8	254.5	104.2	100.0

*Allowing for underestimation of income assessed to income tax. Thus industry and service figures increase more rapidly over the years than they otherwise would.

†Using Tiwari's adjusted price index of 1921–22: 100; 1931–32: 47; 1938–39: 51.

Source. Tiwari, Table 122 facing p. 266, for Cols. 1, 2, 3, 4, 6, 7, 8; Table 121, p. 265 for Col. 9; Table 120, p. 264 for "Total or average" lines.

Note. Total net provincial incomes given by Tiwari, Table 117 facing p. 260 were: 1921–22: Rs. 48,571.9 lakhs; 1931–32: Rs. 24,450.2 lakhs; 1938–39: Rs. 29,742.6 lakhs. It is not apparent who received the income here unaccounted for.

TABLE 12. *Income Per Capita and Per Earner in Urban and Rural U.P.*

Year and class	Income per capita	Index of prices	Real income per capita		Income per earner or equivalent	Real income per earner or equivalent	
			In 1921–22 prices	Index (1921–22 = 100)		In 1921–22 prices	Index (1921–22 = 100)
	(Rs.)	(%)	(Rs.)	(%)	(Rs.)	(Rs.)	(%)
1921–22							
Province	107	100	107	100			
Urban	222	100	222	100	574	574	100
Rural	91	100	91	100	205	205	100
1931–32							
Province	51	47	108	101			
Urban	133	47	283	127	311	662	115
Rural	37	47	79	87	83	177	86
1938–39							
Province	56	51	110	103			
Urban	145	51	284	128	371	727	127
Rural	39	51	76	84	89	175	85

Note. Figures allow for underestimation in income assessed to income tax. If underestimation is not allowed for, real income in urban areas is lower in 1938–39 than in 1931–32, but the urban–rural relationship is unchanged.

Source. Tiwari, Table 119, p. 262 for provincial figures and Tables 126, 127, pp. 270–71 for other figures.

The burden of the Depression fell upon the rural areas, and particularly upon agriculture. This was partly a result of the world-wide drop in the price of agricultural produce and the shift in the terms of trade in favor of urban areas and manufacturing countries, but it was also partly a result of the general decline of agriculture in U.P. The severity of the crisis was caused not so much by a decline in real incomes, or even by the shift of real incomes from rural to urban areas, as by the financial squeeze exerted upon the cultivator. His rents had been negotiated during the period of prosperity and rising prices in the first third of the century, and after the fall in prices the real burden of rent and debt charges increased greatly. It was inability to adjust to this sudden and cruel financial pressure that made the lot of the cultivator miserable.

The fall in prices in the first few months of the Depression was remarkably sharp. From December 1929 to December 1930, the Congress party reported that wheat prices fell from Rs. 5.52 per maund to Rs. 2.64; barley from Rs. 3.90 per maund to Rs. 1.60; gram from Rs. 5.52 per maund to Rs. 2.61; and rice from Rs. 7.62 per maund to Rs. 3.91.[34] The U.P. government index number of retail prices fell from 191 in January 1930, to 102 in January 1931. The price of rice fell 36.2 per cent, of wheat 43.1 per cent, and of gram 48.2 per cent.[35] Both sets of figures[e] show prices halved within a year, and there must have been a heavy increase in the real burden of rents, which accounts for the strains and open conflicts of the period.

Less weight can be given to the suffering caused by price changes in explaining the stagnation of agriculture over a longer period. Quinquennial averages of index numbers from 1881–85 to 1921–25 show increases for each quinquennium except 1901–05, the rise from 100 in 1881–85 reaching 300 in the triennium 1926–28.[36] Annual price series for the years after the First World War show a peak in 1920–22 well above the average for the rest of the twenties, but prices in 1929 and in 1930 were higher than in 1923. The twenties show a decline from postwar prices, but taking one year with another the trend of prices immediately before and during the period of agricultural stagnation was upward, and if not upward in the latter years, was certainly not downward. After the 1931–32 trough there was a slow but steady rise in prices until

e. Misra, pp. 218–19, gives figures for the period 1928–33 that agree more closely with the Congress than the U.P. government figures.

the war; during and after the Second World War prices rose
rapidly, so that by 1947 the official price of wheat was Rs. 12.3
per maund; of gram, Rs. 13.1 per maund; and of rice, Rs. 17.8 per
maund; while the open market price of wheat was Rs. 12.5 per
maund and of rice Rs. 18.5 per maund.[f]

More striking evidence of the inability of fluctuations in price
to explain the long-run failure of the market may be found in the
index numbers of prices, rents, and revenue demand (Table 13).

TABLE 13. *Index Numbers of Prices, Rents, and Revenues in U.P.*

Years	Wholesale prices	Rents of stable tenants	Rents of ordinary tenants	Revenue demand
1901–05	100	100	100	100
1920–24	221	115	137	108
1924–29	220	120	149	109
1930–34	122	121	163	112

Source. Computed from yearly figures in Misra, Appendix A, pp. 260–61.

The wholesale index number for the years 1931–35 (instead of
1930–34) is lower at 112, but the interesting information contained
in Table 13 relates to the earlier courses of prices and rents. Up
to the Depression the prices received by the cultivators rose more
than their rents, and it must be remembered that after the first
blow of the crisis, the government reduced rents to the level existing at the beginning of the century. All told, the price movements
of the twenties and thirties were insufficient or came too late to
account for the chronic distress in rural U.P. Table 13 also supports the argument that it was not the high level of land revenue
that caused the stagnation.

Surprisingly enough, the sharp fall in the prices of agricultural
produce in the thirties did not hurt agricultural cooperative societies, although it slowed their growth.[37] Beginning in 1930, new
loans fell and by 1932 had reached a trough well below half the
pre-Depression level, recovering to their old level by 1938. At the

f. Misra, pp. 260–61 and *Seasonal and Crop Reports of the United Provinces
of Agra and Oudh, 1919–20—1946–47.* The same pattern is shown in the index
numbers for cereals and pulses in Calcutta for 1923 and 1929, although 1930
Calcutta prices for cereals were lower than 1923 prices, perhaps because Calcutta markets reflected the decline in world market prices more rapidly than
did markets in interior cities. See Vera Anstey, *The Economic Development of
India*, pp. 493–94.

same time the amount overdue rose by about 70 per cent; it fell again to the old proportion of 30 to 40 per cent of total loans by 1939, but from 1932 to 1935 the societies had strengthened their financial position by recovering more each year than they lent. Since the fall in new loans reflected a lower price level as well as the worsened position of agriculture, the contraction in real terms was not as great as the money figures indicate. Rs. 20 lakhs would buy a lot more equipment in the thirties than it would have bought in the twenties. The financial position of the cooperatives was maintained throughout the Depression and improved rapidly after 1935. Profits as a percentage of working capital were as high in the thirties as in the twenties, while working capital did not fall below 96.8 per cent of its 1929 level. During the worst part of the Depression the amount of capital owned by the cooperatives increased, and it first exceeded 50 per cent of total capital in 1932. It is hard to draw any firm conclusions from these facts because the cooperative movement was so small. The total working capital never amounted to as much as eight annas per cultivated acre in U.P., and the loans outstanding never amounted to more than five annas per cultivated acre. Nevertheless, it is fair to say that the cooperatives showed that a properly run economic organization was capable of earning profits and expanding despite the Depression. It is a longer step in reasoning, and one not so safe, to say that one cause of their success was that they were extending credit for productive purposes and that the shortage of capital equipment in rural U.P. was so great that the productivity of capital was large enough to overcome the worst the Depression had to offer.

The course of the Great Depression in U.P. looks very like the course of that Depression throughout the world, yet in other areas economic development, though it received a setback, was not brought to a halt. The risks of the market were common to all economies integrated on market principles. The crisis of 1929–34 could explain the troubles of U.P. only if it had had similar results in areas where the market mechanism had been successful in developing the economy. We are still faced with our original problem of how other places could organize their economies around a market and develop, while in U.P. there was always the feeling that the market was not achieving results, even during the period of slow development.

CHAPTER 10

Why the Market Failed:
The Right Reasons

1. IMPERFECTIONS IN THE MARKET

None of the foregoing explanations of the failure of the market to function efficiently is convincing. To see why it did not create prosperity we must look beyond the land market to the logic of the market system itself. An efficient market for factors of production directs them into the uses in which they are most profitable, and therefore in which they will bring the greatest material returns to the society. If a market for factors is to work successfully there must be *alternative* uses for the factors, which means that all the factor markets must mesh. The trouble in U.P. was that alternatives were lacking because the land market was not related to a properly functioning capital market. In a monetarized

market economy the money market allocates capital resources, but
in India the money market was so disorganized as barely to be a
money market at all. In U.P., which has no industrial and financial center such as Calcutta or Bombay, the money market was
even more rudimentary. In consequence, substitutability of land
and capital was never achieved. Furthermore, the cultivator was
only imperfectly connected with the market for agricultural produce; to a great extent he was producing for consumption and not
for sale.[a] Even when the cultivator had to sell a large proportion
of his produce right after the harvest, he sold to the village mahajan, local money-lender, or grain merchant, who might in the
course of the year simply carry the produce and sell it back to the
cultivator. These local transactions appeared to be independent
of the large urban markets. A glance at the prices given in the
appendices of the *Seasonal and Crop Reports of the United Provinces* will make it amply clear that prices in one area were completely unrelated to prices in another. In the central districts prices
of the same food varied by more than two-to-one in different
places, and prices of the same food in the outlying Himalayan
tracts might be a quarter or six times the prices in the central
districts. "Price" was a highly localized phenomenon.

Reference to Table 3 (p. 145) showing "Outturn as a Percentage
of Normal" and Table 14 showing "Farm Income in U.P." will
illustrate the poor response of agriculture to the price mechanism.
There was an absolute increase in the amount of sugar cane produced, and an increase in the amount of wheat produced relative
to the other crops, while there was a sharp decline in production
of barley, gram, and "other" crops. Yet the sharpest decline in

a. "As a way of life Indian agriculture has made for immobility and many
incentives have failed to evoke the normal responses. . . . When the bulk of
food grown is intended for consumption at the site of production, it is difficult
to apply the ordinary price incentives to the same effect" *(Eastern Economist,*
Aug. 15, 1952, p. 248). See also my "Economic Accounting and Family Farming
in India" for a full discussion of the issue. In addition, in a survey of eight
villages in western U.P. (P. K. Mukherjee and S. C. Gupta, *A Pilot Survey of
Fourteen Villages in U.P. and Punjab,* p. 80) it was found that from one-half
to two-thirds of food consumed by the sample families (166 including 23 with
no agricultural occupation and 47 with a nonagricultural primary occupation)
was produced by the consuming family. A survey of another village in western
U.P. (S. C. Gupta, *An Economic Survey of Shamaspur Village,* pp. 63, 64, 124)
shows marketings of agricultural produce varying from 19 per cent of output
for the smallest cultivators to 35 per cent for the largest—about a quarter for
the village as a whole—while 85 per cent of the wage payments were in kind.

TABLE 14. *Farm Income in U.P.*

	1921–22				1931–32				1938–39			
Crops	Acreage (000 acres)	Output (000 tons)	Price (Rs. per ton)	Value (Rs. millions)	Acreage (000 acres)	Output (000 tons)	Price (Rs. per ton)	Value (Rs. millions)	Acreage (000 acres)	Output (000 tons)	Price (Rs. per ton)	Value (Rs. millions)
1	2	3	4	5	6	7	8	9	10	11	12	13
Principal food crops:												
Rice	6,814	2,320	242	5,614	6,554	1,989	110	2,189	7,663	1,975	113	2,232
Wheat	6,609	2,673	174	4,651	7,784	2,610	70	1,827	8,371	2,642	80	2,114
Barley	4,304	2,052	87	1,785	4,049	1,607	49	787	3,900	1,182	65	768
Gram	6,058	2,114	137	2,896	5,686	1,560	57	889	5,529	1,481	82	1,214
Sugar cane	1,152	1,116	270	3,013	1,576	2,199	61	1,346	1,628	2,167	126	2,730
Other	7,419	2,018	144*	2,902	6,884	1,712	47*	812	6,355	1,336	66*	876
Total food crops	32,356	12,293	—	20,862	32,533	11,667	—	7,849	33,446	10,783	—	9,935
Other principal crops				2,074				659				418
Total principal crops				22,937				8,509				10,352
Fruits				990				496				593
Fodder crops				6,409				2,534				3,521
All other crops				3,974				1,198				1,807
Grand total				34,309				12,736				16,274
Deduct: wastage, seed, Interest and maintenance of land, bullocks, and equipment				9,223				4,281				7,059
Net agricultural income				25,087				8,455				9,215
Value of livestock products				5,820				3,602				3,624
Total net farm income				30,907				12,057				12,839

*Computed from Cols. *3, 5, 7, 9, 11, 13* as appropriate.

Source: Tiwari, Table 32, p. 90; Table 35, p. 94; Table 42, p. 103; Table 50, p. 114; Table 117, facing p. 260.

price was that recorded for sugar, and the most stable price was that of barley. The price of gram did not decline appreciably more than the price of wheat. There is no apparent connection between price and production of one crop or another. After the Second World War there was a rise in the amount of rice produced relative to other foods, and this may have been connected with the postwar rise in price, but in the crucial period of the twenties and thirties prices were not directing production.

Dr. Misra's survey of a village in Kanpur points to the same conclusion (Table 15). The discrepancies in profitability are re-

TABLE 15. *Profit Per Acre with Different Crops*

(*R. B. Misra's Survey*)

	Jowar (Rs.)	Wheat (Rs.)	Gram (Rs.)
Gross value of total produce	65.00	66.00	28.00
Expenses of agriculture	11.38	38.25	17.50
Rent	12.00	20.00	10.00
Profit	41.62	7.75	0.50

Source. Z.A.C. *Report*, p. 31.

markable. One wonders why anyone grew any gram, or even wheat. If these figures correctly state the net returns available on the crops, price was almost totally ineffective in organizing production.

Mr. Brij Lal, the registration officer for the United Provinces in the 1920s, discovered that the general level of prices and the number of registrations of property transfers were very closely related. Correlating the movements in prices and the number of registrations, he found a coefficient of correlation of .76 ± .06. He attributed this relationship to the fact that when prices are low people have less need to mortgage or sell their property.[1] One would expect activity on the market for a factor of production to reflect increased earning power of that asset, not the threat of a decrease in the standard of living of the owners of the factor, yet the latter relationship is clearly indicated by the high correlation found by Mr. Brij Lal.

The absence of a meshing, a gearing, an interrelatedness between the markets has a physical and an institutional aspect. On the physical side there was a lack of transport facilities, making hypothetical any price in a market to which there were no roads from a village. When markets are too small to guarantee a continuous supply of food to cultivators who sell their produce, the cultivators will choose to grow for their own needs for fear they will starve if the market supply fails. The lack of industry, which was closely connected with the rudimentary state of the money market, meant that there was no alternative employment for labor or capital outside of agriculture. In the Soviet Union a major problem in development was inducing the peasantry to move from the land to the cities and from the west to the east. England's early and magnificent success with the Industrial Revolution is attributed in part to the mobility of labor caused by the enclosure movements, which threw the rural population off the land. In India, there does not seem to be a problem of labor mobility in this classic sense. Labor will move, as is shown by the emigration from U.P. to Bombay, where a considerable proportion of the labor force is made up of emigrants from U.P., and by the movement of labor from India to Burma and back in the days before Burma was separated from India. The trouble is not that labor will not move but that there are not enough places to which it can move.

There were no institutions to mobilize the savings of the villagers except the post office banks and, after the First World War, the cooperative societies. The rural money-lenders dealt with shroffs, the indigenous bankers of the little towns, who in turn dealt with the smaller banking concerns, but none of these were closely connected with the monetary institutions of the great centers, nor did they have the knowledge or connections to channel savings into the industrial sector or into larger-scale improvements in land management. Savings tend to stay within the family group, even among the industrialists in the cities.

The lack of connection between the rural sector and the industrial and larger commercial markets is illustrated by the course of events following upon the amassing of savings within the rural sector. Typically the savings are devoted to one of three purposes: the purchase of rights in land, the purchase of jewelry, or lending, sometimes via the medium of money and sometimes in real terms. There is of course a corresponding real saving, a reduction in demand for current output on the part of the savers, but this release of resources from the satisfaction of current wants is individual, not social. The seller of land is almost invariably selling in order

to finance consumption or ceremony or in order to repay a debt.
The same is true of the seller of jewelry; while the borrower,
whether of money or of the saver's real savings in foodstuffs, is
usually borrowing in order to finance current consumption. Even
in exceptional cases where the seller of land or jewelry or the
borrower is not in immediate need there is not likely to be an
increase in aggregate savings, for the "surplus" available for real
investment will at a later stage in the series of transactions find
its way into the hands of someone who wants to consume. At no
point does control over real savings come into the hands of people
or groups who in the normal course of their business would devote
it to creating capital. This is what is meant by the absence of a
meshing between the activities of the villagers and the market for
capital. The result is "the unbalanced occupational distribution of
. . . population, the decay of cottage industries, and the consequent
increase in the pressure on land" which the Zamindari Abolition
Committee found the "main reasons for the poverty of the country."[2]

The reasons why there were no satisfactory alternative uses for
factors in the industrial and commercial spheres is a question beyond the compass of a history of the market for land. No doubt
commercial policy had something to do with it. No doubt the failure of the British to develop a money market in the same way that
they created land and labor markets had something to do with it.
In addition, the composition of Indian society was doubtless an
important element. The engineering tradition was absent, and
many people have made much of the lack of a middle class in the
Western sense. The essential point is clear: that India did not
produce any appreciable number of entrepreneurs, did not produce a group of industrial capitalists or any substitute for them.
Whatever the reason, there was no alternative to the land. When
rents rise to the value of the marginal productivity of land, the
next step should be an increase in the quantity of land and of
substitutes for land, but in the absence of money and industrial
capital markets there was no mechanism to make this secondary
reaction to the rise in rents effective.

The inability of the market mechanism to organize and force
the pace of development, combined with its ability to achieve limited results, was a major cause of the failure of tenancy legislation.
Harvey Leibenstein asserts that "a lack of adequate non-agricultur-
al employment opportunities lies at the very root of the economic

development problem."[3] There was the same lack of opportunity to invest outside of agriculture; and what changes and events did take place outside of agriculture had little effect on the conduct of agricultural operations. Toward the end of British rule, activities in the towns did have consequences in the rural sector—the growth of cane cultivation in northern U.P. to supply the new mills, the growth of cotton cultivation in Gujarat to supply the textile industry, jute cultivation in Bengal to supply the Calcutta and Dundee mills, and belts of commercial vegetable farming and dairying around the towns—but these came late rather than early in our history. Perhaps the towns and the countryside, agriculture and industry, commerce and banking, would eventually have formed an integrated whole after a further lapse of time; but during the century and a half of intimate culture contact between Britain and its Indian Empire such developments were at most rudimentary, presaging the future, not characterizing the period.

2. LACK OF CAPITAL

Badly functioning markets are not the private preserve of India, but in more advanced countries the difficulties are not combined with a very low productivity of labor. If, for instance, land is free, as it was for a long time in the United States, the market organization of land does not work in the way the market theorem visualizes, but this failure does not create a chronic crisis. The owner of free land will not receive a differential rent and will have to acquire his income in some other way. But when labor is free, and that is the state approached in U.P., it is not possible to earn a living. In capital, land, or money markets we are dealing with inanimate things; an unproductive machine cannot riot if it is allowed to run down to scrap. In the labor market we are dealing with people, who are the focus of our interest. It is to provide these people with the means of material well-being that economies are organized, and to allow them to run down to the scrap heap defeats the entire purpose of having an economy. Substitutions of cheap land for expensive capital or cheap capital for expensive labor either leaves most people untouched or tends to increase material welfare, but the substitution of cheap labor for other more expensive factors, while economically efficient, is but a recognition of poverty and a seal on the distress of the people. The reflection of this situation in U.P. is "high" rates of interest and "high" rents, but they are really only the obverse of the low productivity of labor. Only an increase in the capital-and-land-to-man ratio will raise the productivity of labor. In reviewing the past or examining present reforms of land tenure this is the point that must be kept constantly in mind. The explanation of agrarian distress is technological, while the cause of the failure of the market to overcome the technological difficulty lies in the lack of alternative uses for labor, and capital is needed to provide the alternatives.

In general terms, the causes of agricultural stagnation and decline were overpopulation and lack of capital. Overpopulation and lack of capital are different ways of expressing the same thing. An area is only short of capital in relation to its population, and a population can only be said to be too large in relation to its supply of capital. It is for this reason that one can call India overpopulated when its population density is only half that of Britain. It is not the absolute rate of population growth that is fearsome, but the rate of growth compared with existing capital resources and the rate of growth of these resources.

It is common to express the problem as a man-to-land ratio. This is legitimate, but to lump land and capital together and to contrast them with labor is better, because land and capital are substitutable one for the other, and the ultimate objective of policy is the return to labor; that is to say, the welfare or standard of living of the people. Whereas there is no absolute limit to capital, there will ultimately be an absolute limit to land, though for the present this difference is not important. Given enough capital investment there is land that can still be brought into cultivation, while the productivity of cultivated land can be increased by the use of more capital. One need only see the terraced orchards on Italian mountainsides to appreciate the first point, or the intensity of British cultivation where, to the foreigner from a land of extensive cultivation, the farms look man-made and nature is apparently buried under centuries of manure and hedging, to appreciate the second. Bringing more land in U.P. under the plow is a matter of capital investment, as is increasing the productivity of land presently cultivated.

Although there is disagreement among economists as to the weightings that should be attached to the various circumstances which encourage or discourage economic growth, there is general agreement that an increasing supply of capital is necessary; virtually no disagreement if capital is considered any use of resources to increase future production rather than to satisfy current consumption. The support for the view that capital is crucial to increasing welfare runs through the spectrum from the orthodoxy of Nurkse ("productivity . . . is a function, in technical terms, of the capital intensity of production")[4] to the heterodoxy of Myrdal ("there is no other road to economic development than a forceful rise in the share of national income which is withheld from consumption and devoted to investment").[5] A socialist, Lewis,[6] and a Marxist, Dobb,[7] take up the same cause. Differences are to be found. Dobb says "that the largest single factor governing productivity in a country is its richness or poorness in capital instruments of production";[8] while Lewis argues that there are three "proximate causes of economic growth . . . economic activity, increasing knowledge, and increasing capital," and treats them as roughly comparable in importance.[9] But if Lewis insists on the importance of attitudes and institutions,[10] he also finds that economic growth does not occur until the proportion of income devoted to capital accumulation rises to 10 per cent or more, and that "one of the main deficiencies of underdeveloped countries is their failure to spend adequately upon research."[11]

Two objections to the emphasis on capital have been raised: that the rate of profits on investments is low in underdeveloped countries and that recent studies of growth in the United States have shown that only a small portion of the American rate of growth can be attributed to the increase in capital. Nurkse has answered the first criticism. Any appreciable increase in one kind of productive capacity will produce more than the market in a poor country can absorb without a marked fall in price and a consequent decline in profit margins, but the increment in the physical flow of goods is nevertheless large.[12] The realizable financial returns to investment in one direction will fall as investment is expanded because the relative utility of any product will drop if production of other goods and services does not expand at the same time. For this reason the return to one or a few firms or industries in an otherwise stagnant economy will understate the potential efficiency of a more general expansion of capital equipment. Moreover, in private accounts the benefits of external economies are not measured. Investment in a spinning mill or a sugar mill may not show unexpectedly high returns, but if the mills draw labor from agriculture a proper evaluation would show the increased returns to agriculture resulting from the larger size of holding cultivated by the remaining ryots. Until the Five Year Plans this was clearly the situation in India; the experience under the Plans shows as clearly that investment on a large scale is not only productive physically but also profitable when the government stands ready to buy the increasing output for its dams, factories, and other developmental schemes.

The second criticism stems from articles by Abramovitz and Solow. Abramovitz constructed indices of output and productivity based upon relative factor shares in a base period and found that only 14 per cent of the increase in American output since 1869–70 could be attributed to increases in inputs—the rest must therefore be attributed to a "rise in productivity." But it should be noted that his per capita indices show net national product rising to 397, capital to 297, and man-hours falling to 94, while the physical volume of capital increased much more rapidly than population (in the ratio of 10 : 3).[13] On these figures it could be argued that the weighting system hid the fact—if fact it be—that almost all the increase is ultimately attributable to capital.

Solow found that in the period 1909–49, seven-eighths of the increase in gross national product per capita was attributable to "technical change" and only one-eighth to the increased use of capital. However, Solow points out that "a lot of what appears as shifts in the production function must represent improvement in the quality of the labor input, and therefore a result of real capital formation of an important kind," and that "obviously much, perhaps nearly all, innovation must be embodied in new plant and equipment to be realized at all."[14]

An interesting if somewhat indirect measure of the importance of capital is found in the relationship of horsepower to productivity, for horsepower is certainly related to capital employed. The average annual rate of increase in output per man-hour in American manufacturing was 3.1 per cent from 1899 to 1949, while the increase in installed horsepower per worker was 2.8 per cent per year. There is a similar close correspondence between installed horsepower per wage earner and productivity in manufacturing industries of different countries.[15]

Finally, capital is necessary to social reorganization. There is a real, material cost to social change, and in the absence of sufficient increments to capital there will be pressure upon the standard of living; for "when there is a *change* from one type of economic and social organization and *way of life* to another, society may require resources to enable it to support itself during the process of transition and while it is engaged on acquiring the new social heritage: resources so utilized are as much 'capital' as are machinery or factory buildings or other kinds of 'saleable' property."[b]

The efficacy of capital in increasing production in India is great. During some of the Mughal period the ruler's share was a third of the crop, but on irrigated lands it was only a quarter. Since we may take it as certain that the ruler suffered no diminution of his share on account of irrigation and that the cultivator would not irrigate if he did not benefit, irrigation must have increased the productivity of land by more than a third. From Table 2 (p. 144) we may derive a measure of the amount by which produce on irrigated land exceeded produce on unirrigated land. For the period 1827–40 an irrigated acre of wheat produced 60 per cent more than an unirrigated acre, while the corresponding figure for barley was 28 per cent. For the period 1897–1921 the figure for wheat was 52 per cent and for barley 50 per cent. There are technological relationships which will further increase the productivity of water, such as that between irrigation and fertilizer: the return on investment in fertilizer and improved seeds will be higher over the years if other capital has already been invested in water storage and irrigation facilities.

A typical example of the problem that lack of capital presents is found in Bundelkhand, where "there is no better and quicker way" of increasing grain production than by the supply of tractor power. The reason is that vast areas are overrun with kans grass, which can only be eliminated by a deep plow cutting the roots two inches beneath the surface.[16] Peasant techniques are incapable of rooting out the grass. It is capital investment or nothing, and in this case the capital investment is not merely a substitute for more land but actually creates more arable land.

Rates of interest are relevant evidence of the productivity of capital. The return on borrowed money should normally be greater than the rate of interest. The notoriously high rates on interest charged on loans to cultivators are often regarded as extortion, and in so far as they are loans for consumption purposes this could easily be true. It is also probable that since some money is devoted to productive purposes the mahajans' rate of interest also reflects

b. Herbert S. Frankel, *The Economic Impact on Underdeveloped Societies*, p. 133. Italics in original.

with some accuracy the rate of interest which the productive return on capital can bear. Bengal Act X of 1859 (Section 20) subjected arrears of rent to a statutory interest charge of 12 per cent per year and this rate was used from that time on. From 1921 to 1936 the agricultural cooperative societies borrowed at 12 per cent and lent at 15 per cent. These rates fell to 9 and 12 per cent in 1937 and to 6 and 9 per cent in 1941, but there is no reason to believe that the productivity of capital fell in those years, and by 1950 the rates charged by cooperatives were again 12 to 15 per cent.[17] The figures hide variations. In 1939 the borrowing rates of cooperatives varied from 8 to 12 per cent and the lending rates from 7 to 15 per cent. When cooperative societies paid dividends, and the well-run ones consistently did, the dividend was 10 per cent. The lower figures already cited for profits include all the badly managed and bankrupt societies.[18] The interest rates paid and charged by cooperative societies probably understate the productivity of their loans. The aim of the cooperative society is to charge its membership lower rates than they would have to pay elsewhere, but high enough to discourage reckless borrowing, to cover the cost of management and bad debts, and to build up the society's surplus.[19] This is a modification of the "strict cooperative principle that all services rendered to members should be charged at cost."[20] The rates of interest fixed by cooperatives have aimed at being "sound" but below the money-lenders' rates.[21] This means that while cooperative societies' rates have not been cheap in the sense of uneconomic or containing an element of subsidy, the rates have tended to follow the cost of supply rather than the demand for credit, so that it is fair to assume that higher rates could have been charged and borne.

During the Depression, real income in the rural areas of the United Provinces fell, while in the urban areas it rose despite the world-wide Depression.[c] Although part of the increase can be attributed to shifts in the terms of trade between town and country, the greater part of the relative prosperity in the towns was due to their industrial and commercial nature.[d] If urban or industrial

c. See Tables 11, 12, and 14.
d. The standard of living of those engaged in industry appears to have improved during the Depression years, while in the rural areas the effect was an adaptation toward subsistence crops while the standard of living was maintained by using up capital and increasing indebtedness (Anstey, *The Economic Development of India*, p. 551).

development of the U.P. were greater, average income would rise
and the average real income of the rural areas would rise too, quite
possibly by more than the rise in the towns, for then the productivity of labor on the land would rise simply because there would
be less labor in the fields.

General indications, such as the high rate of interest paid and
received by cooperative societies, the 12 per cent rate of interest
legislatively enacted for arrears of rent and revenue, and the success of cooperative business lending during the thirties,[e] as well
as specific cases, such as the babar and tarai lands lying below the
Himalayas awaiting drainage, could be multiplied. These are examples of physical relationships and not of legislative unfairness,
social injustice, or the exploitation of the tenant by the zamindar.

The Five Year Plans provide further evidence about the productivity of capital in India. The Planning Commission computed
a capital-output ratio (the number of rupees of investment needed
to create an income stream of one rupee) of 1.8 for the period of
the First Plan and believes that the rate during the Second and
Third Plan periods will be on the order of 2.3 and 2.6.[22] These
ratios are lower, meaning a higher productivity of capital, than the
ratios 3 to 4 suggested as typical by W. Arthur Lewis.[23]

The figures for the marginal return on capital are surprisingly
high. It is probably true that the return to capital employed by
any one firm or industry would be lower and decline more rapidly,
and that these high figures presuppose development throughout
the economy. Studies of marginal capital-output ratios for major
industries by George Rosen show capital productivity varying
from 20 per cent to 59 per cent.[24] However, other computations
by Wilfred Malenbaum indicate ratios of 3.3 to 5.[25] But such computations from historical data do not invalidate the argument
that development plans can operate on the assumption of high
returns to capital.

This explanation of the failure of the market is not an indict-
ment of British policy. It is hard to believe that anyone else would
have adopted better policies during the period of British rule, and
even if one concedes the unlikely possibility that India left to
itself would have forced the pace of industrialization, it is even
harder to see how Britain could have done so without bringing
more calumny down upon its head than it did. While it is always

e. See above, Chap. 8.

possible that if things had been different, then things would have been different, nothing in the record indicates that the hindsight of twentieth-century scholarship would have been given practical effect in the nineteenth century if the Indian subcontinent had been left to itself.[f]

3. SOCIAL STRUCTURE

Perhaps as important as the lack of capital, perhaps underlying the lack of capital and the failure to develop a system of markets, was the structure of family and village ties. The relationships, values, and loyalties that existed before the advent of the British have not disappeared today,[g] and these standards of behavior are different from the standards of public morality and economic behavior on which the Western economic system rests.

The trial of a case in court or the discovery of fact by judicial process assumes that the witnesses giving evidence will, as a rule, tell the truth. They do not, of course, assume that the witnesses know the truth nor that interested parties will be honest, but the processes do assume that there are disinterested parties and that a witness will tell the truth as he sees it if he is not deeply involved in the outcome. The existence of persons whose word can be accepted also acts to lessen the probability that interested parties will lie, for the stories of the interested parties will need to conform as closely as possible to those of the disinterested if they are to be believed. Furthermore, it is not impossible to sort the true from the false when there is a good deal of the truth known.

In India the necessary conditions are not fulfilled. First, it is hard to find disinterested people who know about the matters in dispute. The Indian ryot looks upon his extended family as the group to which he owes the highest obligation and from which he expects the fullest support. Whenever there is a choice between the family and some group outside the family, the ryot will choose

f. This of course completely begs the question of whether India would have been left to itself if the British had not been there. The author doubts it.

g. Thomas O. Beidelman, *A Comparative Analysis of the Jajmani System,* constitutes one large body of evidence that the complex relations outlined in Chap. 3 ("Before the British") still existed at the end of the British period. See also McKim Marriott, "Western Medicine in a Village of Northern India," in Benjamin D. Paul, ed., *Health, Culture, and Community,* pp. 244–45.

to support his family without reservation.[h] He adopts a similar if weaker attitude toward his village caste[1] or faction.

In the West we recognize the strength of the family bond, but there is a difference in degree so great as to be a difference in kind. The wife cannot testify against her husband in Anglo-American law, and a jury will assume that a spouse, parent, or child would be willing to perjure himself to save a loved one. But this assumption does not extend beyond the immediate family: cousins, second cousins, and in-laws are not included within the protected group, certainly not one's servants or banker. The traditional social structure makes no provision for loyalty to the national state or to general standards of public behavior, but it is these more general loyalties that are essential to the functioning of a contract economy.[1]

The size of the "family" would not be an insurmountable barrier even when there are as many as a hundred members of a family in a local area, for there may be twenty times that number outside the family. But family loyalty extends beyond those related by blood or marriage. If the family is a leading family in an area it will have many followers and hangers-on. These people will be willing to perjure themselves in the interest of the family. Conversely, the leading family will support its followers whenever they become involved in trouble. Were there a large number of groups of families-and-followers there would be disinterested people whose testimony would constitute a foundation of truth, but there are not enough groups because the different groups tend to coalesce into factions, with the result that everybody in a village will owe allegiance to one of two or three factions.[2] When a member of Faction A brings a case against a member of Faction B considerations of balance of power and future favors to be won or lost will be sufficiently strong to assure that all members of Faction C will be interested parties and cannot be counted on to tell the truth. The result is that there are no sources of impartial information available to the official trying a case. "The Villagers are generally so connected, directly or indirectly, by ties of blood, marriage, or interest, with both sets of combatants, that plenty

h. An important exception occurs when a deeply felt cleavage splits a family. In such cases the two parts of the family lead opposing factions and the fight becomes as permanent a feature of family relations as was the preceding loyalty.

i. See J. S. Furnivall, *Colonial Policy and Practice,* pp. 303–11, for a discussion of the problem in a Burmese context.

can be found to confuse the traces, while none are concerned to stop this interference with the course of justice."[3] Each person who knows about the case will favor either the plaintiff or the defendant and will testify accordingly.[j]

If testimony were slanted this way or that by every witness, it should still be possible to get at the truth of the matter if the testimony, limited and twisted as it might be, were still not false; but this is not the case. The witnesses will falsify without limit, even without consistency. It is no solution to disregard obviously perjured or inconsistent testimony, for in many, perhaps most cases, that is the only testimony there is.[k] The way to discover the truth in India is not through legal procedure.[l]

Families-with-followers and factions account for the lack of disinterested witnesses. To account for the freedom with which interested witnesses falsify and for the ease with which such disinterested witnesses as there are can be suborned, we must recognize the structures of loyalties and of ethical standards in India. These structures are family centered and, through the family, they are caste, faction, and village centered. As far as the villagers' interpersonal and intergroup relationships are concerned, since there is no concept of loyalty to the state or to a larger society, there is no loyalty to the organs of law enforcement, nor does an abstract ethic of truthfulness for the sake of truthfulness outweigh the ethic of family and faction unity. In the Western state the citizen recognizes obligations that override his obligations to his immediate family. A parent is not expected to help a son evade conscription, falsify a tax return, or commit perjury. It is everywhere believed that there are circumstances in which a man must surrender the interests of his immediate group to the interests of a larger body of which his group is but a small part, so emotions in India and the West are not different—but they are directed toward

j. Professor McKim Marriott (letter of July 19, 1958) says that there are "disinterested witnesses to start with, but that the plaintiff and defendant, or police, bring to court only the well-prepared, interested ones."

k. Two books give excellent accounts of the process. One is a novel by Philip Woodruff (Philip Mason), *Call the Next Witness,* and the other an exposition of a career in the I.C.S. between the wars told in the form of a novelized biography, Penderel Moon's *Strangers in India.*

l. As *Strangers in India* and *Call the Next Witness* make clear, it may be possible to find out the true story, but not through legal processes. One must go to those whom one knows and who trust one, and they will tell the truth, but only because the truth and source thereof will not be made public.

different groups. "My country, right or wrong" reflects the same kind of attitude as "my family, right or wrong." The institution with which one stands in a crisis differs as do the orders of priority among moral imperatives, so that English legal proceedings have no moral foundation and thus no effectiveness in India. It must be emphasized that the difference in ethical attitudes toward judicial processes in India and in England is not a difference in the level of morality. Rather, it is a difference in the phrasing of moral questions and a difference in the rank ordering of noncomparable imperatives. Since the ethic of family loyalty and faction solidarity is subscribed to by all, there is no disgrace in being caught in perjury in India. In fact, a person who refused to support his group would be frowned upon by his neighbors. The voice of conscience requires false, not true, testimony. In these circumstances the corruption of the judicial process becomes a moral act.

The land law of U.P. applied to an area and population greater than that of most European states. The population of a district runs around a million today. The sole points of contact between the villager and the British in the administration were the courts and, in case of difficulties, assistant, deputy, or additional collectors. There was no meeting of minds between the villagers and the administration on the moral imperatives that must underlie any social structure. This is an exaggeration, for much of our knowledge comes from the British administrators—Mackenzie, Thomason, the Lawrences, Bennett—who did understand the society with which they dealt, but these were exceptions. Sometimes the British understood intellectually but could not bring themselves to accept Indian standards emotionally or to believe that their own system would not be accepted, since they sincerely felt it to be superior. Both the scale of operations, district and province, and the difference in outlook placed barriers between the administrative organs of enforcement of land law and the villagers who were to benefit by the system.

The Indian procedure in the settlement of disputes is to achieve a compromise, and in the absence of a compromise "the fiction of a compromise." This differs essentially from British law where decision "is defined in terms of winning or losing." When the Chamars in the village of Madhopur (studied by Bernard Cohn) met to decide a dispute, there were meetings in which people talked and talked without formal procedure or rules, but the meetings eventuated in a compromise. It is this difference in the concepts of judicial processes which caused the Indian ryot to abuse the English court system. "The way a people settles disputes is a part of its social structure and value system," argues Cohn. "In attempting to introduce British procedural law into their Indian courts, the British confronted the Indians with a situation in which there was a direct clash of the values of the two societies; and the Indians in response thought only of manipulating the new situation and did not use the courts to settle disputes but only to further them."[4]

The difficulties in enforcing tenancy legislation were increased by the absence of divergence of interest. Criminal law depends for its enforcement upon the divergence of interest between the criminal and all the rest of society, and a moral repugnance for the criminal's acts substitutes for personal antipathy. Civil law depends for its enforcement upon the divergence of interest between the persons who are to benefit and the persons who are to suffer from the legislation. It is this divergence that brings violations to the attention of the courts. In a simple situation of landlord versus tenant under a rent control law, one can count on the tenant to complain about his landlord's violation.

In U.P. there was no such simple divergence of interests. The legislators and the higher levels of the administration felt a strong moral repugnance to violations of tenancy legislation. Were they the only people involved, the land legislation could have been cast in the form of criminal law; but whether the issue was civil or criminal, the higher echelons did not know the facts of particular cases and so could not enforce their own legislation. In this situation they depended upon others to bring cases to light, but the others were not faced with simple conflict. A tenant might have had an argument over rent with his landlord but that same tenant and landlord might have had satisfactory debtor-creditor relationships which the tenant did not want to endanger. Or the tenant-landlord dispute might have been complicated by joint interests vis-à-vis third parties. An occupancy tenant might have been willing to pay excessive nazrana to a landlord in order to keep his own sharecropping arrangements with subtenants out of the courts. The interests of the faction of which both tenant and landlord were members might have been more important to both than the land issue in dispute.

Such conflicts of interest are not unique to India. What makes them so important in the Indian land problem is that all relationships are restricted to such a small area and small number of people that almost no case is simple.[m] In the West, banker, landlord, wholesaler, retailer, political leader, and social leader are seldom the same person. In U.P. one man is likely to fulfill several and even all of these functions, and disputes in any one sphere must affect relationships in all. "Beyond the multiplicity of relationships, the Indian is apt to regard the use of state laws and regulations as immoral, even as a form of robbery."[5] Cases are therefore not brought. Cohn points out that

> The landlord-tenant relationship is not just a contractual relationship, as it is treated in law, but rather it is a hereditary relationship having important social and ceremonial concomitants which cannot be treated as contractual relations. Two Thakurs disputing over a piece of land are not only buyer and seller with a contractual tie, but in classificatory kinship terms are brothers or uncle and nephew. . . . some of these ties cannot be summarily cut by a decision of a court. People must continue to live and work together in a multiplex society.[6]

The argument that peasants are so awed by and fearful of authority that they dare not bring cases is often true, but it is unnecessary to explain the failure of the administration to enforce legislation. There is also some reason to doubt that peasants would not complain if they felt the issue to be clear-cut: witness the support for the Congress movement and for the "No-Rent" campaigns after 1919. The riots over a linguistic state in Bombay in 1956 show a willingness to fight authority, but the same Marathas accepted evasion of the 1948 tenancy legislation.[7]

Although the acts of the Imperial government indicate no intention to take away by procedure that which the law granted in substance, nevertheless the mechanics of judicial administration made it hard for the ryot to appear in court and present his grievance successfully. Perhaps a selection of comments by the British officials to whom it fell to carry out the law will show how helpless the courts were in their efforts to make the principles of legislation

---

m. Marriott (letter of July 19, 1958) argues that absentee landlords are "the exception which proves the rule" because tenants do try to steal land from absentees.

effective. First, there are Carstair's views formed at the turn of
this century:

> In England, justice goes to the people; in India, the
> people had to come to justice. . . .

> [The litigant] had to find his way to this strange tribunal
> in an unknown land as best he could, in charge of the po-
> lice, whose tender mercies he dreaded, or alone.

> If he went alone, it was not for long. Around the Courts
> were swarms of petty lawyers, who had their touts on the
> roads and in the villages. Long ere he came within hail of
> the Court he had been fastened upon by several of these,
> and persuaded that his only chance of success was to put
> himself in their hands; say what they bade him; pay what,
> when, and to whom they told him; and above all, to be-
> ware of telling the truth: it would never be believed. . . .

> In those strange cases there was no common ground.
> Whatever one side asserted the other denied; all the wit-
> nesses were tutored; and whether true or not to begin with,
> the case as presented on both sides was invariably concocted.
> . . .

> I for one came to the conclusion that nearly all, save a
> few of the graver cases, were episodes in some dispute not
> before the Court. The parties were not the real parties, but
> puppets of others, who remained in the background, pay-
> ing for and directing the proceedings.

> Most of the genuine disputes never reached our Courts
> at all, but were settled at some earlier stage and in other
> ways. . . .

> While we dispensed justice as best we could to those who
> came before us, we knew that an enormous number of in-
> jured persons never came to us at all. Many were deterred
> by difficulties in the way; many dared not come for fear of
> offending the local despot, who by threats of injuries—
> threats which he could carry out—was able to prevent them
> from complaining, and to stop the mouths of their witnes-
> ses. [n],[8]

n. R. Carstairs, *The Little World of an Indian District Officer*, pp. 13–15. See
also' Cohn, p. 91:
    Very often, even in the caste meetings, the case which is ostensibly the

Penderel Moon, who served during the last decades of British rule, held similar opinions:

> A layman, still more an illiterate peasant, who endeavored to prosecute his own complaint or conduct his own defence in one of our Indian Courts had not the remotest chance of success. The procedure and rules of evidence were so elaborate that even educated persons did not understand them; and the proceedings were conducted in a language unintelligible to the majority of the litigants. The Courts were a sham and a mockery in which police, witnesses, lawyers and judges all played their part in producing or using evidence which they knew to be quite false. . . .
>
> Everyone who had anything to do with the criminal administration was aware of this and deplored it. But as the system was now well established and supported by the vested interests of the lawyer class, no one showed the slightest inclination to alter it. Most English officers simply washed their hands of the whole matter. Having worked as ordinary magistrates for a short while during their early years of service, and having decided that hearing criminal cases was a futile waste of time, they put all this behind them at the earliest opportunity.[9]
>
> A simple people had become habituated to systematized perjury, had been corrupted by unscrupulous lawyers, had been taught to flock to the law courts, and to revel in the tainted atmosphere of bribery and chicanery that surrounds them. Litigation had become a national pastime and the criminal law a recognized and well-tried means of harassing, imprisoning and even hanging one's enemies.[10]
>
> In Indian conditions the whole elaborate machinery of English law, which Englishmen tended to think so perfect, simply didn't work and had been completely perverted . . . myriads of Indian magistrates daily spent hours in their

---

crux of the dispute is only a minor expression of a long-standing antagonistic relationship between two families or groups. . . . The caste meeting can and does deal with the string of disputes. . . . The British court, given the nature of the adjudication process, can deal only with the specific case presented by the contending parties.

Courts solemnly recording word for word the evidence of illiterate peasants, knowing full well that 90 per cent of it was false. Even if the events described had actually occurred, the alleged eyewitnesses had not seen them. Even if the accused were guilty, it was perjury which proved their guilt. False evidence was always in demand as much to prove what was true as to establish what was false, against innocent and guilty alike it was equally necessary.[11]

If the plaintiffs, defendants, and witnesses made impartial justice difficult, the lower officials of the administration made it impossible. Sir Cecil Walsh spent his career in U.P.:

[The village chaukidar] is a Government employee, and a sort of cross between the old English night watchman and the modern village constable. He is often a rogue, and almost invariably supine or corrupt. His evidence in court, especially if it differs from the report to which he has made himself a party, is frequently bewildering, and the effort to sift it, and to separate the wheat from the chaff, is one of the most trying tasks of a sessions judge.[12]

When giving evidence before the Simon Commission at the end of 1928, the Inspector-General of Police for Bihar and Orissa said that 99 per cent of the constabulary, 75 per cent of the Sub-Inspectors, and 50 per cent of the Inspectors were probably corrupt, due partly to inadequate pay and partly to the standard of morality of the classes from which the police were drawn. . . . The corruption spoken of generally takes one of three forms: the extortion of small payments or *baksheesh* for performing an act of ordinary duty; the extortion of gifts, large or small according to the means of the individual, for not following up a charge; and the levying of blackmail by threats of false charges.[13]

It can be argued that there were good motives—that is, understandable motives—for the falsification of evidence by the police: to enforce truth in cases of perjury; to secure convictions, partly to maintain law and order and partly to earn promotion; and to avoid accusations of bribery if evidence was not produced in court.[14] According to Walsh, judges did not think it worthwhile to prosecute for perjury. The only English judge who did so in Walsh's experience "so congested his court with arrears that it

became a by-word in a province where the number of appeals
awaiting decision in the High Court is usually in the neighborhood of 5000." When the courts feared that more pressing cases
would suffer if perjury were prosecuted, it is hardly surprising
that perjury thrived.[15]

The conscientious policeman did not in the long run help the
government. Carstairs tells the story of investigating a complaint
about a sub-inspector of police. It turned out "that in searching for
stolen property the sub-inspector had pulled to pieces a limekiln
for burning shell-lime, which he had left in ruins." Carstairs remarked "that certainly a good deal of damage had been done," to
which the sub-inspector replied that the "great Bakaulla" knew
how to search, for this mentor of the sub-inspector in searching a
house "used to pull it to pieces, walls and thatch and all, and dig
up the ground on which it stood to a depth of three cubits. Nothing could escape a search like that."[16] It is probable that public
faith in government could not stand many such searches either.

The enforcement of land law in particular faced one other immense obstacle, the character of the patwari or village record-
keeper. His record of right was *prima facie* evidence in any revenue, tenancy, or title case and the only written evidence against
which to test oral testimony. Yet there is Walsh's description of the
U.P. patwari:

> In the United Provinces there are 30,000 *patwaris,* each
> of whom has usually charge of three or four villages. It
> has been found extremely difficult in practice to ensure the
> accuracy of the *patwari's* papers. Maps and records are not
> kept up-to-date, and public and private interests alike suf-
> fer. Changes occur every year under all the heads of records
> which the *patwari* has to prepare: field boundaries are al-
> tered; waste land is brought under cultivation; parts of
> holdings are relinquished by tenants; tenants are ejected;
> new tenancies are created; rents are raised or lowered; pro-
> prietors die and their lands are divided among the heirs;
> sales and mortgages take place; irrigation and crops vary
> perpetually with season and market. The scope for error
> is practically unlimited. But the neglect and stupidity of
> *patwaris* are not the worst evils against which the illiterate
> cultivator has to struggle. The *patwari* is an institution. He
> has survived many dynasties and every change and improve-

ment which the organizing genius of British rule has devised for the development of local administration. Heaven and earth may pass away, but the *patwari* will not pass away. He has been threatened too often. The importance of his work to the village community explains his opportunities, and his reputation, for corrupt practices. He keeps, and ought to keep up-to-date, the *khasra* or field-book, the village map with its numbered plots and its corresponding entries in the register, and the *jamabandi* or rent-roll. . . .

. . . upon the simple issue as to which of two persons has cultivated a plot, or is in actual possession of it, it is quite common to find a number of witnesses on either side flatly contradicting one another, each backed by strong corroborative detail in support of his assertion. In such a contest the *patwari's* official entry, supported by his sworn testimony, and his normal means of information ought to be conclusive; and the side which he supports has *prima facie* a strong card to play. His own position is certainly a strong one. His opportunities are not to be measured merely by the influence ordinarily exercised by a person who can read and write, however imperfectly, over a heterogeneous crowd of tenants and cultivators who can do neither. An absentee landlord, whose rents depend upon entries made by the *patwari,* is obviously very much at his mercy in matters of detail which form the basis of the pecuniary calculation. On the other hand, a community of cultivators defending themselves against the greed of a shrewd and grasping landlord, whose demands are enforced by the unknown terrors of the law, have every motive for keeping the *patwari* in a sympathetic and reasonable frame of mind. It would be idle to expect the average *patwari* to accept his slender salary as adequate remuneration for his exacting and varying duties. It is unlikely that anyone ever attempted to compel him to do so.

A *patwari* would probably be astonished, if not indignant, to meet a landlord, or a cultivator, who expected him to work for his pay alone; and a plentiful supply of grain at harvest time, sufficient to provide for the food of a large family, free of charge, or a cultivatory area held at a rent which is never collected, may be regarded as the minimum of his requirements by way of perquisites. While it is due to him to recognize the value of his indispensable services, his opportunities for extortion are considerable, and the methods of dishonesty pursued by the various occupants of his office differ as widely as their habits of thought. It is not difficult for such a man to command a circle of friends; it is impossible for him to avoid making irreconcilable enemies.[17]

When the patwari was not at work corrupting the record, there was someone else to take his place. "More serious still [than perjury], of course, are the astounding forgeries of birth registers, deeds, and other documents, in cases involving property; but this form of crime is more a local industry, with its schools and apprentices and wholesale dealers, to be found in more populous centres amongst educated men."[18]

The landlords did take advantage of the situation. To the dense fog of falsification which obfuscated justice they added the threat of personal violence. Of the Bengali landlord Carstairs says:

> The lord of each estate was as much its lord as our own medieval baron was of his. The law prevailing in it was not the law of the land, but the will of the landlord, who was master within it.
>
> Every landlord had his force of retainers, armed (since fire-arms were a State prerogative, and only carried by license)—armed usually with heavy, iron-bound bamboo clubs. They were needed for lawful purposes, such as guarding treasure, going messages, and the like duties. They were also his instruments for overawing the villagers and for punishing those who had incurred his wrath. To "pleasure the laird" they would go to any lengths—would even kill a man, destroy his house, plough up the site, and sow it with salt.
>
> He could have cattle driven through his enemies' fields; filth thrown into his courtyard; the women of his house insulted; his house or stacks set on fire; his cattle driven away. No man who valued life and comfort dared offend the all-powerful lord.
>
> What was there to interfere with the landlord?
>
> The District Officer, indeed, loomed like Fate in the background, and was as little heeded in every-day life.

The Police—he was their local head, and they were in his pay.

The Courts could do nothing. If any man had the rashness to complain against him, no witness dared give evidence. And if so extraordinary a breach of discipline took place, his servants and money and lawyers brought him safely off, and he was free to deal with the man who had cared to invoke the protection of the Court.

The landlord's Courts—his administration of justice in them—were indeed illegal and punishable at law. Who cared?

The breaches of the law went on, and were not punished.

The authorities never heard of them officially unless the title of the landlord was itself being disputed. . . . But in the flood of fake charges that poured in at such times an occasional true one passed unnoticed.[19]

The abuse of legal proceedings by landlords is illustrated by the tale of the brothers Mookerjea. Joykissen Mookerjea did not want anyone intermediate between himself and his villagers, so he drove out the middlemen and middlemen-tenants by the use of law suits. "It mattered little to him whether he won or lost in the end. He would never own himself beaten until he had exhausted every process of every Court that was open to him, up to the Privy Council in distant London. He, a rich man, was fighting with poor men, who could seldom last out the contest, and it came to be generally understood that the man whom Joykissen Mookerjea attacked was bound in the end to get the worst of it."[o]

Joykissen's brother Harihar decided to raise the rents which a court had declared fixed by custom. First he talked his tenants into paying the rent in monthly installments on each plot of land separately. This established the practice and therefore a precedent. Next he refused to accept the rents when offered and proceeded to sue for arrears of rent, item by item for the whole year. A tenant who held five plots thus found himself involved in sixty law suits (five plots times twelve months). The total in the one

---

o. Carstairs, pp. 88–89. See also Bernard S. Cohn ("Some Notes on Law and Change in North India," *Economic Development and Cultural Change*, 8 [1959], 93) for a description of how Thakurs regarded courts as battlegrounds for prestige, not through "one quick case" but through "a series of cases, appeals, adjournments, and counter-appeals."

village of Makla was twenty thousand suits. If the tenant did not appear to answer each suit he lost by default; if he appeared the court did not believe him because it did not believe a landlord would refuse payment. To extricate themselves the tenants conceded a small increase in rent "voluntarily." But now the rents which the court had found fixed by custom were no longer fixed, for there were contracts to show that the rents were freely negotiated. The barrier of customary precedent broken, Harihar doubled the rents within a few years.[20]

The forms of abuse of privilege were multitudinous. Eighty years ago a settlement officer was complaining that "in fact the Indian landlord seems to consider that a resident of his village should pay for permission to do any conceivable action, even for eating, drinking, and sleeping";[21] while at the same time in another district another official found that charges were made for a boil on the landlady's leg.[22] A list of names (or excuses) for the exaction of nazrana has been compiled by H. D. Malaviya:

> Bhusavan: husk for the landlord's cattle
> Motorovan: money to buy the zamindar a car
> Hathiyavan: money to buy an elephant for the landlord
> Bhagavan: money to help the landlord plant an orchard
> Petpiravan: a gift to the landlord when his wife conceived
> Janmavan: another gift when the landlord's child was born
> Holiyavan: a gift on Holi, and gifts similarly entitled on other holidays.[23]

The origins of the attitudes and powers of the leading zamindars went back to the days before British rule, and the mixing together of politics and economics did not end with English law, for many zamindars "derived important status" from "their role as settlers of disputes and judges, and from their claims to be kings in a traditional social order." In their judicial capacity these landlords settled property and inheritance cases and inter-caste disputes. They thought of themselves and were thought of by those below them in the hierarchy as "lords." "The Thakur attitude was summed up by one elderly Thakur, who said 'we took this land with the sword, these people are our dependents.' "[24]

The line between those who ruled the village and those beneath them was not the only line of social cleavage accepted by people on both sides of the line. Cultivators and artisans were members of clean castes while laborers were from the untouchable groups. Between the cultivating kisan (peasant) and the laboring Harijan (untouchable), "although the community of interest may appear very large, there is a steep social barrier."[25] The rare untouchable who tries today to buy land, Thorner argues,

> may find insurmountable obstacles in the way of the purchase. For he is up against the deeply entrenched tradition of rural inequality—a tradition which goes back centuries if not millennia. To a considerable extent, the belief that low castes are born to labour with their hands, and high castes to enjoy the fruits of others' labour, is accepted by the former as well as the latter. The separation between proprietorship and physical cultivation both draws sanction from and serves to reinforce the caste structure of rural society.[26]

The north Indian idea of men in society is the opposite of the idea of equality before the law. "When Indians go into a court, they are supposed by definition to lose their outside statuses. . . . To an Indian peasant this is an impossible situation to understand. The Chamar knows he is not equal to the Thakur. He may want to be equal, but he knows he is not. The Thakur cannot be convinced in any way that the Chamar is his equal."[27]

Lastly, there was the failure of the administration to enforce the criminal law. Violence against the persons and property of opponents in disputes was common. Inquiries around Allahabad and Lucknow by the author about the actions of landlords frequently elicited the explanation that they enforced their wills by "murder." To explain the success of landlords in terrorizing peasants one must return to the loyalties and factions that characterize villages in U.P. All law was unenforceable as long as the persons whose relationships the law was to govern were more strongly devoted to village ways and village standards than they were to ideas of abstract justice on a provincial scale. Violence outside the law was not something different from the failure of land law in the Indian social structure; it was only another manifestation of the lack of acceptance of English legal processes by Indian society.

Until recently the upper caste Thakur (Rajput) landlords enforced their decisions by beating members of the lower castes. In one case a leader of the Chamar (untouchable) caste in a village explained his acceptance of a beating: "I told my Thakur that I did not strike him back because he was my Thakur, otherwise I would not stand to be beaten. . . . I thought BBS was my Thakur and therefore equal to my mother and father and he should not be insulted."[28] During the nineteenth century the idea of a dispute between a Thakur and his Chamar follower did not arise because the only way in which the latter could break the master-servant relationship was to flee from the village and to find a protector elsewhere. On the other hand, a feeling of obligation to feed, clothe, and house the tenant, an obligation enforced by the social pressure of the other Thakurs, existed at the same time.[29] The rise of a rebellious peasant movement after the First World War stemmed in part from the disappearance of the idea of obligation to one's underlings.

In the case of "A Police Pantomime," recounted by Walsh,[30] Ishway Nath, a Brahman thekedar of U.P., was behind a plot to "frame" people for dacoity (robbery) in order to give prestige to the police inspector and to provide himself with money. He offered to release suspects for a fee of from Rs. 10 to Rs. 50 and threatened to have others arrested. His business was blackmail and extortion. Walsh explains that he was a type—the "bazaar bully"—who lives by hooliganism and violence, and says that once such a person starts terrifying people, including the police, no one dares to stop him. Other cases in Walsh's book illustrate the extreme distaste of villagers for getting themselves mixed up in cases from fear of vengeance, and illustrate the fact of vengeance as well.[31] John T. Hitchcock studied a Rajput village a few years ago and was told that the village was full of robbers within living memory and that "within the memory of middle aged men" merchants were in danger of losing their wares if they came to the village.[32] It was not much longer ago that "an old, wise, and much respected landlord" told Carstairs, when they were discussing legislation to protect the tenants, "Whatever you do . . . we have ways of forcing them to do our pleasure."[33]

Where the law failed to protect the tenants or to change the rules of land management, it was not the fault of particular laws. It was a fault common to all laws imposed by an administration whose standards and methods were not accepted by the society. It was not a peculiarity of foreign administration, for the same problems arose under the Indian provincial legislatures and arise today, when India is independent: the failure of tenancy legislation in many states in India;[34] the failure of age-of-marriage legislation; the failure of prohibition; the great difficulty in ending untouchability.

One must conclude that the ineffectiveness of legislation was as much, if not more, due to the nature of Indian village society than to the law and to its officers of enforcement. Perhaps we should regard the conversion of tenancies-at-will to occupancy and hereditary tenancies in the twenties as triumphs over great odds and not as evidence of cowardice, inefficiency, or wrongheadedness on the part of the British administration.

PART IV

CHAPTER 11

The Arguments of the
Zamindari Abolition Committee

1. THE ARGUMENT FOR ABOLITION

To appreciate the Zamindari Abolition Committee's *Report,* on which the reform of 1951 was based, it is necessary to grasp the political motives and philosophical conceptions behind the Committee's work, its thinking, and its recommendations. The political bias or philosophy underlying the *Report* is a faith in what might be called rural cooperative socialism. In its view the artisan and cultivator lives an essentially satisfactory life making decisions, seeing his work completed, and taking pride in it, while the factory worker is a cog with few satisfactions. Economic efficiency should be secondary to the democratic development of the full personality, and large-scale organization, whether capitalist or socialist, is

a threat to individual independence and initiative and causes
the destruction of an ethos of cooperative fellowship. The Committee fears the need for coercion when the state goes beyond
"mere palliatives and minimum reforms."[1]

> It is widely admitted that in cases where large-scale produc-
> tion is inescapable, as for instance, in heavy industries, a
> socialist organization is superior to a capitalist organization.
> The difficulty is, however, that after an industry has been
> organized on a democratic basis and the inequitable distri
> bution of wealth corrected, the industry as a whole would
> still continue to be essentially a capitalist unit, in the sense
> that its collective production and marketing would still be
> governed by capitalist motives. It would continue to over-
> produce, sell at the maximum profit and compete with
> other units, in a manner inconsistent with the general wel-
> fare of the community as a whole.[2]

The quotation is a confusion of socialist beliefs, anti-industrial
emotions, ethical concepts of proper motives, and underconsump-
tionist business cycle theory with classical monopoly theory. It
gives little ground for belief that the Committee's thinking was
characterized by logical clarity.

Realizing the need for new organizations in agriculture to
achieve the minimum needs of the population, yet fearing organizations so large that their members would be out of touch with
one another, the Committee decided that a pyramidal form of cooperative organization would avoid the evils feared. At the base of
the pyramid would be the village cooperative societies, democrat-
ically responsible to the membership which would be co-extensive
with the village citizenry. Above the village cooperative would be
the district cooperative banks, the associated land mortgage cooperatives for long-term credit, and above these the central state
bank. The top of the pyramid would set only a general plan,
with application, methods, and initiative at the base. The small
groups at the base would provide the social control, social morality, and training for cooperative democracy which the Committee
desired to see take shape in U.P.

This version of small-scale rural cooperative socialism is not
unusual, and if one grants the right of a legislature to hold such
a political philosophy, then a committee of the legislature cannot

be criticized for basing its recommendations on the philosophy to which the legislature subscribes.

The Committee devoted a good deal of space to a horrifying history of the zamindari system, partly to justify the abolition of the system and partly, it appears, to give vent to its collective spleen. The Committee's uncontrolled hatred of the British led it into ridiculous charges simply in order to use words with bad connotations. Thus the statement that "the feudal system of land tenure and the high market value of the land lead to rack-renting and illegal exaction"[3] ignored the difficulty that market values and rents do not exist under a feudal system. It might better be argued that rack-renting and illegal exactions lead to the high market value of land. The Committee argued that the economic interests of the pre-British classes were carefully adjusted and their relations controlled by custom. In spite of specialization and the hereditary division of labor, the villages were on the whole homogeneous and essentially democratic, according to the Committee. Economic and social conflicts were represented as reduced to a minimum—a strange picture of the caste system—but "the establishment of a feudal order has broken down the social organization of the village, and the policy of *laissez faire* has intensified economic maladjustments."[4] It is true that the old village organization had broken down, but the zamindars under British rule were not feudal, the pre-British conditions were not idyllic, and the British did not follow a laissez faire policy in U.P., as the tenancy legislation amply illustrates.

The Committee's arguments against the zamindari system were actually not necessary, since the Committee was operating under a directive to devise a way in which to end the system and not to look into its merits or historical justification:

> This Assembly accepts the principle of the abolition of the Zamindari System in this Province which involves intermediaries between the cultivator and the State and resolves that the rights of such intermediaries should be acquired on payment of equitable compensation and that Government should appoint a committee to prepare a scheme for this purpose.[5]

In view of the Committee's terms of reference—both the terms of the abolition resolution and the general philosophy of the legislature—it is not fair to judge the *Report* by the standards of historical scholarship. Rather one should ask to what extent the Committee grappled with the basic agricultural and economic problems of U.P. in its effort to reform the system of land tenure.

The Committee did not attack the problem from the point of view of discovering what went wrong with the British-sponsored system. On the contrary, considerations of ethics, of income distribution, of the behavior of zamindars, and of financial loss to the state dominated its reasoning.

Instances of the ethical approach are easy to find in the *Report:* "Agricultural production is the winning of wealth from the land by means of labour and only those can have the right to such wealth as work to produce it and only for so long as they continue to do so." John Stuart Mill was quoted to the same effect, and the conclusion drawn that "zamindars and other rent receivers" have no "judicial principle in favour of the continuance of their rights."[6] The same ethical argument was broadened to:

> He who does not make a return in the shape of produce or social service equivalent to or more than what he consumes is a drone and a drag on social and economic progress. Every section of people must perform a definite economic function. Experience has shown, however, that the various classes of intermediaries functioning as rent receivers, whether zamindars or taluqdars or underproprietors or other subordinate holders, have done nothing to improve the land and have left the land and the tenantry where they were, and indeed in a plight worse than before.[7]

The charge against the zamindars was true, but the Committee also argued that "thinkers and economists" have been forced to "the conclusion that in India, as in many other parts of the world, landlordism is an inequitable anachronism; that land can no longer be allowed to be treated merely as a source of income; that it is for use, and therefore, it should be regarded as a definite and limited means for supplying labour to a category of citizens whose occupation in life is the tilling of the soil."[8] The step was made from the argument that to the tiller belongs the produce, to the argument that the primary function of the land is not to provide produce for the members of society, but to provide work for some of society's members.

Inequity of income distribution also offended the Committee. It pointed out that since land revenue was assessed on the valuation of the land, the share of land revenue paid reflected the share of the land owned, and that the share of the land owned reflected to some degree the distribution of income. Eight hundred and four zamindars, or .0014 per cent of the population of U.P., owned 27 per cent of the land, while 1,986,641 zamindars owned only 42 per cent of the land (Table 16). The inequality was perhaps better shown by the fact that 1.5 per cent of the zamindars owned 58 per cent of the land. The 98.5 per cent of the zamindars owning 42 per cent of the land each paid a land revenue of less than Rs. 250, and of these, 86 per cent paid land revenue of less than Rs. 25.[9] The Committee felt that not only would abolition reduce the inequalities of land distribution, but would actually help the small zamindar. "The petty zamindars suffer more at the hands of the moneylender than a tenant of equal status. Many petty zamindars are also tenants and as such subjected to exploitation by the bigger landowners."[a] Because the small zamindar was not essentially a rent receiver but relied for his support primarily on his sir and khudkasht which he would keep, he would not suffer from the abolition of zamindari.[b] Tables 17 and 18 show the distribution of sir and khudkasht and the proportion let.

It appears that letting of sir land was not as common as one might have supposed. Only the richest zamindars and those holding large areas of sir and khudkasht let an appreciable proportion of their holdings, and even among these groups the area let did not average half the total sir and khudkasht. The evils of zamindari sir and khudkasht may have been overemphasized.

The Committee was on shaky ground when it argued that the small zamindar might gain, "for as a result of direct impact between the tiller of the soil and the state, large and small works of land improvement and land reclamation will gain impetus. The State proposes to spend large sums to effect technological improvements by undertaking comprehensive schemes of development."[10] The gain here would not be a result of the abolition of the zamindars but of the developmental works undertaken by the state, and these works could perfectly well be undertaken without abolishing the zamindars.

a. Z.A.C. *Report*, p. 243. An indication of the multiple status of cultivators is found in the fact that there were 12,278,289 individual holders of land but 21,556,617 separate interests in land. Z.A.C. *Report, 2: Statistics*, Statements 5, 6, pp. 6, 8.

b. Ibid., p. 343. Also, see below, Table 19, for scales of compensation.

TABLE 16. *Distribution of Zamindars by Amount of Land Revenue Paid*

Class of land revenue		Number of zamindars	Percentage of all zamindars	Amount of land revenue payable (Rs.)	Percentage of all land revenue payable	Average land revenue payable (Rs.)
Rs. 25 or less		1,710,530	84.81	10,049,725	14.76	5.88
Exceeding Rs. 25 but not Rs.	50	142,890	7.09	5,002,021	7.35	35.01
" " 50 " " " "	75	53,288	2.64	3,251,796	4.78	61.02
" " 75 " " " "	100	28,369	1.41	2,457,362	3.61	86.65
" " 100 " " " "	150	27,861	1.38	3,405,055	5.00	122.22
" " 150 " " " "	200	14,473	.72	2,482,548	3.65	171.53
" " 200 " " " "	250	9,230	.46	2,068,434	3.04	224.10
Subtotal for Rs. 250 or less		1,986,641	98.51	28,716,941	42.19	14.47
Exceeding Rs. 250 but not Rs.	500	16,758	.83	5,919,934	8.70	353.26
" " 500 " " " "	1,000	7,491	.37	5,172,919	7.60	690.55
" " 1,000 " " " "	1,500	2,362	.12	2,875,894	4.22	1,217.57
" " 1,500 " " " "	2,000	1,076	.05	1,867,686	2.74	1,735.77
" " 2,000 " " " "	2,500	588	.03	1,318,882	1.94	2,243.00
" " 2,500 " " " "	3,000	393	.02	1,073,639	1.58	2,731.91
" " 3,000 " " " "	3,500	242	.012	785,148	1.15	3,244.41
" " 3,500 " " " "	4,000	179	.009	671,590	.99	3,751.90
" " 4,000 " " " "	4,500	135	.007	571,335	.84	4,232.11
" " 4,500 " " " "	5,000	114	.006	539,491	.79	4,732.38
" " 5,000 " " " "	10,000	414	.021	2,928,888	4.30	7,074.61
" " 10,000		390	.019	15,626,679	22.96	40,068.45
Subtotal exceeding Rs. 250		30,142	1.49	39,352,085	57.81	1,305.56
Grand Total		2,016,783	100.00	68,069,926	100.00	33.75

Source. Z.A.C. *Report, 2: Statistics*, Statement 1, p. 1.

The Committee went on to the three strongest economic arguments for land reform. First, there was no inducement under the existing system to farm well and to invest in improvements. "The cultivator does not only lack the means of improving his land, what he lacks very much more under the present system is incentive. The radical alteration of the present land tenure system by the removal of intermediaries between the tiller of the soil and the State will in itself go a good way towards the rehabilitation of agriculture."[11] It is upon the truth and importance of this reasoning more than upon any other grounds that the justification of land reform rests.

Next in importance, the Committee asserted that the zamindars deserved no "praise or sympathy" for an unproductive investment in zamindari rights. "Their money should profitably have gone to industrial concerns and enriched the country." Since the policy of the Indian government was one of central control and partial socialization, the abolition of the zamindars was within the spirit of Indian policy. "Moreover, private enterprise in industry has some justification for the *entrepreneur* provides organization and takes risks. The zamindar, however, is not an organizer of agricultural activities in the sense in which an industrialist or businessman is. Apart from the money that the zamindar invests in acquiring land, he invests almost no capital for increasing agricultural production and does nothing to improve the land or the standard of cultivation."[12] This argument points to a crucial failure of the zamindari system. The British made a bargain with the zamindars and talukdars: a title in exchange for enlightened and effective land management. The landlords did not keep their part of the bargain.[c]

On the financial side, the Committee had an eye to increasing the revenues. The state and local authorities collected Rs. 682 lakhs in land revenue and Rs. 71 lakhs in local rates, while the zamindars were left with Rs. 1,000 lakhs of income.[d] When governments need additional sources of revenue for developmental

c. *Eastern Economist* (Feb. 15, 1946, p. 258) cites an illustration of entrepreneurial lethargy: the refusal of a landlord to install a well—maximum cost of Rs. 10,000—although irrigation would have increased his rental income from Rs. 3,000 to Rs. 5,000.

d. Z.A.C. *Report*, p. 341. But on p. 541, the Committee visualizes revenue collections after abolition of Rs. 2,000 lakhs, or more than the totals above: either the present tenants were to pay even more or we have a wide choice of figures.

TABLE 17. *Distribution of Sir and Khudkasht by Area Held*

Area of sir and khudkasht held by zamindars	Number of zamindars	Sir and Khudkasht Possessed by Zamindars in Col. 2					Average area per zamindar in acres
		Area in acres	Percentage of total area	Area let in acres	Let area as a percentage of Col. 3		
1	*2*	*3*	*4*	*5*	*6*		*7*
Not exceeding 5 acres	1,579,365	2,767,152	38.82	396,988	14.35		1.75
Exceeding 5 but not 10 acres	189,227	1,288,426	18.08	170,714	13.25		6.81
" 10 " " 25 "	96,903	1,402,248	19.67	194,902	13.90		14.47
" 25 " " 50 "	23,482	764,362	10.72	127,064	16.70		32.55
" 50 " " 100 "	6,746	450,521	6.32	84,775	18.82		66.78
" 100 " " 250 "	1,921	280,084	3.93	60,983	21.77		145.80
" 250	406	174,507	2.45	50,655	39.03		429.82
Total	1,898,050	7,127,300	100.00	1,086,081	15.24		3.76

Note. At least 118,733 zamindars, or 5.89%, held no sir or khudkasht.

Source. Z.A.C. *Report, 2,* Statement 3, p. 4. Cols. *4, 6,* and 7 were computed.

TABLE 18. *Distribution of Sir and Khudkasht by Size of Holders' Revenue Payment*

Class of zamindar by blocks of land revenue	Number of zamindars in class	Sir and Khudkasht Possessed by Zamindars in Col. 2				Average area per zamindar in acres
		Area in acres	Percentage of total area	Area let in acres	Let area as a percentage of Col. 3	
1	2	3	4	5	6	7
Not exceeding Rs. 250	1,858,325	5,114,251	82.77	784,854	13.30	3.17
Exceeding Rs. 250 but not Rs. 300	14,238	184,143	3.22	45,265	19.73	16.11
" " 300 " " " 350	6,332	125,179	2.19	31,027	20.00	24.67
" " 350 " " " 500	6,410	147,004	2.62	39,757	21.29	29.13
" " 500 " " " 1,000	7,646	195,053	3.59	60,498	23.67	33.42
" " 1,000 " " " 5,000	4,213	174,436	3.35	64,166	26.89	56.63
" " 5,000 " " " 10,000	430	36,209	.72	14,976	29.26	119.03
" " 10,000	456	64,944	1.55	45,538	41.22	245.52
Grand total	1,898,050	7,127,300	100.00	1,086,081	15.24	3.76

Note. At least 118,733 zamindars, or 5.89%, held no sir or khudkasht.

Source. Z.A.C. *Report,* 2, Statement 4, p. 5. Cols. *4* and *6* were computed.

purposes as badly as the Indian states do, any move likely to provide the state with a larger income has a *prima facie* justification.
The 1,000 lakhs ($20 million) is 1 per cent of the annual outlay of
all India's Second Five Year Plan. It is to be observed, however,
that if the state took this revenue the cultivator whose rents were
"too high" could not enjoy a reduction in his rental burden.

2. THE ARGUMENT FOR PEASANT PROPRIETORSHIP

As important to a reform as the evils it ends are the virtues it
creates. The justification for a face-lifting operation is that the
patient looks handsomer afterward, not that he was ugly before.

The Zamindari Abolition Committee went through the list of
possible alternative forms of agricultural organization, dismissing
state farms on the Russian model because they had not been successful in Russia and because the U.P. Department of Agriculture
was reckless,[e] and dismissing collective farms on the grounds that
productivity per acre would be lower than on peasant plots and
would not provide a large demand for labor. As large-scale capitalist farming was not permissible on doctrinal grounds, the remaining alternatives were peasant proprietary holdings or some
form of peasant village cooperative organization. Clearly, the U.P.
legislature would have preferred cooperatives if feasible. The only
way to bring agricultural incomes up to the level of industrial incomes, the Committee felt, was to have a large mechanized farm
with a skilled manager, but the scale involved was impossible in
U.P.[13]

Because of the paucity of figures, the Committee had to gauge
the advantages of mechanized farming by measuring the advantages of size in advanced countries where mechanized farming is
related to size; it found no proof that mechanization increased
productivity per acre, although it evidently did increase productivity per man. Peasant farming at its best was found to grow the
most per acre.[14] But this may have been a result of the economic
need to conserve labor, rather than land, in developed countries.
Australian, Canadian, and American farms have been worked on
an assumption of virtually free land, so there has been little pressure to increase yields per acre. It does not follow that advanced
mechanical techniques cannot be developed for achieving high

e. Z.A.C. *Report,* pp. 487–88. The objection to the State Department of Agriculture is indeed peculiar in a socialist document.

yields per acre, and as a matter of fact, yields per acre have been rising in the United States as a result of more capital-intensive farming.

The discussion of new farming techniques prior to the recent development of Community Projects suffered from the tendency to equate capitalization, mechanization, and size. This tendency revealed a misconception of the problem, which is not a combine harvester, or even a tractor, versus a bullock. From the technological point of view the need is to apply more capital, and it is wrong to prejudge the issue of what form the capital should take. It may be better feed for the bullocks. It may be a bullock instead of no bullock. It may be better breeding. It may be more wells, or more manure, or crop rotation, or better seeds, or more irrigation ditches, or more tanks for storing water, or steel-tipped plows, or iron harrows. In some places tractors may be the proper investment, as in the kans tracts of Bundelkhand. In other places, diesel or electric pumps may be the most productive form of capital investment. Capital in these uses is virtually infinitely divisible. Pumps, for instance, are expensive, but they water much land and the cost per cultivator is not high. Capital for seeds, manure, or animal feeding stuffs can be spent in any amount down to the *naya paisa*.

Some striking examples of capital development on a small scale can be found. In U.P., areas totally at the mercy of the monsoon can be assured a year-round supply of water by the construction of tube-wells, each irrigating about five hundred acres. Even before the Five Year Plans two thousand tube-wells protected a million acres.[15] In Etawah, improved wheat over 92 per cent of the area increased the crop yield by eight times the recurrent cost in two years, while health improved and education expanded. A project in Gorakhpur increased paddy yield by twice the recurrent expenditure in the first year.[16] In Coimbatore, a district in South West Madras, "gardenland" farming was introduced on a large scale. Mechanization and the concentration of large areas in one holding *increased* the demand for labor. Before the introduction of electricity, five- to ten-acre holdings were irrigated from mhotes (bullock-powered lift wells), and a pair of bullocks could supply water to only three or four acres. An electric pump handled fifty acres, while twenty-five-acre holdings became common. The cost of the well, Rs. 10,000, was financed by the increased productivity and the savings in labor and animal costs. The proportion of manual labor cost to total cost fell from 32 to 12 per cent, and the number of draught animals was halved. Even so, the demand for labor rose. Stony land was turned into gardenland by blasting boulders, picking up the stones by hand, and spreading tank silt six to nine inches deep. The diversity made possible in the farming pattern evened out the demand for labor over the year. Financing, however, did not come from small cultivators but from highly efficient agriculturalists who had made their fortunes in the cotton industry, and the holdings were sometimes as large as one or two hundred acres.[17]

Cooperative farms, the Zamindari Abolition Committee argued, have virtues other than the possibilities of mechanization: "if the capital of individual cultivators were pooled in the joint stock of the village community, financing would be easier than if the State were dealing with the individual cultivators. Besides this, joint management by the village could in any case lessen the cost of production and increase the purchasing power of the agriculturalist."[18] The first point is concrete and doubtless true. The state would find it easier to lend to and recover from one cooperative than a hundred or two hundred cultivators. It is not clear why cooperatives would lessen the cost of cultivation or increase the purchasing power of the cultivator. His purchasing power depends on how much he produces and how much it costs him to produce, so the essence of the matter is whether cooperatives would cut costs. There is reason to believe that cooperatives would reduce the cost of credit, perhaps of purchasing supplies, and probably of selling.[19] But beyond this, and the recommendation was that all activities be cooperative, the reduction in costs would depend upon radical reorganization of work and an increase in the capital employed. Neither follows directly from the creation of cooperatives. Both can happen without cooperatives.

Cooperative farming in U.P. had already shown some success. Two large cooperative farms were started in Jhansi district after the war. Eighty-one families on 489 acres at Nainwara had been making a profit of Rs. 30 per acre, and a 412-acre farm at Darauna had made a profit of Rs. 22.5 per acre.[20] The Nainwara farm, averaging six acres per family, produced a profit after wages of Rs. 181 per family, a good sum in U.P.

The Committee pointed out obstacles to be overcome before cooperative farming could become a success in U.P. First was the strong attachment of the cultivator to his land. This would prevent rapid growth if the cooperatives were voluntary. Second was a lack of managerial and technical skill. This deficiency could be met by recruiting and training personnel, by establishing demonstration farms, by propaganda, and by permitting cooperative farms smaller than village size, although one cooperative for the whole village would be ideal. To induce the cultivators to join cooperatives, the Committee thought the state should reduce rents, provide funds at a low rate of interest, provide seeds, insure against crop failure, provide social services, and make grants of waste and vacant land.[21] All such aids, it might be noted, have a strong element of bribery in them. If cooperatives are more efficient, they should be able to progress without state help.

Cooperative farms face one great difficulty in India. The divisions between caste and factions and even between families are accompanied by attitudes of strong distrust. So far, cooperative organization has had its successes where there has been a homogeneous equalitarian society: in Scotland, the north of England, Scandinavia, the rural districts of New York state, and Ceylon. In India, social unity is lacking. Perhaps this is the basic reason why thirty years of intensive effort failed to stimulate cooperatives.

In principle, as we have seen, the Committee preferred cooperatives even though it realized that the yield per acre on small peasant holdings was high. Recognizing, however, that cooperative farming on a voluntary basis would not spread even with all possible inducements, the Committee finally recommended small peasant holdings, with the hope that ultimately the state might develop a strong state-wide system of cooperative farms.[22] Again the stumbling block was lack of capital, for the training of competent cooperative farm managers and technicians involves a real saving in some part of the economy. Also, as long as the state is poor, the training of manpower will strain its resources. The normal expectation is that while there are few good technicians, the training of more will be slow, and that technical and managerial skills, like the absolute amount of capital equipment, will increase in geometric progression, so that beginnings will be small.

Actually, whatever the legal form they take—from sharecropping tenancies through proprietary holdings to plots in a large cooperative—the operational farms in U.P. must be small peasant holdings. Neither skilled manpower resources nor social structure nor political demands permit any other result.

It is important to remember that peasant cultivation on small plots is highly productive per acre. The returns to the peasant are low because the marginal productivity of his labor is low. Likewise, the small, labor-intensive holding is a poor commercial proposition; profits will be low. But in grading the merits of an agricultural system we have three measures: productivity per acre, productivity per man, and profitability. A system that ranks high by one measure may not appear so advantageous by another. With India's development problems—the need for increased agricultural output and shortages of foreign exchange—there is much to be said for maximizing gross output. Small holdings will do this.

To favor peasant proprietorship did not settle the problem; the system had existed in India for a century and a half. A proprietary peasantry was the solution in central and south India, where it is called the ryotwari system. *The Eastern Economist* makes the point that on grounds of efficiency "there is nothing to choose between the *zamindari* and the *ryotwari systems*," arguing that a change in ownership can be no more than a precondition for capital investment or for a program of agricultural development. Of itself a change in ownership has no effect upon production, and any beneficial effects of a change occur only because the new owner is encouraged to invest.[23]

The Zamindari Abolition Committee was aware of the danger of substituting the ryotwari system for the zamindari system. It pointed out that the ryotwari system had "itself developed some of the worst features of the zamindari system." There was as much fragmentation and renting at high rents in the ryotwari areas as in the zamindari areas, and perhaps more since the tenants in the ryotwari areas were not protected by legislation. In ryotwari areas peasant proprietors bid up land prices as much as they did in zamindari areas.[24]

The Committee therefore decided that the state should retain the land. It argued that "agriculture is no doubt a means of earning a livelihood for the peasant. None the less the peasant holds the land in trust for the nation. . . . Land was not created by man's efforts. It is nature's gift to man, and is vital to the community. It cannot, therefore, be looked upon as property owned and possessed by individuals to be used or abused at their will."[25]

CHAPTER 12

The Zamindari Abolition Act

Since the principle of zamindari abolition was widely accepted, the zamindars did not fight the abolition bill strongly during the legislative process, but instead took the issue to the courts on constitutional grounds. Article 24 of the Constitution required that compensation be paid when the state acquired private property, and Article 25(1) said that the right to compensation was justiciable in the courts. It was thought that the courts would regard as "unfair" the compensation which the states intended paying. With an eye on expediency rather than on what a fundamental right must be if it is to be fundamental, the difficulty was overcome by amending the Constitution. The Amendment, Article 31A, stated that zamindari abolition or agrarian reform laws should prevail notwithstanding any fundamental rights, provided they received the assent of the president of the Indian Union. The zamindars carried a case to the Supreme Court, which finally upheld the abolition legislation of Bihar, Madhya Pradesh, and Uttar Pradesh,[1] and so on the last day of June 1952, the government of U.P. took title to the land.

The Uttar Pradesh Zamindari Abolition and Land Reform Act I of 1951, Section 4, states that as soon as possible after the commencement of the act all estates in U.P. shall vest in the state free of all encumbrances, and Section 6(c)(i) reads: "all rents, cesses, local rates and sayar . . . which . . . would be payable to an intermediary, shall vest in and be payable to the State Government." It created three permanent kinds of tenure: bhumidhari, sirdari, and asami, roughly comparable to the owners, hereditary tenants, and statutory tenants of earlier acts. Adhivasi tenure was devised as a transitional measure to take care of tenants of sir.

The bhumidhar has exclusive possession of his land and may use it as he pleases, sell it, or transfer it in any other way, provided the recipient will not thereafter hold more than thirty acres or that a mortgagee will not take possession. A bhumidhar may not lease his land unless the person is an unmarried, divorced, or widowed woman; a minor, a lunatic, or an idiot; physically incapable of managing his land; a student under twenty-five years old; a serviceman; or in jail. The penalties for evasion of the restrictions upon transfers and leases are severe, and will probably be effective since it will be advantageous to others to enforce them. Where a transfer is made illegally, the Gaon Sabha (local village government) may sue to eject the transferee and acquire the land as vacant land. Where the bhumidhar lets his land illegally the lessee automatically becomes a sirdar if the area let is less than thirty acres, but is liable to ejectment if the area exceeds thirty acres.[2] The local government, which is responsible for the land revenue and the management of vacant lands, has a vested interest in enforcing the penalties, while the lessee has nothing to lose if he has leased less than thirty acres.

Bhumidhari tenure was granted to the intermediaries in respect of their sir, khudkasht, and grovelands; to permanent tenureholders in respect of their grovelands and land personally cultivated; to fixed rate tenants and rent-free grantees; and to any occupancy, hereditary, patta dawami or istamrari tenant having the right to transfer by sale.[a] The recipient of bhumidhari rights did not receive these rights on all the sir and khudkasht he held,

---

a. I of 1951, Sec. 18. The last two were a form of rent-free grantee on sir. There were very few of the last four types of tenant who had the right to sell.

but only upon his proportionate share in a joint holding. If he were cultivating more than his share, the excess land was to be held at exproprietary rates. The bhumidhari tenure was also granted to those given a declaration under Section 6 of the U.P. Agricultural Tenants (Acquisition of Privileges) Act X of 1949,[3] passed in anticipation of the abolition of zamindari tenures. This act permitted a privileged tenant to pay ten times his annual rent to the government, after which he would not be liable to ejectment and had to pay only one-half his former rent. The other half of the rent was to be paid by the government to the landowner.[4]

It was also made possible to acquire bhumidhari rights after the passage of the act. A sirdar can become a bhumidhar by paying to the government ten times his annual rent in one lump sum, or twelve times his annual rent in four installments over two years; if a sirdar is newly admitted to vacant land at any time he can acquire bhumidhari rights by paying ten times his annual rental within a year after being admitted to the holding. The purchaser of bhumidhari rights reduces his payments to the government by 50 per cent.[5]

The sirdar has exclusive possession of his land as long as he uses it for agricultural or horticultural purposes, which include animal husbandry, poultry farming, and pisciculture. He may let the land on the same conditions as a bhumidhar, which in most cases means he cannot let his land, but there is no provision for any other form of transfer except inheritance. In the case of any illegal transfer by a sirdar the transfer is void, the transferee may be ejected, and the sirdar automatically loses all rights in the land, including the right to claim compensation for the improvements he has made.[6]

Sirdari tenure was granted to tenants holding on special terms in Oudh, exproprietary tenants, occupancy tenants not already eligible for bhumidhari rights, hereditary tenants, grantees holding at favorable rates, groveholders, and subtenants of sir and khudkasht owned by landowners paying revenue of more than Rs. 250. (The provision that tenants of such sir become hereditary tenants for purposes of this act appears to create the possibility of two claimants to sirdari rights on the same land.) In addition to acquiring sirdari rights by virtue of these provisions, a person admitted to land after the passing of the act becomes a sirdar, and a person may also come into the right by virtue of other provisions such as the penalty on bhumidhars for letting.[7]

The asami is a cross between a sirdar and a protected subtenant. Asami rights are granted to nonoccupancy tenants of an intermediary's groveland, subtenants of groveland, subtenants protected under Act X of 1947, a mortgagee of someone acquiring bhumidhari rights, and nonoccupancy tenants of pasture land, land devoted to the cultivation of singhara, land under shifting cultivation, and other land on which sirdari rights cannot accrue, a thekadar (lessee of all rights of ownership and management) cultivating the sir and khudkasht of his lessor, anyone admitted as an asami under the act, and legal tenants of bhumidhars and sirdars. A tenant of sir or khudkasht who holds the land in lieu of maintenance is considered an asami while his right to maintenance continues.[8]

The asami has the same rights over his land as a sirdar, and is subject to the same restrictions. However, his rent "shall be such as may be agreed upon" although it may not be varied thereafter. If a rent is not agreed upon at admission, the courts shall fix the rent one-third higher than the hereditary rate for the plot. The produce of the land of an asami is hypothecated for the payment of rent, and he may be ejected whenever he falls in arrears on his rent or when the terms of his holding expire. This provision differentiates the asami from the bhumidhar, who cannot be ejected, and the sirdar, who can be ejected only for illegally transferring the land or misusing it. On ejectment the asami can recover the value of any improvements he has made.[9]

The sum of land revenue payable by bhumidhars and sirdars is the land revenue assessed upon the village, and the payment of the revenue is the first charge on all land, rents, profits, or produce of the village. All land held under bhumidhari or sirdari rights is liable to revenue, and all bhumidhars and sirdars are jointly liable for the revenue if a notification in the gazette is made to that effect. If a bhumidhar or sirdar is required to pay more than his share he can recover from the other holders in the courts.[10] A bhumidhar must pay in revenue whichever of the following amounts is appropriate to his case:

> The land revenue payable before vesting day
> The rent paid by a fixed-rate tenant
> The sum fixed for a grantee formerly holding rent-free
> The rent payable before vesting day by any tenant entitled
>   to become a bhumidhar on vesting day

One-half the rent paid before buying exemption under
Act X of 1947
One-half the former rent paid by a sirdar who buys bhumid-
hari rights
The sum to be fixed in the future for adhivasis who become
bhumidhars.[11]

The revenue payable by a bhumidhar shall not be changed for
forty years unless the size of his holding changes. The sirdar has
to pay in revenue the rent he paid before vesting day, an amount
to be determined "on principles to be prescribed" if admitted by
the Gaon Sabha, or the rate paid by the preceding sirdar if the
preceding sirdar's right expires while another person is on the
sirdari land, but no sirdar admitted after July 1, 1948 is to pay
less than the hereditary rate.[12]

Forty years after the commencement of Act I of 1951, the state
may direct an "original settlement" of any district, and a fresh
settlement may be made forty years after that.[13] This provision
seems a little too farsighted. It takes revenue policy up to the
year 2032, and unless repealed binds the government's hands. The
period is so long that one must assume that the government will
choose to repeal its guarantee long before 2032. Since the next
forty years of agricultural development are to take place at present revenue and rent rates, the settlement provisions of the act
would not be of much interest were it not for the fact that the
legislature reverts to the system of Regulation VII of 1822. While
the other provisions of the sections on settlement follow the usual
form,[14] Section 264 states that the settlement officer shall base his
settlement on the estimated average surplus after deducting the
estimated costs of cultivation. Despite years of experience and a
great deal of completely justified criticism the legislature decided
to adopt the defunct assessment on pure economic rent.

A temporary adhivasi tenure for tenants of sir and for subtenants was created for cultivators who did not acquire one of the
regular tenancies. Adhivasi rights were to disappear as adhivasis
purchased bhumidhari rights or surrendered the land,[15] but in
1954 adhivasis were granted sirdari status.[16]

Although the act established a system of peasant proprietors,
it made provision for the growth of cooperative agriculture. Any
ten or more bhumidhars or sirdars owning thirty or more acres
may register a cooperative farm. All land held by the members of

the cooperative, whether held under bhumidhari, sirdari, or asami
tenure, is deemed to belong to the cooperative society, and the society can use it for any agricultural purpose or for cottage industries. The cooperative farm shall consolidate the area held by it,
and the assistant collector can order holders to exchange land
with the cooperative for this purpose. The state may grant a
number of facilities and concessions to cooperatives, including a
reduction in the revenue, reduction in or exemption from agricultural income tax, free technical advice, financial aid, admission
to other land by the Gaon Sabha, and priority at state irrigation
works. If at least two-thirds of the bhumidhars and sirdars with
uneconomic holdings totaling at least two-thirds of the area in
uneconomic holdings apply to the collector for the establishment
of a cooperative farm, the collector can force all holders of uneconomic holdings to join the farm.[17]

The legislature seemed to have very little faith in the ability
of the cooperatives to manage themselves. The state's power to
make rules for cooperatives gives it virtually complete control over
them. The state shall make rules concerning "the rights, privileges, obligations, liabilities and duties of members; the admission, resignation, and expulsion of members. . . . The contribution
of land funds and other property by members, their valuation and
adjustment"; wages, payment of expenses and dues, the distribution of produce and profits; "the conduct generally of the affairs
of the farm and its working," and "directions for agricultural
development and for controlled or planned agricultural production."[18] This leaves very little if any autonomy to the cooperative
except in so far as the state refrains from exercising the rule-
making power or exercises it in a vague way.

The incidental matter of mining rights was handled by nationalizing them in form but leaving them private in fact. Existing
leases of mining rights were accepted by the government, and
where the mining rights were exercised by the owner of the land
a fictional lease was assumed, after which its actual terms were to
be negotiated between the intermediary and the state, or set forth
by a mines tribunal.[19]

The difficulty of managing the land and collecting the revenue
was increased by the new system of tenures. The work involved
in admitting new cultivators to holdings was greater, and the number of cultivators enjoying direct relations with the state was
larger. To meet these difficulties, the old revenue system and the

new tenure system were fitted into the new system of local government. The village organization itself was established by the U.P. Panchayat Raj Act XXVI of 1947. A Gaon Sabha consisting of all the adults in a village or group of villages meets at least twice a year. It is the supreme organ of local government. It elects a president, a vice-president, and a Gaon Panchayat of thirty to fifty-one members. The Gaon Panchayat is in charge of common property, local public health, education, local amenities, local problems in general, and the administration of criminal and civil justice. To raise money for the Gaon Fund the Gaon Panchayat may tax the rentpayer one anna in the rupee, the rent-receiver six pies in the rupee, and the holder of sir and khudkasht one anna in the assumed rental value. The Gaon Panchayat may also tax trades and professions and buildings not covered by the taxes on rents. The budget for the Gaon Fund must be approved by the Gaon Sabha. The Panchayati Adalat (local council and court) tries minor cases and can levy fines up to Rs. 100. The decisions can always be reversed by the subdivisional magistrate, Munsif, or other officer. The Panchayati Adalat consists of five members (panches) from each Gaon Sabha in a circle (a small revenue assessment area of land similar in quality), and the panches elect their own chief or Sarpanch. The government may always override the Panchayati Adalats, inspect them, and make rules to govern them.[b,20]

The Zamindari Abolition Act fitted the new tenures into the framework of this village system. In each village, or larger or smaller area to be called a circle, there is a corporate body, the Gaon Samaj, consisting of all adults who ordinarily reside in the circle and hold land in the circle as bhumidhars, sirdars, or asamis. At any time after title to estates vests in the state the state may vest in the Gaon Samaj:

1. All land outside holdings and groves
2. All trees except those in holdings, groves, the abadi, and on the boundaries of holdings
3. All forests
4. All public wells

b. Recently the Union government has asked the states to introduce a three-tier system of local government so that the organizational levels of local government will parallel those of the Community Development blocks and the districts. The U.P. system of Gaon Panchayats will fit into the new system as the lowest (village) tier without significant change.

5. All fisheries
6. All hats, bazars, and melas (different kinds of permanent and occasional fairs and markets) except those inside the boundaries of bhumidhari holdings
7. All tanks, ponds, private ferries, water channels, pathways, and abadi sites.

The state may keep such uncultivated area as it decides is in excess of the Gaon Samaj's ordinary requirements, and if the state takes back land it has vested in the Gaon Samaj, the latter shall not be entitled to compensation. In other words, the act makes the Gaon Samaj the trustee of the state's interest in land. The act goes on to make the Gaon Sabha a trustee for the Gaon Samaj. For and on behalf of the Gaon Samaj the Gaon Sabha shall superintend, manage, and control all Gaon Samaj lands in order to improve the lands, to develop cooperative farming, to consolidate holdings, and to develop cottage industries. Hats, bazars, melas, ferries, and water channels may be transferred from local control to the district boards,[21] or Zila Parishads as they are likely to be called in the future.

The Gaon Sabha's functions shall be performed by the Gaon Panchayat through a committee to consist of the Gaon Panchayat members from that circle plus enough persons elected by the Gaon Sabha to make up a membership to at least ten. All money received on behalf of the Gaon Panchayat, its committee, the Gaon Sabha, or the Gaon Samaj, and other prescribed sums, shall be credited to the Gaon Fund, which shall be used to finance the Gaon Panchayat's duties. Sums realized on behalf of the state do not go into the Gaon Fund. The state has the right to issue orders to the Gaon Panchayat, to turn over the duties and authority of the Gaon Panchayat to a person or some other authority if the Gaon Panchayat cannot carry out its duties or "it is otherwise expedient or necessary," and to make rules governing the Gaon Panchayats.[22]

By this series of trusteeships the act gives administrative power over local lands to the village government. When an interest in land is extinguished, the Gaon Sabha is to take possession and may admit anyone to the land as a sirdar where the land can be held sirdari, or as an asami where the land cannot be held sirdari. In admitting new holders to village land, priority shall be given to cooperative farms, to bhumidhars who hold less than six and one-quarter acres so that their holdings may rise to six and one-quarter acres, to other holders of land on the same conditions, to landless laborers residing in the circle, and lastly to any other person.[23]

The method of collecting arrears of revenue had to be altered somewhat to fit the new tenure and local government system. The state government reserves the right to use any method it likes to collect the revenue, but in practice delegates collection to the Gaon Sabha or the collector of the district. The methods of recovering an arrear are:

1. A writ of demand
2. Arrest and detention up to fifteen days
3. Sale of movable property
4. Attachment of the holding
5. Sale of the building
6. Sale of other immovable property.

The Gaon Sabha may employ only methods 1, 3, and 4, but the collector may employ them all, and in addition may attach a whole village or part of a village for up to three years, or lease a holding to some new party for up to ten years, in order to realize the arrears.[24] These provisions do no more than adapt the old system to the new tenures and to the Gaon Sabha organization.

Since the rental market never worked well, and since so many customary ways and different attitudes existed, some of which were frozen by the tenancy legislation, rents for like pieces of land varied so widely from place to place, within as well as between classes of cultivators, "that it is difficult to find any apparent justification for it." Because there was no justification for these variations, the Committee thought that rents should be equalized as far as possible, but that the process should await new settlement operations when there could be no objection in principle.[25] Equalization of rents is a reasonable objective, but if the cultivators themselves were to re-allocate the revenue to keep the burden on individuals fair, then the state could not fix new rents for the cultivators. The best the state could do would be to alter the total assessment on a village if the total were thought to be too high or too low. The sacrifice to reality which the Committee, and to an extent the legislature later, was unwilling to make was to realize that if the village were to govern itself, then the state would have to resign itself to what the village did, for if the state would not resign itself to letting the villages carry on some administration

and make some decisions, there would be no point or substance
to the complicated system of local government.

In her dissent to the *Report,* Begum Aizaz Rasul interpreted
the equalization of rents to mean that holders of sir and khudkasht
now paying a revenue of Rs. 1 per acre on the average would be
raised to the hereditary rate of Rs. 4 to Rs. 6 per acre.[26] The Committee's recommendations do not seem to mean this, and in any
event Act I of 1951 provides that a bhumidhar shall never pay
more than one-half the sirdari rate.[27]

Compensation presented a problem. On the logical plane it
was not clear how values should be computed: as a multiple of
land revenue, as a multiple of net rents, at market value, or as a
scaled multiple or proportion of one of these. For each there was
an argument, and against each there was an objection. Land revenue on different holdings had been assessed at different times
over half a century, although it had the legal advantage that it
represented an agreed assessment of 40 per cent of rentals. Rentals
were the logical choice but were difficult to discover.[28] Market
values were also hard to determine[29] and reflected a "prestige
value" over and above earning value, and the government was in
principle unwilling to accept this element.[30]

On the policy plane, one purpose of zamindari abolition was
to increase the revenues of the state. It followed that the costs of
compensation should be kept below the expected increase in government revenues of Rs. 678 lakhs.[31] The act provided for payment over forty years in 2.5 per cent bonds[32] at an annual cost
in interest and capital of Rs. 630 lakhs.[33] This leaves only Rs. 48
lakhs of uncommitted net gain to the state, but the interest charge
alone declines from an original maximum of Rs. 392 lakhs, so that
the state's debt or accounting position improves steadily until it
receives the full gain in the year 1992. The administration of the
abolition was estimated to cost an additional Rs. 154 lakhs.[34] The
compensation figures are shown in Table 19.

It is interesting to note that despite strong feelings against the
zamindars it did not occur to either the Committee or the legislature to convict the zamindars with their own evidence. The
zamindars recorded rents received in the siyaha record, which
showed collections varying from 51 per cent to 71 per cent of
recorded rent over the years 1930–46.[35] On the zamindars' own
evidence, the base for compensation could have been radically
reduced.

In accordance with the socialist aim of equalizing incomes and wealth, the Committee wanted to grade compensation in order to pay the richer zamindars proportionally less than was paid the poor ones.[36] The legislature avoided any legal difficulties involved in differential compensation by paying each zamindar eight times his net rentals,[c] and then paying "rehabilitation grants" graded to benefit the small zamindar. Whereas creditors of mortgage loans could collect from compensation, the "rehabilitation grants" were exempt from attachment except for unsecured personal loans.[37] Legally "compensation" was eight times "net assets"; the "true" multiple is shown in column 9 of Table 19 which also shows in column 10 the distribution of the total compensation of approximately Rs. 157 crores. Instead of thinking of a rate of return of 2½ per cent, which was all the Committee wished to see paid on compensation bonds, the Committee might have argued that the rate of return on an investment was much higher. Had the Committee argued that the zamindars could take the proceeds of their compensation and invest it in improving their own lands and lending to others and so earned a return of 25 per cent, the gross compensation would have been on the order of Rs. 36 crores, and it might have been possible to raise this amount of money. The Committee could easily have held that the zamindars could lend to cooperative societies at 10 per cent and the gross compensation would then have been around Rs. 100 crores.

The Committee bit off its nose to spite the zamindars' face in another respect. While the Provincial Congress Committee in 1932

c. I of 1951, Secs. 27–29, 37–40, 54, 60, 68, and Schedule I. Net rentals were the sum of the rents, cesses, and local rates in cash or in kind; undetermined rents at exproprietary or hereditary rates; the rents on proprietary cultivation at exproprietary rates; the rents on sir on which hereditary rights accrue at hereditary rates; patta dawami and istamrari sir at the rents actually paid; the average value of sayar income over the past 10 years; the average income from building sites over the past four years; the income from forests based upon the income over the past 20 to 40 years and the present yield; and the average mining royalty income over the past 12 years; minus all sums payable to the government or superior holder in the preceding year for land revenue, rents, cesses, or local rates; the agricultural income tax in the preceding year, if any; 15 per cent of gross revenue to cover costs of management and irrecoverables; the value of land under personal cultivation, or held as sir, grove, or khudkasht, computed at hereditary rates, less the sums payable as revenue, rent, cesses, rates, agricultural income tax, and 15 per cent for management; the income tax on royalties; and 95 per cent of the gross income of directly worked mineral rights.

TABLE 19. *Estimated Compensation of Zamindars under Act I of 1951*

Classification of zamindars by blocks of land revenue	Number of zamindars	Gross assets (Rs. millions)	Total deductions for land revenue, leases, cost of management, and irrecoverables (Rs. millions)	Net assets or income (Rs. millions)	Average net income per zamindar (Rs.)	Compensation multiple enacted by Act I of 1951
1	2	3	4	5	6	7
Not exceeding Rs. 25	1,710,520	28.0	13.0	15.0	9	8
Exceeding Rs. 25 but not Rs. 50	142,890	13.8	6.7	7.4	52	8
" " 50 " " 100	81,657	15.8	7.3	8.5	104	8
" " 100 " " 250	51,564	21.9	10.1	11.8	229	8
" " 250 " " 500	16,758	16.3	8.4	7.9	471	8
" " 500 " " 2,000	10,929	27.9	14.7	12.7	1,162	8
" " 2,000 " " 3,500	1,223	8.9	5.0	3.9	3,189	8
" " 3,500 " " 5,000	428	5.5	3.1	2.4	5,607	8
" " 5,000 " " 10,000	414	8.0	4.5	3.5	8,454	8
" " 10,000	390	42.1	23.7	18.4	47,179	8
Total	2,016,783	187.7	96.2	91.5		
Subproprietors and Underproprietors		8.6	2.4	6.2		

Source. Z.A.C. *Report*, pp. 419–21 for Cols. 2, 3, 4, 5, 6, and Act I of 1951, Schedule I for Cols. 7, 8.

Classification of zamindars by blocks of land revenue	Rehabilitation grant multiple of Act I of 1951	Total compensation multiple of Act I of 1951	Compensation under Act I of 1951 (Rs. millions)	Average compensation per zamindar under Act I of 1951 (Rs.)	Net assets as a percentage of total net assets (%)	Act I of 1951 compensation as a percentage of total compensation (%)
1	*8*	*9*	*10*	*11*	*12*	*13*
Not exceeding Rs. 25	20	28	420	246	16.7	27.0
Exceeding Rs. 25 but not Rs. 50	17	25	185	1,295	8.1	11.9
" 50 " " 100	14	22	187	2,290	9.3	12.0
" 100 " " 250	11	19	229	4,348	12.9	14.4
" 250 " " 500	8	16	126	7,543	8.6	8.1
" 500 " " 2,000	5	13	165	15,107	13.9	10.6
" 2,000 " " 3,500	3	11	43	35,132	4.3	2.8
" 3,500 " " 5,000	2	10	24	56,075	2.7	1.5
" 5,000 " " 10,000	1	9	32	76,087	3.8	2.0
" 10,000	0	8	147	377,436	20.1	9.5
Total			1,553	770	100.1*	99.8*
Subproprietors and Underproprietors			137			

*Cols. *12* and *13* do not add to 100.0% because of rounding.

TABLE 20. *Recorded Rents and Profits Compared with Actual Rents and Profits*

Year	Total recorded rental, cash, and grain including sayar and siwai income (Rs. millions)	Total collections of rental demand of current and previous years (Rs. millions)	Collections as a percentage of recorded rent (%)	Land revenue (Rs. millions)	Nominal margin of profit—Col. 2 minus Col. 5 (Rs. millions)	Actual margin of profit—Col. 3 minus Col. 5 (Rs. millions)	Actual profit as a percentage of nominal profit
1	2	3	4	5	6	7	8
1926–27	192	156	81.3	69	123	87	70.8
1927–28	192	154	80.1	69	123	85	68.9
1928–29	193	131	67.7	69	124	62	49.6
1929–30	194	143	73.8	70	124	73	58.9
1930–31	193	98	51.1	71	122	28	22.7
1931–32	188	112	59.7	71	117	41	35.2
1932–33	189	110	58.2	71	118	39	33.0
1933–34	187	99	53.0	71	117	28	24.2
1934–35	188	120	63.8	71	117	49	41.7
1935–36	188	126	67.0	71	117	58	46.9
1936–37	187	117	62.3	70	116	45	39.1
1937–38	183	120	65.7	70	113	50	44.3
1938–39	181	111	61.6	70	111	41	37.1
1939–40	181	122	67.4	70	111	52	46.8
1940–41	174	119	68.6	69	105	51	48.0
1941–42	171	107	62.8	68	103	39	38.1
1942–43	172	120	69.9	68	104	52	50.1
1943–44	174	124	71.4	68	106	56	52.9
1944–45	175	127	72.2	68	107	58	54.5
1945–46	175	115	65.5	69	107	46	43.4

Source: Z.A.C. *Report*, 2, Statement 21, p. 87 for Cols. 2, 5, and 6 and Statement 22 (iii) p. 92 for Col. 3. Other columns computed.

quoted the siyaha records of the rents actually paid, in order to support the contention that it was impossible to pay the nominal rents, the Zamindari Abolition Committee, also made up of Congressmen, insisted that the siyaha records were notoriously inaccurate, in order to support the contention that the zamindars were exploiting the tenants and that the incomes of zamindars were rising much faster than their revenue payments.[d] Table 20 shows the relationship between the nominal rents and the rent receipts recorded in the siyaha records. From the information provided by the Committee, columns 4, 7, and 8 may be computed. These show that from the beginning of the Depression onward, rental collections ran under two-thirds of rental demand; but even more important for purposes of computing the compensation to be paid, the actual net income ran well under half the nominal net income.[e] The Committee would have been justified in taking the figures which the zamindars claimed as their actual receipts and in fixing the compensation on the basis of these figures. The saving in compensation would have been enormous. If the siyaha figures were correct, this would have been the proper thing to do, and if they had been fraudulently understated, the wrongdoer would have had no right to cite his own wrongdoing in his own favor. If the recorded rental collections for the years 1941–42 through 1945–46 are averaged, the net income from landed rents was Rs. 5.03 crores. The Committee could thus have justified compensation as low as Rs. 20 crores, and could even have justified lower compensation by deducting from the rental collections the cost of collecting the rent.

d. Z.A.C. *Report,* p. 403. On page 415 the Committee says that between 1893–94 and 1944–45 land revenue rose by 15 per cent from Rs. 593 lakhs to Rs. 682 lakhs while rents rose by 43 per cent from Rs. 1,224 lakhs to Rs. 1,753 lakhs, and added that the figures did not contain concealed rents, levies, and cesses common in the thirties.

e. The zamindars argued that 15 per cent of rents was spent in the process of collection, and that, all in all, not more than 10 per cent of the rents remained in the zamindars' hands *(Eastern Economist,* March 28, 1947, p. 596). *The Eastern Economist* comments that "surely all will not agree with these percentage estimates."

CHAPTER 13

What Zamindari Abolition Accomplished

While the state government has been substituted for the zamindari as landlord, figures on the areas under different tenures and the distribution of zamindari ownership will not support the thesis that a major change has been made. Daniel Thorner lists U.P. among those areas of India in which there is "some perceptible change" but in which the agrarian structure remains basically the same.[1] Table 7 shows that virtually all tenures in U.P. had been brought under legislative protection by the 1920s, and that by the 40s nearly all holders of land had hereditary rights to their holdings. At the beginning of the century over half the cultivators held land on whatever terms the market provided. Forty years later only one-thirtieth held under these conditions.

It is not possible to give exact figures for the areas that became bhumidhari, sirdari, and asami under the Act of 1951, and it will not be possible to do so until all the resurveys have been completed under the land consolidation procedures—perhaps not until 1970. However, we can make a close approximation. When the percentages in Table 21 were computed for the *Report of the Revenue Administration in Uttar Pradesh for 1953*, the Revenue Administration had listed 94 per cent of the area paying 92 per 'cent of the revenue under one or another of the headings "bhumidhar," "sirdar," "asami," or "adhivasi." Since the transformation of adhivasis into sirdars, the total of sirdari land has risen to a total of two-thirds of the area of U.P. The results differ from those that one would have anticipated from the tables used by the Zamindari Abolition Committee, which indicated that only about a fifth of the area would become bhumidhari. The difference is accounted for by the acquisition of bhumidhari rights through purchases.

TABLE 21. *Percentages of Land Held and Land Revenue Paid by the New Tenure-holders*

Class	Percentage of acreage in 1953	Percentage of revenue in 1953	Acreage in 1957	Percentage of acreage in 1957
1	*2*	*3*	*4*	*5*
Bhumidhars	31	17	14,091,000	31.3
(by conversion of pre-1951 rights)			(8,135,000)	(18.1)
(by payment of a multiple of rent)			(5,965,000)	(13.2)
Sirdars	63	75	30,293,000	67.2
Asamis	1	1	290,000	0.6
Adhivasis	5	7	382,000	0.9

Source. Cols. 2 and *3, Report of the Revenue Administration of Uttar Pradesh for the Year Ending September 30, 1953*, computed from Statement 34—Z.A.; Cols. *4* and *5*, Singh, *Next Step in Village India*, p. 20, citing Shri Piyare Lal Rawat's unpublished Lucknow University thesis for which he compiled the data from the Register of Holdings and Rentals, 1956–57, Board of Revenue, Lucknow.

The first thing to be noted in comparison of the pre- and post-reform laws is the disappearance of a rental market and of a mortgage market. The end of the mortgage market goes part way to defeat the purpose of allowing transferability of land. The Committee reluctantly recommended that land be transferable in order to mobilize the financial resources of the rural areas, but this is now difficult since it is not possible to mortgage land.[2] These changes in status could have been accomplished without abolishing the zamindari system if existing law had been amended to prohibit the renting or mortgaging of land.

The abolition of the rental market was not completely effective. Professor Baljit Singh believes that land reforms have "failed in preventing subletting and renting. Quite many of those who till the soil have no land rights whereas many of those who do not cultivate still own and possess land. The latter let out their land to the former. . . . Besides letting and sub-letting, many carry on cultivation through permanent outside labour." In a survey of six villages it was found that 8 per cent of farmers cultivated "mainly through hired labour" and in one of the villages 9 per cent of the land was sublet and another 26 per cent farmed by sharecroppers.[3] S. C. Gupta of the Agricultural Economics Research Section of Delhi University found that 10 per cent of the land in Shamaspur village was sharecropped,[4] while Mukerjee and Gupta found that from 0.2 to 19.1 per cent of the land in cultivating possession in eight villages of western U.P. was let out.[5] These figures illustrate both the difficulty of differentiating hired labor from sharecroppers in enforcing the law and the strength of local relationships in subverting the law.

The second thing to be noted is that those zamindars who have now become bhumidhars retain absolute control over their holdings, a third of the total area, except that they cannot let it. In other words the land market is still functioning in regard to bhumidhari land, and the market may be more effective now than it was during the turmoil of the debt relief and tenancy legislation of the twenties and thirties.

The history of the Zamindari Abolition Fund shows how little the cultivators valued bhumidhari rights. The Committee had noted that the two classes of occupancy tenants in the Central Provinces and Berar had been able to purchase their land since 1940 by paying the landlord 10 or 12.5 times the rent, depending upon their classification, yet "tenants have not taken advantage of this provision to any great extent."[6] In 1949 the U.P. Minister of Revenue, Thakur Hukam, said that the Zamindari Abolition Fund set up by the purchase provisions of Act X of 1949 and continued in the same provisions of Act I of 1951 should raise over Rs. 170 crores from more than a crore of cultivators. Six months later, despite intense propaganda, only Rs. 16 crores had been raised, and the government was thinking of extending the time during which the cultivators could pay and raising the payment to eleven times the rent. By June expectations had fallen to a belief that Rs. 19 crores could be raised, and the government expressed a definite intention to extend the provisions of the 1949 Act and raise the rent multiple to eleven. *The Eastern Economist* said that the expectations that the peasants were eager and able to purchase bhumidhari rights had been disappointed, and that hope of being able to pay Rs. 50 crores of the compensation in cash were being given up. By August of 1950 the idea that purchase of bhumidhari rights would make the abolition of zamindari self-financing had been dropped. Rs. 26.81 crores had been collected. The sum was respectable, said *The Eastern Economist,* for 2.7 million people had paid an average of Rs. 100, and this was also evidence of a fair degree of prosperity in the countryside.[7] After three years Rs. 35 crores had been subscribed,[a] but by 1957 only a sixth of the sirdari area had been converted to bhumidhari (see Table 21). The lesson to be drawn is that the cultivators did not regard bhumidhari rights as worth ten times their annual rent. It may have been that the cultivators were unable to raise the funds; Sen thinks so[8] but neither the government nor *The Eastern Economist* thought this was the reason.

One can compute the return on money invested in the acquisition of bhumidhari rights. A reduction of one-half the revenue is bought at a cost of ten times the revenue, or $(.5R) \div (10R) = 5$ per cent. On delayed purchases at twelve times the revenue the return is 4.16 per cent. As a business matter it seems hardly worthwhile—a cultivator would do much better to invest in agricultural equipment—[9] but Thorner argues that there is much satisfaction in enjoying the "prestige and prerogatives of ownership."[10]

Two-thirds of the land is now held on sirdari tenure, and it is difficult to see how this new title alters the content of the old status. Most of this land was formerly held under occupancy or hereditary rights. It is no longer possible to sublet, but most of the land was cultivated by the occupancy and hereditary tenants anyway. Both before and after reform, the land was and is heritable but not transferable, and, both before and after, the land

a. Bhowani Sen, *Indian Land System and Land Reforms,* p. 90. A year later Thorner (*Agrarian Prospect,* p. 48) said that one-third of those eligible had purchased bhumidhari rights.

had to be, and has to be, used for agricultural purposes. Instead of paying a regulated rent to a private landlord, the cultivator now pays the same rent to the state. The complicated provisions for getting permission to make improvements no longer exist, and this is probably the greatest change in the terms of the sirdar's tenure. Amendments to the old tenancy legislation to allow an unrestricted right of improvement by the tenant would have been a significant alteration in the content of ownership rights, but considering the changes the tenancy laws made, such an amendment to these laws would not have been exceptional.

Of all the groups, the asamis benefited most from the reform, for they acquired permanent status. From being tenants-at-will the asamis became hereditary tenants and recognized holders of land, although a few lose their rights as claims based on pre-reform contracts expire. That they do not hold the same plots in perpetuity is a result of the uncertain character of the land they cultivate and is not a threat to their security. In the future, as one plot is forced out of cultivation they should be assured of another as a result of their permanent membership in the community of cultivators. The change in status is not merely an increase in their security of tenure, but extends to the substance of their position in the community under the new system of village government. However, only 5 to 10 per cent of the land is involved.

Two developments in remolding the agrarian structure of rural India have begun to affect the villages since the land reform legislation. The first is the Bhoodan Yagna or land-gift movement of Vinoba Bhave; the second is the network of Community Development Projects and National Extension Blocks that will extend over all of rural India. The former has not been an economic success, whatever may be said for its moral effects. Three-quarters of the land donated in U.P. was unfit for cultivation, and the total amount given was not great.[11]

In the longer run the Community Development Projects will probably prove the effective agent in transforming rural India, but in concept and administration they are a completely different matter from the land reform movement. If one wishes to peer into the future, the Community Projects should be the current point of departure.[b] For the purposes of a study of the history of land tenure in U.P. and the postindependence efforts to change that

b. The best source of information, and a fascinating book, is Albert Mayer, McKim Marriott, and Richard L. Park, *Pilot Project, India.*

system, however, the hope for the future inherent in the Community Projects is irrelevant.

Personal impressions of the results of a law are dangerous evidence on which to rely. The author interviewed civil servants in the revenue, land reform, cooperative, and panchayat branches of the U.P. government and some extension workers south of Allahabad in the summer of 1955 and came away with a mixed bag of views. There was wide agreement that the abolition had added to the dignity of those who became sirdars and asamis, and that the reforms were a "good thing." There was much less agreement on the extent to which it had resulted in nonpsychic benefits. In fact, there was only one uniformity: each interviewee credited any measurable gains to the work of his own department. But the "departmental views" emphasized the equalitarian and attitudinal benefits of reform and did not lend strong support to the argument that land reform helped agricultural productivity, except indirectly.

The act did lead to one crisis in administration. During the war and in the seven years following, owners could earn more by managing their holdings than by letting them, and tenants and sharecroppers were evicted and then hired as laborers. Toward the end of this period "the preliminaries to, and the stately legislative progress of, zamindari abolition gave to the patwaris of the U.P. an opportunity such as had never before occurred to them, even in their fondest dreams. They did not fail to avail themselves of it." The patwaris falsified accounts to such an extent that "one cannot go to a U.P. village today without hearing from ryots about land over which they should have sirdari rights but which went to the former landlord as bhumidhari land, courtesy of the patwari."[12]

Then in 1953 the patwaris asked too much. They demanded more pay; the government turned down the demand; and the patwaris called a strike. This gave the U.P. government an opportunity to rid itself of undesirable patwaris, and all were fired. Many lost the job permanently; others were rehired as lekhpals, the new title for village record-keepers and panchayat secretaries. However, the effort to "clean up" the servants of the local governments failed because the lekhpals, whether renamed patwaris or new men, proved as venal as their predecessors. Despite the new name the lekhpals are still commonly called patwaris; they are as disliked and distrusted as the old patwaris. It was not possible to hire literate men of a new sort at the salary of a lekhpal and within the social situation existing in the villages.

It is peculiar that the Land Reform Act tied the hands of the government well into the next century so far as concerns the power to raise revenue and thereby capital resources from the rural areas. While it is always possible to repeal the sections of the act fixing the revenue demand at its 1951 level, enacting these sections indicated an attitude of indifference toward possible sources of development capital. With the freedom to pay what compensation they wanted, with the opportunities opened by general agreement to revolutionize land tenure, and with the freedom from prior commitments implicit in India's new independence, the legislators left the revenue mechanism virtually untouched. With the abolition of the zamindari, new systems of land taxation and revenue assessments could have been adopted. The history of land tenure under British rule shows that many of the attributes of ownership had been transferred to the privileged tenant, but the legislature contented itself with nationalizing the rights remaining to the zamindars. At no point was the idea of varying the revenue with an index of agricultural prices even touched upon. Nothing was done about the possibility of varying revenue demand with the financial needs of the state. Despite the great advantages of government holding and manipulation of stocks in order to stabilize prices, and despite the real economic need for warehouses and graneries, there was no consideration of the possibility of collecting revenue in kind. No provision was made for relating land revenue or security of tenure to the development of capital resources on or off the land. Certainly remissions of revenue related to capital investment could provide a quicker start toward the solution of the problems of the cultivators than provisions to register cooperatives under stringent government regulation. The sanads of the talukdars said that they had to develop their lands. The grant of rights in Act I of 1951 allows bhumidhars to do anything at all with their lands except let them, and guarantees sirdars security of tenure no matter how ruinous their farming may be. Further inflation, a likely possibility in a developing country, could wipe out a large portion of the real value of land revenue. The reforms did not change tenures much. Neither did they change the revenue system much.

· Table 22 shows the revenue demand and collections immediately before and after the Zamindari Abolition Act. The gain in reve-

TABLE ·22. *Revenue Demand and Collections, 1952 and 1953*

Year (ending Sept. 30)	Demand (Rs.)	Collections (Rs.)	Percentage collected (Col. 3 ÷ Col. 2)
1	2	3	4
1952	70,689,053	66,329,898	94
1953	189,072,438	182,183,616	96

Source. *Report of the Revenue Administration of Uttar Pradesh* for the years ending September 30, 1952 and 1953 (Allahabad, Supt., Printing and Stationery, U.P.), Statement I. My computations for Col. *4*.

nue demand of Rs. 11.84 crores exceeds the additional cost falling upon the state consequent upon the reforms by Rs. 2.01 crores. (Table 23). The net gain is not great. Thorner was disturbed to find the cultivators paying the whole cost of abolition, when the purpose of the reform was to lighten their burdens. "If, indeed, the zamindars were parasitic, the question can be asked as to whether they were entitled to any compensation at all."[13]

Land revenue, and particularly land revenue in kind, seems to be an excellent way to combat the insufficiency of a marketable surplus of grain during industrial development. The classic case of a crisis in the marketable surplus of agriculture was the scissors crisis in Russia in the 1920s. Food does not necessarily follow labor to the towns, for with fewer mouths in the village each mouth may decide to eat more. Maurice Dobb believes that

> if there is any factor to be singled out as the fundamental limiting factor upon the pace of development, then . . . it is the *marketable surplus* of agriculture: this rather than the total product, or the productivity, of agriculture in general. . . . The surmounting of this limit is accordingly a matter, not of providing appropriate financial policies and institutions, but of the appropriate organization of the social and economic life of the village, of agricultural production and of commercial exchange between village and town.[14]

Of all possible forms of organization, small peasant holdings are least likely to provide a large marketable surplus. In Russia, although by the late twenties agricultural production had revived to the pre-World War I level, the marketable surplus was still at

TABLE 23. *Liability of State Consequent upon Zamindari Abolition*

Item	Cost (Rs. millions)
Installments of interest and principal	576
Annuities to charities	60
Subsidy in lieu of local rates and cesses to district boards	139
Cost of collecting revenue	80
Assessment and administration of compensation	78
Loss in agricultural income tax	50
Total	983

Source. "An Account of the Land Reforms Legislation in Uttar Pradesh" (mimeo., U.P. Govt., 1954?), p. 20.

one-half the pre-World War I level.[15] It would be much easier in U.P., and much more in line with the customs of its people, to increase the quantity of food reaching the towns by levying a high land revenue, or collecting a large part of it in kind, than by the more drastic measures that Soviet Russia found necessary.

The problem of a marketable surplus is not one that is merely likely to arise in the future. It has plagued India for many years. Procurement of food through official channels from 1944 through 1947 remained constant at about five million tons. This amounted to 10 per cent of a total production of fifty-five million tons, or 20 per cent of the marketable surplus of twenty-five million tons. Village retention of produce increased because high prices and the scarcity of consumers' goods made it necessary for the farmer to sell as much as before, and even the high prices were regarded by the cultivators as "inadequate." Compulsion was needed, and went so far as shooting in exceptional cases, but the compulsion needed was too great for popular governments to employ.[16] The government of U.P. made a survey during the war and found out that 40 per cent of the cultivators had no surplus at all to sell; that 33 per cent had to part with practically all their wheat in order to pay their rents and other charges; and that only 27 per cent "may be presumed to be in a position to withhold the disposal of their surplus."[17] This is not only evidence of poverty. It is evidence of a very dangerous situation, for the lucky quarter who can withhold their surplus can cause untold difficulty, and the other three-quarters can only be induced to sell because the charges made upon them are so great. Since agriculture in U.P. is not organized for the sole purpose of selling its product, some means must be found to induce the peasant to sell if he has a surplus. It is surprising that neither the Zamindari Abolition Committee nor the legislature attempted to assure a food supply for the towns when they were revising the system of land tenures. There can be no doubt that U.P. and the rest of India face a problem of moving food from the surplus to the deficit areas; from the rural to the urban areas. It is not necessary to regard this as *the* major threat to the development of the country to see that the tendency of the cultivator to consume all his produce is a major threat to development.

There were a shade over two million zamindars. If we assume that the zamindars' families averaged five members, the zamindars and their families constituted ten million persons or one-sixth of the population of the state.[c] This is too large a group to be treated as a lesser breed outside the law. In addition, it is wrong to imply that one-sixth of the population owned the land while the other five-sixths had to serve the one-sixth. Only 75 to 80 per cent of the population is dependent upon agriculture, so the zamindars and their dependents constituted over a fifth of those dependent upon agriculture.

But even this figure gives a misleading idea of the number of cultivators who stood to benefit. The Committee said that there were in U.P. four hundred landless laborers for every one thousand cultivators.[d] Assuming that a fifth of the population was not engaged in agriculture, that a sixth were zamindars, and that there were four hundred landless laborers to every thousand cultivators, 40 per cent of the population is unaccounted for and may be called "cultivators other than zamindars," as in Table 24. If we assume four members in a zamindar's family, the zamindari percentage would fall to 13 and the cultivators other than zamindars would rise to 44 per cent, but in either case the figures indicate that a minority of the population of U.P. benefited from the

c. Begum Aizaz Rasul in her dissent from the *Report,* p. 601, notes that the original returns to the Committee showed 2.9 million zamindars, and says that a quarter of the population was made up of zamindars and their dependents.

d. Z.A.C. *Report,* p. 503. The figure for all India in 1931 was 417 landless laborers per thousand cultivators and both R. K. Mukerji and Gyan Chand believe the figure doubled by 1947 (Ibid., p. 550). Although the evidence in support of the contention is not given, the Committee felt that the ratio of 400 to 1,000 was about right for U.P.

TABLE 24. *Occupational Distribution of the Population of U.P.*

Occupation	Percentage of the population
Nonagricultural population	20
Zamindars	17
Landless laborers	23
Cultivators other than zamindars	40

reforms. To put it another way seventeen zamindars had to be abolished to help forty tenants. Sill another way of stating the implications of Table 24 is to say that 60 per cent of the people were hurt or were unaffected by the abolition. Certainly it is not true that a large majority of the people in U.P. are benefiting from the reduction in status of a small minority.

However, one can have very little faith in the figures given in Table 24 for they are in gross disagreement with the figures for the number of cultivators in U.P., the population of U.P., and the population living in towns in U.P. Figures of the occupational distribution of the Indian population sometimes appear impossible to use. The Thorners have found in analyzing the data that the census enumerates 2.36 million agricultural laborers in U.P. whereas, using different definitions, the Agricultural Labour Enquiry's most comparable figure would be 4.70 million.[18] Earlier, Thorner had shown that the census figures were unreliable because they depended on classifications that were not operationally defined.[19]

The total number of holdings was over twelve million including holdings under all kinds of tenure.[20] Except for the count of all zamindars, on which Table 24 is based, the figures compiled for the Committee counted zamindars and other persons more than once if they held land in more than one pargana, but the secretary to the Committee thought that the margin of error was "for all practical purposes negligible."[21] If the Committee's twelve million holdings represent twelve million families, one cannot account for landless laborers. If each cultivator had five dependents, the cultivators and their families totaled sixty million, or the entire population of U.P. If we assume families of four including the cultivator, the cultivators and their families made up about 80 per cent of the population, but since we know that the other fifth is not dependent upon agriculture there is still no margin to account for the landless laborers. To assume a smaller size for the cultivator's family would deny all estimates of the typical Indian family.

There is evidence from recent village surveys of a high degree of duplication in occupational status. In three villages of Bulandshahar District (in western U.P.) just over one-third of the households had subsidiary occupations, roughly divided between agriculture and other employments. In the district of Meerut (also in western U.P.) the proportions of households with subsidiary occupations varied from two-thirds to three-quarters in the five villages surveyed.[22] In Saharanpur District one village of 67 households had 112 occupations, and only one of nineteen households classified as "agricultural laborers" depended entirely upon agricultural labor for a living. A third of the households combined nonagricultural and agricultural occupations; of twenty-three bhumidhari households, seven had subsidiary occupations; and of twenty-seven sirdari and (illegal) tenant households, fourteen had subsidiary occupations.[23]

To solve the dilemma we must make a choice: we can assume a large landless labor problem only by ignoring the land records; or we can deny the existence of a large landless labor problem. However, a better way out of the dilemma is to revise the concept of the landless laborer. A man with a small plot appears in the figures as a nonowning cultivator, or even as a zamindar, and yet the major part of his income may have come from wages or shares in the harvest. There may also have been several adult and adolescent males in a family, one of whom farmed the holding while the others undertook wage labor. In fact, both these cases occurred, and double counting is the only explanation of the figures—the only way of reconciling the twelve million cultivators with the assertion that there were a large number of landless laborers.[e]

However we choose to reconcile the conflicting figures, it is necessary to reduce the dimensions attributed to one or another of the social problems. One cannot have it both ways. If it is asserted that the great problem is the large number of cultivators with very small plots, then one cannot also assert that there is a great problem of landless laborers. If one asserts that there is a

e. The intricacies involved in attempts to differentiate laborers from laborers with cultivation as a subsidiary occupation from cultivators with labor as a subsidiary occupation from earning dependents from "helpers" are made clear in Daniel and Alice Thorner, "Agricultural Manpower in India: Labourers," *Economic Weekly*, Nov. 9, 1957.

great landless labor problem, then one cannot assert that there is also a bad crisis among the very small tenants. One can choose to treat these people either as cultivators on impossibly small plots or as landless laborers (more properly, as laborers largely or mostly dependent upon wages), but not as both. If either problem is solved, the other problem disappears because the same persons are involved in both. If they are provided with economic plots, then they stop earning wages and the agricultural laborer disappears. If the conditions of agricultural labor are brought up to a satisfactory level, it is no longer necessary to worry about their small supplementary holdings.

When the figures, estimates, and guesses are reconciled by assuming fifteen million families, of four members each, in U.P., three million of which were nonagricultural, two million zamindari, and ten million nonowning cultivators and laborers, we find that a large number of people in the U.P. were zamindars, and that an even larger number could not benefit directly from the reform of the land tenures. In consequence, it is to be feared that zamindari abolition may prove less astute politically than has been hoped, and may well contribute less to the sum total of welfare and happiness than has been believed.

The second striking fact emerging from Table 24 is that most zamindars were extremely small holders. Eighty-five per cent paid on the average Rs. 5.88 in revenue. If they were taxed at 40 per cent of net assets, the average rental value of their holdings was Rs. 14.7. If they were taxed at, say, a third of net assets since their holdings were so small, the average rental value of their holdings came out to Rs. 17.64. The Zamindari Abolition Committee treated payments of revenue under Rs. 250 as evidence of the status of "small zamindars." This group constituted 98.5 per cent of the zamindars, and with two-fifths of the net assets of an estate going to revenue, the average rental value of these estates worked out at Rs. 36. It is immediately apparent that there is very little point in talking about exploitation by the zamindars as a class. Only a few thousand zamindars were in a position to exploit anyone, and only about eleven hundred received gross rental incomes of over Rs. 10,000 (the salary of a very well paid professor). About fifteen hundred zamindars received net incomes of over Rs. 5,000.

These figures show that the troubles of U.P. could not be blamed upon the zamindars. At best the troubles could be blamed upon the large zamindars, but then the criticism of the system was a criticism of large properties and not of zamindars. Since the large properties were divided into many small holdings, the criticism should have been directed at the management of the large properties, and this in turn could only mean the failure to invest in the improvement of the property, for after the twenties that was the major managerial function of the landowner. We find ourselves back at the proposition that the difficulty lay in the lack of real savings and investment or in the social structure of village life, with the possibility of charging a few thousand zamindars with a large share of the blame for this state of affairs. But once this point is reached, the crux of the matter is seen to have been the investment habits of these men, and not the zamindari system. The next step in reform should have been directed toward assuring that more of their resources went into investment. Only incidentally, as one possible part of a method, would the abolition of zamindari become part of a solution of this problem.

The question, then, to be asked about zamindari abolition is: to what extent was it likely to result in directing more resources into real investment? Would the removal of large private landlords, owning from a quarter to a half of the land, depending upon where one draws the line for large landlords, result in a larger amount of real investment? Investment will increase only if the state employs the rental income for investment, or if cultivators individually receiving much smaller incomes than the zamindars whom they are replacing make larger investments. There are evidently many gaps between abolition and the solution to the problems of agriculture.

The question whether land reform will lead to an increase in investment by the cultivators breaks down into three subsidiary questions:

1. Will it provide larger resources to the cultivators for investment?
2. How will it affect the cultivator's propensity to save and to invest?
3. How will it affect the forms in which the cultivator chooses to invest?

The answer to the first question is that the cultivators gain only the amount previously extracted from them illegally. The purchase of bhumidhari rights either uses up liquid capital that could have been used for investment in real capital or puts the cultiva-tor into debt.[f]

The incentive effects are positive. The question really is, how important are they? Thorner argues that insecurity of tenure left the cultivator and the laborer with no reason to undertake im-provements, and "seeing before them little prospect of betterment of their condition, concentrated rather on warding off a worsen-ing." On the other side, the proprietors, finding "it more profitable to rent out their lands than to manage them personally," did not think it worthwhile "to invest capital in agricultural operations so long as these operations were to be left in the hands of the most backward and ill-educated villagers." This complex he calls "the built-in depressor."[24] The positive effect involved in giving the cultivator hope of betterment must be offset to some degree by his "backwardness," and of course the reforms did nothing for the landless laborer. Furthermore, what moves the Indian peasant is not, or at least not most importantly, the drive toward economic efficiency. "The primary aim of all classes in the agrarian struc-ture," says Thorner, "has not been to increase their income by adopting more efficient methods, but to rise in social prestige by abstaining insofar as possible from physical labor."[25]

In the 1930s Doreen Warriner made an impressive study of ag-riculture and land reform in eastern Europe. The results, inter-preted in the light of conditions in U.P., are not encouraging. She found that the volume of savings among the peasantry was larger than it was on the estates: "peasants in all regions where a money economy is established tend to save a very high proportion of their income, even when the income is much smaller than that of a wage earner."[26] The peasant holdings were more capital-intensive than the large estates. The trouble arose from the facts that wide dispersion of ownership tended to lead to overinvestment in land at the expense of capital accumulated for industry; and that the savings were not mobilized but misdirected into uneconomic in-vestment and high land prices, creating a capital shortage amidst high savings. The more heavily populated the area, the more pro-nounced were these effects, and in areas of low rainfall (under 24 inches) there were too many draft animals per acre and no way in which to grow fodder.[27] These are the conditions which obtain

f. Thorner (Agrarian Prospect, pp. 24–25) says that the result of zamindari abolition is to leave the cultivator with no more resources than he had before abolition.

in U.P. There is a likelihood that the incentive effects of zamindari abolition will exhaust themselves in uneconomic forms of investment, and in "investments" for which the ryot has a high propensity—jewelry, purchases of rights in land, ceremonies, conspicuous leisure—but which do not raise the level of capital intensity.

On the other hand Bernard Cohn, in his study of a village in eastern U.P., reports that the ex-zamindars are not investing their savings in farming but rather in the education of their sons so that the sons will be able to get and hold urban jobs and so support the family. Their secondary outlet for investment funds is in contract building and commerce. These same Thakur bhumidhars are trying to raise Rs. 60,000 in order to qualify for a matching government grant to start a cooperative sugar mill.[28] Until after the event it is probably impossible to tell whether the effect of abolition will be to increase investment in farming, to cause misinvestment in farming, or to encourage investment outside the agricultural sector. While no one would disapprove of the devotion of funds to the furthering of education or the development of cooperative processing enterprises, India is almost notorious for the degree to which its citizens have already overinvested in commercial activity.

There are other standards by which to judge the reforms: those of social equality and democratic process. Here perhaps is the strongest argument for abolishing zamindari tenure, but the abolition may be as much an effect as a cause of increasing democracy. The tendency of the separate hierarchies of caste, of landownership, of wealth, and of political power to coalesce makes free and equalitarian social and political life difficult to achieve.[g] It is for this reason that Thorner insisted on the necessity for a much more thoroughgoing land reform than U.P. had experienced. The demand to take land from those who do not work it and to give it to those who do "is the one most frequently made in most parts of rural India by the working peasants themselves. It does not originate from outside, but from the very core of village realities. The heart of power, prestige, and standing in the village lies in land. Put the land in the hands of those who are working it and

g. Thorner (Ibid., p. 76) says that a small minority "enjoy an effective concentration of local economic, social, and political power," and although this minority owns less than half the land, it controls the most valuable land and gives out the most land to others.

you crack the existing concentration of power."[29] This is social reform, however, not economic improvement. It may be more important for the soul of man—this writer is sure it is—than economic efficiency, but it is not an economic argument for land reform. And this is largely Myrdal's argument when he asserts that "land reforms have their significance in the national plan not only as a precondition for raising productivity in agriculture but, more primarily, as a means of shattering the foundations of the stale class structure of a stagnating society."[30]

But in U.P. the abolition of zamindars has not led to social and political equality and was unlikely to have done so. The vision Thorner had of the results of thorough reform was belied by his experience in U.P., where six to twelve families still controlled the cultivators and laborers in the village, where the resident landlords-become-bhumidhars were the backbone of the Congress party which administers the state, and where "now that the great absentee zamindars have been removed, the resident zamindars and big tenants have come up to take their place; today they strut around as lords of the land."[31] One effect of the abolition may have been to consolidate the middle castes in defense of a new and common vested interest against the Harijans, who were not benefited by the reforms. By 1951 the conflict between peasants and laborers had led to the formation of communal organizations. Malaviya's account of the first and second elections to the local panchayats cites evidence that these elections tended to become struggles between communal or caste groups.[32]

In the village of Madhopur the abolition was having its intended effects during the middle fifties so far as the low but clean Noniya caste was concerned, but the Harijan Chamars had been dispossessed and had no recourse but to go to the city to join the "emerging working class." The Noniyas became "increasingly independent of their old landlords" and built their own school and now celebrate the ritual holidays in their own hamlet. But the lowest levels did not benefit from the act. The claims of permanent tenants who should have become sirdars were not entered in the records. Some stayed on as tenants; others were ejected. Only a few of those who had the right to sirdari tenures took advantage of the abolition act. The rest were suffering a "marked" deterioration in their standard of living—were in fact going hungry, so hungry that marriages were breaking up for lack of food. The Chamars were being driven to the towns, much against their tastes, whatever the ultimate advantage might be. Cohn believed that a new rural society was emerging, but not the one "that the Planning Commission and those concerned with revitalization of village life may want." The continuum of social life between town and country was disappearing. "In a generation's time . . . a gap will have developed which is new to Indian history, and paradoxically enough India will develop a peasantry in the middle of the twentieth century such as we are familiar with in European history of the eighteenth and nineteenth centuries. . . . The village will be in the hands of small peasant proprietors, with a floating group of landless workers."[33]

The success of the reforms in establishing a new social and political society depends, however, not upon the gift of the legislature but upon the willingness and ability of the lower orders in the hierarchy to assert themselves and to take upon themselves the powers and responsibilities of that new society.

> No society has ever substantially reformed itself by a movement from above: by a simple voluntary decision of an upper class, springing from its social conscience, to become equal with the lower classes and to give them free entrance to the class monopolies. Ideals and social conscience do play their very considerable role, which should not be forgotten. But they are weak as self-propelled forces, originating reforms on a large scale—they need the pull of demands being raised and pressed for.
>
> When power has been assembled by those who have grievances, then is the time when ideals and social conscience can become effective.[h]

The movement from below had been taking place in U.P. for some time before the passage of the Zamindari Abolition Act, actually since the Congress began its appeal to tenants and laborers in 1919. By 1931 "the country" was "seething with such a deep spirit of agrarian discontent that it" would require "only a touch of sympathy on the part of anyone to inflame it," said Gangulee in a letter to *The Englishman;* and "we have already the signs of it in the United Provinces."[34] There has undoubtedly been an acceleration of the rise of the lower classes, but this process was becoming effective in the organization of the Harijans against the

h. Gunnar Myrdal, *Rich Lands and Poor,* p. 71.

higher castes in the early panchayat elections[35] before land reform became effective.

The changes in U.P. were presaged three-quarters of a century ago in Bengal by determined ryots, long before zamindari abolition. When Carstairs went to Tipperah district in 1874, he found "a new influence—that of the peasantry." The landlords and their clerks were not natives of the district. The ryots had begun "to pluck up spirit" and "became able to hold their own against physical violence."

> Litigation they did not fear. They were themselves well versed in the trickery of the law, and met the landlord even there on equal terms.
>
> The peasantry had learnt to unite. They formed for the purposes of common action and common defense . . . leagues, thousands strong, having common funds, and employing, when necessary, the best lawyers.[36]

Land reform does not make new men of peasants. New men make land reform.

PART V

CHAPTER 14

Consolidation and Economic Holdings

Characteristic of all India has been the increasing fragmentation of holdings, in ryotwari as much as in zamindari areas. It does not arise from a hierarchical tenure system and is not prevented by land reform in the specific sense of the abolition of landlords. In a wider sense, it does require "reform," and following upon the Abolition Act of 1951 the U.P. government undertook to re-arrange the many plots in single holdings into solid blocks.[1]

The division of single holdings into many plots can be traced back to the ancient idea of fair shares, when each member of the village community could expect to have some of each kind of land. Since then the religious laws of inheritance have made matters progressively worse. Not only is the holding divided among the sons, so that with each generation the size of holdings becomes smaller, but each son takes a plot of each kind, so that the individual plots multiply even faster than the number of holdings. In ryotwari areas there is only one main tenure, but even so, attempts to check fragmentation have not been successful.[2]

"The evils of fragmentation need no emphasis: waste of time and effort, the impossibility of rational cultivation are obvious effects. Nonetheless, the consolidation of holdings is not an easy reform to carry through. The conservatism of the peasant is one obstacle, the high cost per acre of surveying and exchanging many small plots is another. Even in a country so advanced as Switzerland the process of consolidation has been slow,"[3] although the "Indian experience proves that consolidation can achieve definitely good results in increasing production and that it can be linked with an impetus towards better living."[4]

Throughout the nineteenth century the British felt that if subdivision persisted beyond the rational limit, the cultivators would fall into hopeless poverty, decay, and debt, and would sell their land. "Many of them then become mere tenants under the purchaser, who by virtue of his sale title reaggregates the various shares he has bought up."[5] This does not seem to have happened to a noticeable extent, because the reaggregation of title did not mean that the plots were reaggregated into compact farms. Tenants continued to till the plots as they had before. F. G. Bailey's study of an Orissa village[6] showed that subdivision, fragmentation, and reaggregation followed changes in family size and not in farming efficiency. Families with a number of sons and grandsons often lost their lands by the third generation, while new, larger holdings were created by single men or men with "only sons." Distribution of land thus became a function of fertility rather than economic rationality. The market mechanism did not provide an automatic correction to fragmentation.

Increasing efforts have been made to prevent fragmentation and to reduce the number of plots in existence. A first permissive measure was to allow tenants of the same class to exchange their land and retain their rights if the landlord or landlords agreed,[7] but it was finally decided that stronger legislative measures were needed. The U.P. Consolidation of Holdings Act VIII of 1939 provided that any proprietor, any lambardar, or the cultivators cultivating a third of the village area might apply for an order of consolidation, whereupon all cases for the partition of holdings were halted. When the records were in order a consolidation scheme was drawn up. Each cultivator was given land suitable for each of the principal crops of the village. Where equality of value between the old and new holdings was not possible, the losers received compensation. When possible, cultivators were given any land on which they had made improvements, and where this could not be done the cultivator received compensation. All rights and liabilities on the old holdings ceased, the rights and liabilities following the cultivator to his new holding.[8] The Tenancy Act of 1939 also permitted landholders, underproprietors, permanent lessees, or tenants to apply to the assistant collector for an order to exchange lands, the encumbrances following the cultivators to the new land.[9]

Beginning in 1923, a campaign was conducted to consolidate holdings through cooperative societies.[10] The growth of these societies was steady but not rapid. Only twenty to thirty new consolidation societies were added to the rolls each year.[11] In consolidating, it was not possible to put all the fields of one cultivator into one block. The most that could be accomplished was to put all the fields of one kind into a single block.[12] By the start of the Second World War, the Registrar of Cooperative Societies felt that the advantages of consolidation were "increasingly being realized,"[13] and 218 societies had consolidated 100,000 bighas and reduced the number of plots in the consolidated areas by about 90 per cent.[14] At this time the cooperative effort was combined with the legislative effort, and a drive was made which by 1947 had reduced 57,000 fields to 7,000 and added 3 per cent to the cultivated area by eliminating boundaries. In 1947 the emphasis was shifted to developing cooperative farming, at first on an experimental basis.[15] The main effort seems to have been on reclaimed land. Twenty-two thousand acres in the Ganga Khadir and 80,000 in the Naini Tal tarai were colonized in self-supporting schemes.[16]

The Zamindari Abolition Committee argued that the zamindari system obstructed the consolidation of holdings not only because it was necessary to convince both owners and tenants of the advantages of consolidation but also because the existence of so many different tenures with different rights made it hard to re-allocate land. For this reason consolidation in the Punjab, where a single form of peasant tenure prevailed, was successful, while in East Bengal the landlord system prevented the cooperative consolidation movement from making headway.[17] The Punjab tenancies were essentially tenancies-at-will, and only one step was required to revise the records. In U.P. the tenants with rights would have had to exchange plots along with the zamindars, and an administrative problem would have arisen since the tenants held under different kinds of rights and under different zamindars. This meant, first, that within the solid blocks tenants would have had differing rights to different plots; and, second, that consolidation would have been incomplete unless a scheme was devised to exchange tenants among landlords.

Since abolition the process has become much simpler since most ex-tenants now hold under a uniform sirdari tenure. The U.P. Consolidation of Holdings Act[18] of 1953 provides for compulsory consolidation whenever the government decides it is ready to consolidate an area.[19] The procedure is to turn the recording and adjudication of rights over to a settlement officer (consolidation) and his assistant consolidation officer (A.C.O.), who checks the maps and records for errors, corrects them, and arranges to partition joint holdings if the co-sharers wish to do so. The A.C.O. then draws up a statement showing all plots of each tenure-holder with area, soil classification, hereditary rent rates, and rental value; and another statement showing the total area, total rent or revenue payment, and total rental value of the holdings of each tenure-holder. An arbitrator appointed by the consolidation officer settles all disputes over the accuracy of these statements.[20] The next stage is the preparation of a statement of the lands to be held publicly by the village for roads, trees, pasture, fisheries, manure pits, khaliyans (granaries), cremation grounds, graveyards, abadi, conservancy, and "works of public utility and other common use."[21] The Consolidation Committee drawn from the Village Land Management Committee advises on this and other proposals of the A.C.O.[22] The village land is demarcated in no more than three blocks on the basis of "(i) The kind and number of crops grown in the village; (ii) The quality of soil; (iii) The existence or absence of irrigation facilities; and (iv) The presence of land subject to fluvial action of any river."[23] The tenure-holders are to receive no more chaks (plots) than there are blocks, preferably as close as possible to the old plots and to the plots of relatives.[24] The "allotment of plots . . . shall be made on the basis of the rental value thereof," within the limitation that the new acreage must be within 20 per cent of the old.[25] Any rights or obligations attaching to the old plots move with the cultivator to the new plots. With the completion of these stages the cultivators acquire their new holdings; a new record of rights and village map are drawn up, and the operation is completed with a division of the costs among the beneficiaries.[26]

The state government is moving slowly in implementing the Consolidation Act.[a] There is a shortage of personnel, so that areas in only two tehsils (subdivisions of districts) were taken up in 1954–55, and while operations are expanding it requires more than a year to consolidate holdings in a small area. Compulsory consolidation is still in progress in the Punjab after a decade, and there it has been found to take upwards of three years to reach satisfactory accords in some villages.[b] To the problems of verifying and correcting records, some of which are forty years old and out of date,[c] one must add the need to achieve a high degree of consensus among the cultivators if fights and litigation are to be avoided. It will of course be difficult to evaluate the effectiveness of the consolidation schemes until the mid-1960s at the earliest. Meanwhile, it has been noted that immediately prior to and during consolidation operations credit facilities disappear because moneylenders fear loss of funds. It is not clear why this should be so— mortgages are illegal anyway and obligations follow the man to the new land—but it is said to be the case.

Ralph Retzlaff says that the consolidation conducted in a northern U.P. village under observation by the India Project of Cornell University was welcomed and the resulting reallocation of land approved, but this may in part reflect already existing caste unity in the village.[d] The common view appears to be that compulsory consolidation is a popular measure among all parties,[e] although Professor Baljit Singh argues that consolidation of holdings benefits only the cultivators with larger holdings. Furthermore, once their holdings are consolidated the larger landholders are less

a. Except where otherwise noted, the information about consolidation since the act was gathered from conversations with revenue, panchayat, cooperative, land reform, and consolidation officials in the departments at Lucknow during August 1955.

b. Conversations with proprietors in the Punjab, March–July 1956.

c. Village patwaris are supposed to keep them up to date, but a sloppy and frequently corrupt job has been done.

d. Interview with Ralph Retzlaff of Cornell India Project, April 3, 1958.

e. Interviews as above in U.P.; Ralph Ratzlaff; correspondence with Dr. Edward E. LeClair, Jr., of Cornell India Project; my own interviews with proprietors in the Punjab who are of the same Jat and Rajput castes as those common in western U.P.; and correspondence with Professor Willis D. Weatherford of Swarthmore who has studied the Punjab consolidation proceedings.

willing to pool their lands in cooperatives, Singh's primary objective. Even within the limits of these severe strictures, he does not believe consolidation is particularly helpful. Despite the redrawing of boundaries the old field dikes are still used, and in an investigation of three villages in one district he found that consolidation had not reduced the number of plots and in one case had increased them from 268 to 389 "as it involved division of certain old plots."[27]

While the problem of consolidating existing split-up holdings has now been tackled, the problem of preventing further fragmentation has not been fully solved, nor the closely allied problem of subdivision of holdings. The major difficulty is inheritance, because religious tradition requiring equal sharing among sons is reinforced by a father's natural desire to provide for all of them.

Bhumidhars and sirdars may sue for the partition of joint holdings,[28] but if the aggregate area of the holding is less than six and a quarter acres the court shall sell the holding and distribute the proceeds. If the partition would create holdings of less than six and a quarter acres the court may dismiss the suit or divide the land "in accordance with such principles as may be prescribed," but in any case a co-tenure holder who has acquired bhumidhari rights under the 1949 act may have his land split off from the rest of the holding. When a sale is ordered in lieu of partition, the court shall fix a price and offer the holding to the co-sharers, and if there are two co-sharers with equal rights the land shall go to the highest bidder. If no one will pay the price fixed by the court, the land shall be sold to the highest bidder.[f]

Although the provisions designed to prevent excessive subdivision are strong, they are weakened by the fact that there is nothing to stop the co-sharers from subdividing the holding informally and cultivating it in the same way they would have if partition had been granted. Furthermore, the antipartition clauses do not solve the problem of inheritance. The bhumidhar may bequeath his holding in any way he wishes. No sirdar or asami may bequeath his holding, and the holdings of sirdars, asamis, and of bhumidhars who die intestate devolve by a special succession. This succession gives precedence to male lineal descendants, widows, fathers, and so on through a wide list of relatives,[29] causing further subdivision and fragmentation upon the death of the holder.

f. I of 1951, Secs. 178–81. With the exception of these provisions, the right of pre-emption is ended entirely. See Sec. 336.

There will be some slight opportunity to consolidate further and to build up larger holdings when interests in land are extinguished. This will happen when sirdars or asamis surrender their holdings or lose their land because they have not used it for agricultural purposes for two years. Interests of sirdars, asamis, and intestate bhumidhars are extinguished when there are no heirs, and the interests of the first two lapse with ejectment, surrender, or abandonment.[30]

Fragmentation of holdings is only part of the problem of the uneconomic use of land. The other part is the small size of holdings. Most holdings in U.P. are too small to achieve full efficiency even with primitive methods of agriculture. Since there is not much more land to be had, the only solution is to remove a large number of cultivators from the land, and this *must* mean the *development of industries* to absorb the surplus population on the land. There is no way to evade this problem or to avoid this solution. Industrialization requires an increase in the capital resources of industry and commerce, so that wherever one looks in seeking to improve the lot of the cultivators, one comes up against the technological necessity of increased real investment.

Two criteria of an economic holding have been used in India. In the nineteenth century, Keatinge defined the economic holding as one that allowed a man to produce enough to support himself and his family in reasonable comfort after paying his necessary expenses.[31] The United Nations group thought that

> In many under-developed countries, however, the question of what acreage constitutes a minimum economic holding, in the sense of what acreage will permit full utilization of the farmer's equipment, is less important than the question of what acreage provides a subsistence minimum, either directly by growing food or indirectly by providing an income from commercial crops. The standard is measured not in terms of a necessary scale of operation, but of a minimum standard of food consumption.[32]

The U.P. Provincial Banking Enquiry Committee used a similar criterion: the minimum holding needed to support a family at its accustomed standard of living.[33]

On the basis of its criterion the U.N. group decided that the minimum holding in India is 5 acres of which 2.3 must be well watered.[34] The Banking Enquiry Committee computed minimum

TABLE 25. *Derivation of the Size of a Minimum Economic Holding*

| | Cultivator's expenses | | | | Rent per acre | | Minimum economic holding | | |
Division	Value of outturn per acre (Rs.)	Food* (Rs.)	Clothes (Rs.)	Other† per acre (Rs.)	Statutory tenant (Rs.)	Occupancy tenant (Rs.)	Statutory tenancy (acres)	Occupancy tenancy (acres)	Average holding (acres)
Meerut	75	218	54	10	13.5	6	5.3‡	4.6	7.8
Jhansi	27	143	45	5	3	2.5	10.0	9.6	13.1
Gorakhpur	78	198	45	12	5	4.5	4.0	3.9	3.8
Lucknow	63	175	45	9	7	—	4.7	—	7.2

*Includes food for self, family, and cattle.

†Includes wages of labor and cost of irrigation.

‡Source gives 5.5, but this is an arithmetic error.

Source. *U.P. Provincial Banking Enquiry Comm., 1,* Tables I and II, pp. 25–26

economic holdings by the method shown in Table 25. It found that more tenants were below the line than above, but that relatively few below the line were without a subsidiary occupation. Six million six hundred thousand persons merely held allotments, another half million considered agriculture a subsidiary occupation, and a further million supplemented their incomes by working as agricultural laborers. The Banking Enquiry Committee found that the average holding exceeded the minimum needed in most cases, and concluded that the surplus was usually large enough to tide the cultivator over a calamity and leave something over. Although holdings in Gorakhpur were small, many cultivators were of good farming castes and specialized in market gardening. The cultivators in Gorakhpur received large emigrant remittances; a third of them, as against a provincial average of 12 per cent, engaged in subsidiary occupations.[35] In any case, the Banking Enquiry Committee's minimums exceeded the present average holding for the state, which is three and a third acres.

The trouble with the criterion of a minimum standard is that a complacent conclusion is almost inevitable. The cost of cultivation and the standard of living are results of the size of the holdings, not causes. If the standard of living were twice as high because the holdings were larger, the Committee's figures for minimum economic holdings would have been higher. In exactly the same way, if the cultivators had been even more impoverished, the minimum holding would have been smaller. The arithmetic result of using the standard of living as the basis is that the minimum standard holding is close to the actual average. Since the criterion used by these groups assumes a norm in the present standard of living, it allows for no economic development: the agriculturalists could continue to subsist and there would be nothing left over for capital development, or for feeding people in industry.

Since it permits development as a policy objective and is not dependent upon the very data used for judgment, the criterion adopted by the Zamindari Abolition Committee is far better. "An economic holding may . . . be defined as a unit of holding which under given conditions of agricultural technique makes for maximum production, i.e., involves an optimum combination of the factors of production. . . . An economic holding should, then, provide full employment for one indivisible factor of production, i.e., the minimum agricultural equipment that a cultivator must maintain and the labour of an average peasant family." The minimum

TABLE 26. *Relation of Average Holdings to Economic Holdings*

| Division | Value of outturn per average holding (Rs.) | Cultivator's expenditure | | | | Surplus (Rs.) | Average as a percentage of minimum economic holding (%) |
		Food and clothes (Rs.)	Rent (Rs.)	Other (Rs.)	Total (Rs.)		
Statutory tenants in:							
Meerut	585	272	105	78	455	130	142
Jhansi	354	188	39	65	292	62	131
Gorakhpur	296	243	19	46	308	−12	95
Lucknow	454	220	50	65	335	119	153
Occupancy tenants in:							
Meerut	585	272	47	78	397	188	170*
Jhansi	354	188	33	65	286	68	136
Gorakhpur	296	243	17	46	306	−10	97

Source. *U.P. Provincial Banking Enquiry Comm., 1*, Tables I and II, pp. 25–26.

*Source gives 142%, but this is an arithmetic error.

or indivisible combination of productive factors was set at two agricultural workers and a yoke of oxen, and the smallest plot which would keep them fully employed was considered to be at least five to eight acres and very probably ten.[36] According to the Committee's figures, 86 per cent of the cultivators had holdings of less than 6.25 acres, and 94 per cent had holdings smaller than 10 acres; most cultivators had uneconomic holdings (Table 27).

The number of uneconomic holdings was itself a strong case for redistributing land. Nine thousand zamindars each held sir and khudkasht of over 50 acres, averaging about 100 acres each, while 2,300 held sir and khudkasht averaging 150 acres each. The 115,000 zamindars and tenants with over 25 acres held 13 per cent of the total area, while 81 per cent of the cultivators had less than five acres and 67 per cent less than 3 acres each.[g]

However, redistribution would not even have come close to solving the problem of uneconomic holdings. The Committee thought that a maximum holding of less than 25 acres would be too small "for a certain amount of inequality is inherent even in a communist society." Taking the six districts of Bijnor, Mainpuri, Sitapur, Banda, Basti, and Ghazipur as representative of the natural divisions of the state, it was found that to bring all holdings of more than a half and less than 10 acres up to 10 acres each would require 11,800,000 acres, while if all holdings in the districts were limited to 25 acres there would be available for distribution less than 700,000 acres. Redistribution of sir and khudkasht by limiting holdings of sir and khudkasht to 25 acres would have provided a surplus of less than 300,000 acres, while it would have required almost 1,700,000 acres to bring holdings of sir and khudkasht below 10 acres up to economic size. Redistribution of large holdings would have had a negligible effect on the size of small holdings.[37]

Other disadvantages of redistributing large holdings were the opposition of the zamindars and large tenants; the increased difficulty of adjustment which would be faced by the zamindars; the fact that smaller farmers would market a smaller proportion of their output than large farmers, and the reduction in sales would cause famine in the towns; and the fact that redistribution would displace a large number of agricultural workers who could not find alternative occupations. On balance it was thought that

g. Z.A.C. *Report*, pp. 385–86. Other groupings of the small zamindars may be derived from Table 27.

TABLE 27. *Distribution of Cultivators in U.P. by Size of Holding*

Size of holding in acres	Number of persons	Percentage of total number of persons	Area in acres	Area as a percentage of total area	Average size of holdings in acres
Not exceeding .5	2,643,431	21.5	925,457	2.2	0.35
Exceeding .5 but not 1	1,995,900	16.3	1,555,708	3.8	0.78
" 1 " " 2	2,205,597	18.0	3,361,180	8.1	1.52
" 2 " " 3	1,429,860	11.6	3,573,178	8.7	2.50
" 3 " " 4	992,496	8.1	3,457,670	8.4	3.48
" 4 " " 5	703,472	5.7	3,150,323	7.6	4.48
" 5 " " 6	514,655	4.2	2,816,963	6.8	5.47
" 6 " " 7	378,480	3.0	2,446,436	5.9	6.46
" 7 " " 8	283,200	2.3	2,112,053	5.1	7.46
" 8 " " 9	215,980	1.8	1,830,090	4.4	8.47
" 9 " " 10	170,729	1.4	1,617,358	3.9	9.47
" 10 " " 12	206,345	1.7	2,264,957	5.5	10.98
" 12 " " 14	138,002	1.1	1,776,344	4.3	12.87
" 14 " " 16	95,620	0.8	1,423,674	3.4	14.89
" 16 " " 18	68,040	0.6	1,151,958	2.8	16.93
" 18 " " 20	51,415	0.4	972,086	2.4	18.91
" 20 " " 25	70,412	0.6	1,570,473	3.8	22.30
" 25	114,655	0.9	5,310,572	12.9	46.32
Grand Total	12,278,289	100.0	41,316,480	100.0	3.37
Not exceeding 1	4,639,331	37.78	2,481,165	6.01	.53
" " 2	6,844,928	55.75	5,872,345	14.14	.85
" " 6¼*	10,580,031	86.17	19,462,088	47.10	1.84
" " 10	11,533,800	93.94	26,819,416	64.91	2.33
Exceeding 2 but not 6¼*	3,735,103	30.42	13,619,743	32.96	3.65
" 6¼ but not 10	953,769	7.77	7,357,328	17.81	7.71
" 10	744,489	6.06	14,497,064	35.09	19.47

*By interpolation of "exceeding 6 but not 7."

the results to be achieved by redistribution would not be commensurate with the hardships and discontent caused by such a measure.[38] This is, of course, but another illustration of the peculiar mixture marking the whole of the Zamindari Abolition Committee's *Report:* radicalism in philosophy and realism about U.P. politics somehow combining to justify a policy of leaving the status quo undisturbed.

Some additional figures will give a fuller idea of the magnitude of the difference between present conditions and the economic minimum for efficiency. To give each cultivator six acres would require the preliminary displacement of 5,300,000 out of 12,200,-000 cultivators. To give each cultivator 10 acres would require the displacement of two-thirds of the cultivators.[39] If cultivators on uneconomic holdings were forced to join cooperative farms, 87 per cent would be affected if the limit were 6.25 acres, and 94 per cent if the limit were 10 acres. (See Table 27.) This would clearly be the equivalent of forced collectivization. The same percentages would of course apply to a rule making holdings of 6.25 or 10 acres impartible. If holdings of less than 6.25 acres were made impartible it "would displace all the younger sons of the lowest class of peasants . . . (85%) . . . [and] would have social and economic consequences that cannot be contemplated with equanimity." Family ties are so strong that the resistance might exceed that in the U.S.S.R. during collectivization. Since land is the "only refuge" and the social security of the cultivator's children, the Committee saw no gain in fully employing some if others were to be left totally without work.[40]

The question of the proper size of peasant holdings is not a straightforward one. There are three possible criteria other than the minimum standard of living. One could wish to maximize total output; to maximize commercial profitability; or to employ fully the time of the cultivator. Each criterion can lead to quite different results. Output can probably be maximized on very small holdings intensively cultivated. Output per acre is usually highest in backdoor gardens. But these are also the least profitable form of agriculture and hence provide the lowest standard of living. Commercially profitable operations will produce less per acre and while providing some peasants with a higher income will leave many without any income. Between the extremes, as much but no more land than a peasant can till will employ more people than profitable agriculture but at a lower level of income. In fact, the aims of India conflict, for the achievement of higher levels of output called for in the Five Year Plans can hold down the levels of income of the cultivating peasants. Were the Indians willing to equalize holdings at a very small size, output would rise, but at the same time the marketable surplus available to the towns would fall. Were marketable surplus to be maximized, employment opportunities in rural areas would fall. The virtue of peasant holdings of six to ten acres is not that they are economic—they maximize neither output nor profitable employment of resources—but that they are a workable compromise between conflicting ends. It is not, however, clear why the size should be that which fully employs the cultivator's and his family's time. What is unemployed time from the planners' and the national point of view is leisure from the cultivator's point of view. Perhaps, too, his wife would like more time with her children and neighbors. Perhaps, again, the family would rather have more income. Certainly the question cannot be answered by defining an "economic holding" legislatively.

Large holdings were feared as much as uneconomically small ones, not only on account of socialist objections to "exploitation of hired labour" but also because large holdings would make it more difficult to protect and organize rural labor. It was for these reasons that the abolition act prohibited the creation of new holdings of over 30 acres as well as the partition of holdings of less than 6.25 acres.

It should be emphasized that there is very little land at present uncultivated which can be brought under the plow. It is difficult to tell exactly how much additional agricultural land there is, but it is not great, and some of it can be made suitable for cultivation only at considerable expense. We have seen that in the 1930s about 35 million acres were cultivated. By the end of the Second World War the figure was 36.5 million acres according to the *Seasonal and Crop Reports* and 37 million acres according to Chaturvedi.[h] In 1950 the net sown area was up to 39 million acres. The *Statistical Abstract, India, 1950,* says that there are only 662,000 culturable acres still uncultivated.[41] Culturable waste certainly

h. *Seasonal and Crop Report,* 1946–47, statement II. Chaturvedi, p. 95, Table 33. Exact figures are in any case doubtful. For instance, Chaturvedi (p. 96, Table 33) gives the total area of U.P. as 68 million acres while the *Statistical Abstract, India, 1950* gives the area as 72.6 million acres by survey and 71.4 million acres by village papers.

falls far short of the 9.7 million acres needed, while most reclaimed land is granted to refugees from Pakistan.

The statistics on land can be misleading. Land classified as "not available for cultivation" and "other uncultivated land excluding current fallows" totals twenty million acres, but "little does the agronomist realize that this imposing figure is made up of components such as old fallows, groves, sites, land under water, roads, railways, and canals, none of which merit a moment's consideration from the point of view of better utilization or extension of agriculture. The only area which need detain us is composed of what is known as 'culturable waste' and 'otherwise barren'. It amounts to about 13 million acres."[42] Some of these thirteen million acres are rock-strewn, sheets of rock, or swamps. Nearly four million acres are barren for these and similar reasons.[43]

At the moment U.P. may be overcultivated. Chaturvedi felt that forests, woodlands, and pastures should be built up to prevent erosion and provide firewood to replace the manure now being burned. In employing "culturable waste" the 98,000 acres in the Himalayan hills "should be left strictly alone" to prevent erosion. In the bhabar and tarai areas at the foot of the hills, only 100,000 of the 340,000 acres should be cultivated, and the remaining 240,-000 acres left to trees and grass. The entire area of culturable waste in the Gangetic basin, 5,663,000 acres, "must be considered as sacrosanct and set apart for the creation of grazing grounds, fuel reserves, and scattered tree growth. Any further clearance of jungle must be prohibited by law." To the south on the central Indian plateau (Bundelkhand) there are 2,081,000 acres of culturable waste. The gentle slopes consisting of 697,000 acres can be cultivated with bundhing (long dikes or mounds of earth designed to prevent the run-off of surface water), but the rest should be managed as woodlands and pasture. In addition to the general benefits from afforestation and pasturage, the usar (alkaline) soils can only be reclaimed at "costs entirely disproportionate to the returns" that could be obtained. Altogether Chaturvedi believed that no more than 797,000 acres should be added to the cultivated area.[44] In short, more new land is not to be had.

This conclusion must be modified in one respect. To the eye of one who has seen intensive agriculture on the continent of Europe, there is much unused land in India. The underutilization occurs in small patches and cannot be remedied by reclamation or resettlement programs, but only by improved local planning of land use. There are strips and bits and patches by roads and paths and houses, and there are building sites at present unused. While often too small for plowing, or too rough and uneven, they are suitable for a tree or two, for fodder, or for a minute pasture in which to tether an animal. Where the land is public the panchayat could derive a small income; where private the owner could increase his outturn. But so far as the problems of land redistribution and consolidation are concerned, these plots are too small and isolated to make a contribution.

A closer examination of Table 27 brings to light aspects of the distribution of cultivators by size of holdings that may indicate the Abolition Committee and the legislature have not taken the proper approach. The magnitude of the problem of uneconomic holdings is overwhelming when broad averages are used and it is assumed that all cultivators should be treated alike. But if we break the cultivators into groups, it seems that the crisis problem concerns less than a third, and the real problem of uneconomic holdings can be handled by changing the condition of less than 40 per cent of the cultivators.

A large number of the small holdings are beyond redemption, and a great number of these are probably not really farms. Most occupiers of an acre or less carry on agriculture as a subsidiary occupation.[45] These cultivators, 38 per cent of the total, are really allotment holders and not farmers. It is more realistic to look upon them as a part of the problem of the rural proletariat than as a part of the problem of the cultivators. Another 20 per cent of the cultivators hold between one and two acres. It is likely that a good many of these have some other occupation. Even if many do not, it is better to face the fact that there is no easy way to bring their holdings up to 6.25 or 10 acres. Whatever program is adopted, the cultivators in this group will not be helped appreciably, and if they cannot be helped there is no point in pretending that they can be helped. In so far as these cultivators are true agriculturalists, they will have to leave agriculture (which means that industry must be developed) or go on being very poor.

Let us ignore these allotment holders. This leaves us with the true agriculturalists who do not have enough land for efficient cultivation—the cultivators holding between 2 and 10 acres. Of these, the cultivators holding from 2 to 6.25 acres are the cultivators-in-crisis about which something can perhaps be done. It will require an additional 23,731,000 acres to bring their holdings up to 10 acres each, or 9,725,000 acres to bring their holdings up to 6.25 acres each. If the cultivators holding from 2 to 3 acres were eliminated, the average holding would rise to almost 6 acres, and if the holders of 2 to 4 acres were eliminated, the average holding of those remaining would rise above 10 acres each. To achieve the lesser aim would require the removal of 1,430,000 cultivators from the land, and to achieve the greater objective would require the removal of 2,422,000. If the greater objective were achieved, it would be necessary to find less than two million acres to bring these left in the 6.25 to 10 acre group up to 10 acres, or the elimination of another 218,000 cultivators of this group or a smaller number from a group with larger holdings.

While the movement of almost a million and a half cultivators (the lesser objective) from farm to town is large enough to give the greatest optimist pause, the movement is not nearly as large as the movements required to take care of all holders of land. Whereas the removal of 5,617,000 cultivators (the number that must be removed to raise the average holding of all to 6.25 acres) would require a complete industrial revolution, one can conceive of development drawing a million and a half people into industry and commerce. Put another way, the regrouping of cultivators to solve the problem reduces the magnitude of the surplus on the land from almost one-half the cultivators to less than an eighth, or less than a fifth in the case of the greater objective. This suggestion for regrouping is not meant to belittle the absolute size of the problem to be faced but only to show how the immediate problem can be reduced from astronomical to manageable proportions. In illustrative terms, it would require the creation of a new metropolis the size of Bombay or Calcutta.

If those who hold less than two acres are left on the land to follow their present allotment farming, laboring, and other pursuits, a movement of one and a half million cultivators selected from the "crisis" group or from those with larger holdings will give all true farmers holdings of an economic size. The most difficult part of the program is to remove the right cultivators. If the 10 per cent of the cultivators who moved were to be those holding less than half an acre each the gain in area available to the remaining cultivators would not be nearly enough. The larger the holding of the man who decides to leave the land, the better off will be the remaining cultivators, but the cultivators most likely to leave the land and to move to new industries would be those with the smallest stake in the land. On the other hand, some of those with agriculture as a subsidiary occupation might remain at their main occupation and continue to cultivate, so that others without an alternative nonagricultural source of income might decide to leave their holdings to go to the new industries.

A solution along these lines might require some form of labor direction. It might be possible to avoid the necessity of a labor draft by subsidizing the movement of cultivators in the two to four acre group (or above) and putting obstacles in the way of the movement of others. Since sirdars can abandon their land without loss, the obstacles, such as a fine on the sale of land, could only be applied to small bhumidhari holdings. The writer fully recognizes the drawbacks involved in the suggestions set forth here and is not hopeful about the success of the proposals, much less the probability of adoption, but he does not see that they are worse than leaving too many people on the land or siphoning off the surplus population without regard to whether the land they leave is going to do much to improve the holdings of those that remain. Since it is true that the larger the holding left, the greater the benefit, instead of concentrating on the two to four acre holders, the state might provide subsidies or bonuses to larger holders based on the size of the holding they leave. Since the problem of uneconomic holdings in U.P. cannot be solved until a large number of cultivators leave the land, it may be easier in the long run to select and regulate those leaving the land so that they leave with the greatest benefit to others.

CHAPTER 15

People, Land, and the Market Mechanism

The story of the market for land in Uttar Pradesh has been told. The analysis of that story has shown that the market failed because there were no alternative uses for the factors of production—no place for the cultivators to go if they did choose to leave the land; because there was so little connection between the land and capital markets; because the market for land did not react to the stimulus of productivity alone but to tradition and custom and to the prestige attached to land; and because the hierarchical and factional organization of village life warped administrative efforts to change the rural social structure. The 1951 reform of land tenures was much less revolutionary than many supposed. A study of the history of the market for land and of the reform of land tenures shows that it was not so much the concept of a market mechanism or the existence of zamindari landlords that were to blame for the poverty of Uttar Pradesh as it was the lack of capital development and the failure of the market mechanism to function under existing conditions. It is therefore likely that the reform of land tenures will help in the alleviation of poverty in rural U.P. only to the extent that it makes effective or replaces the stimulus of the market and assures an increase in the capital resources of the people of the state.

In the first stage of the history of the land market, from 1801 to 1822, the British assumed that a market existed, and in so doing destroyed the remains of a decaying Indian system based on the village grain heap and the ruler's share therein. For the next eleven years the British tried to correct their earlier misunderstanding by recording and defending the subsidiary rights of cultivators, but at the same time they assumed the existence of the market mechanism in their assessment of land revenue. Regulation VII of 1822 in fact required the assessing officer to discover the true economic rent of the land. The requirement was impossible when there were no markets and prices for all the factors entering into production, nor for all the produce of the farms. For the rest of the period of British rule, policy was directed toward recording, protecting, and increasing the rights of cultivators, but in 1833 the British stopped trying to compute the true economic rent, and on the basis of such data as was available tried to find a "theoretical rent rate" which would approximate the rent that would have occurred if the market had been functioning properly. The techniques were gradually refined until in the latter half of the nineteenth century the record of rents became sufficiently accurate—or so it was thought—to base assessments upon the actual rent rates charged, adjusting the figures for fraud or to make them approximate more closely to the market ideal.

By assuming a market at the very beginning of their rule, the British implicitly assumed the system of ownership existing in the West. The closest approximation to ownership in India was the right to shares in the produce of land—the right to a share attaching to a specific social function. After 1822 the British recognized that there were many kinds of rights, but they treated the multiplicity of rights in the same way they treated a sole owner; the right was personal, and the recognition of subordinate rights was achieved by transferring part of the total bundle of ownership rights from the superior to the inferior claimants. Inferior rights established by Bird's settlements of the 1830s were codified into the written law by Bengal Act X of 1859, and the next century saw the expansion of the rights of inferior owners at the expense of the rights of superior owners. By the end of the period of British domination, at least half of the rights of ownership had passed from the "owner" to the "tenant." The market for superior ownership rights was curtailed but little. The range of possible buyers was restricted in Bundelkhand and Oudh by the alienation of land and settled estates acts, but elsewhere in U.P. holders of superior rights could sell them freely until the 1940s. Thereafter sale of the land of smaller zamindars required the consent of the collector. The major curtailment of the market for the sale of land was the inalienability of occupancy rights, which in time came to include a large proportion of all rights in land.

Like the market for the sale of land, the market for the letting of land was implicitly recognized from the beginning of British rule. For half a century the efficacy of this market was limited by the customs and traditions of the country, slowly reinforced by the recording of the rights of the cultivators. Then in the second half of the nineteenth century the freedom of an owner to let at whatever rent he could charge was restricted in respect to an increasingly large class of tenants. The area held by occupancy and expropriety tenants was extended as the number of cultivators falling into these classes increased when proprietors lost their superior rights and became expropriety tenants, and when more cultivators acquired occupancy rights under the twelve-year rule. Next, enhancements of rents were limited to once in seven years, and collectors and settlement officers fixed the rents of those tenants in suits for enhancement and abatement, and at the settlements. In the twentieth century much stronger restrictions were placed upon the rental market when, in 1921 in Oudh and 1926 in Agra, almost all tenants were granted a life interest in the land at rents determined by rent officers. In 1939 the life interest became hereditary, so that by the end of the period of British rule most rents had been put under the control of the revenue officials.

The change from the determination of rents by the market to the determination of rents by the revenue officers could have been a revolutionary change, but it was not. The revenue officers were not asked to develop a new system for fixing rents, nor to abide by a special set of criteria—based upon social class, let us say, or upon ancient Indian traditions, or upon popular ideas of fair incomes. Rather, the revenue officers were in essence told to imitate the market, to achieve those rents which the market had not been able to achieve because it was imperfect. The result was that the revenue officers adapted their rents to market forces and to those rents that were still arrived at by market processes. Throughout the period many rents were arrived at in the market: the rents of subtenants, or tenants on sir, and of tenants newly admitted to land. After 1939 these market rents applied to perhaps 10 per cent of the cultivated area, but before 1939, with some hereditary tenants dying each year, the figure was probably about 15 to 20 per cent.

The British did not pursue a laissez faire program in regard to the sale and rental markets for land. On the contrary, from an early date and increasingly as time went on, the British interfered with the market, protected the tenants, and transferred many of the substantive rights of ownership to the tenants; but the British policy of interference did not significantly alter market relationships, although it did significantly alter ownership relationships. Until 1939, and even thereafter to a lesser extent, complete rights of ownership could be exercised in the market if the owner and tenant agreed to combine their rights for purposes of subletting.

The Zamindari Abolition and Land Reform Act of 1951 completed the process of taking rights away from the landlords. The act did not give these rights to the tenants, except the right to improve the land without interference, but instead vested the remaining rights of ownership in the state, allowing the village communities to exercise these rights in trusteeship. The state did not take over the owner's rights on land he cultivated himself, so that the new tenure system created two types of landholder: the bhumidhar, who is the owner of his land in more or less the Western, Roman sense, and the sirdar and asami, who are tenants on the state's lands. The revenue paid by the bhumidhar and the rent paid by the sirdar are the same as the respective revenue and rent paid by the former owner and tenant.

The act virtually abolished the rental market for land as far as private owners are concerned. However, even this reform was not very revolutionary because the rental market had already been restricted and because the land management committee of the panchayat admits new sirdars to vacant land. The crucial question here is the method of arriving at the terms upon which new sirdars will be admitted to vacant land, and there is nothing in the act implying that the method will differ significantly from the market method. The rents of new sirdars will probably approximate, with variations due to local circumstances and personalities, to the hereditary rents fixed by the revenue officers, and the revenue officers, unless there is some great change, will arrive at these rents in the same way as they have arrived at hereditary rates of rent in the past. This will mean that the method of arriving at the rents of sirdars newly admitted will approximate as closely as administration permits to the rents that would be paid if a rental market for tenants with special privileges existed.

The market for the sale of land will be virtually unrestricted in regard to bhumidhari lands. Other land will not be alienable, but the proportion of land held bhumidhari is appreciable and may grow as sirdars newly admitted elect to purchase bhumidhari rights. It is not possible to tell how much of the land will be held bhumidhari when the transition to the new tenure system is complete, but one can guess. About a fifth of the land became bhumidhari land automatically under the act, and after sirdars contributed to the Zamindari Abolition Fund a sixth of the sirdari land became bhumidhari land, so that a third is now held bhumidhari. This proportion will increase slightly in the coming years. In any case, it is clear that the market for the sale of land will remain important.

The abolition of the zamindari system and the reform of land tenures in Uttar Pradesh was not a reversal of British policy, nor was it a radical change in the direction of policy. The reform measures were a continuation of a policy that had been going on for more than a century. The difference between British policy and the policy of the state today is that British policy transferred rights of ownership from the owners to the tenants, while the policy today is to transfer rights of ownership from the owners to the state and then to allow the localities to exercise the rights.

To see that the land reform policy of the state government does not alter the trend of policy, it is only necessary to consider the amendments to the old system which would have accomplished the substance of the abolition reforms. The law on renting and subletting could have been amended to bar all subleases and leases of sir except in the usual cases of widows, lunatics, and so forth. Another amendment could have permitted the tenant to make any improvement he chose, while a third amendment could have required the collection and payment of rents through the agency of the village community. These amendments would have accomplished what the act set out to accomplish, except that the sirdars and asamis may now feel that they are in some sense owners and so take a greater interest in the improvement of their lands; and except that the state's income from the land is now greatly increased at the cost of the burden of paying compensation. Purchases of bhumidhari rights will barely cover compensation and rehabilitation grants for the land involved, and will reduce the state's income from land. At the end of forty years the state will have its increased income free and clear, but until the forty years are over the state will pay in interest and amortization almost as much as it receives in increased revenues. For longer than the crucial period of Indian development planning, the benefits to state finances will be small.

If land reform is to reverse the process of agricultural stagnation and decay, it must do so because it leads to "a real burst of enthusiasm, a genuine release of energy among the working peasantry."[1] Hopes based on reform in Uttar Pradesh rest on this one hope, for the resources at the disposal of the cultivators have not been increased. And this one hope assumes that talent for farm management is widespread among cultivators—in contrast to the normal distribution of all other talents—and that enthusiasm creates effectiveness, probably a naïve assumption.

Even the hopes and expectations of the Zamindari Abolition Committee existed under the shadow of the scarcity of capital resources. The problems of agriculture, the Committee said, "rule out any facile optimism that the abolition of zamindari will, by itself, bring an era of plenty and prosperity by removing all the impediments to increased production and assuring the cultivator of a high standard of living." The Committee was sure that a more efficient and progressive system of tenures was a prerequisite to progress, and that no progress was possible until the obstacle of the zamindari system was removed, for only then would the cultivator have security and incentive. But "the necessary capital and organization are not present today and cannot be supplied if the size of holdings and the methods of production remain after the abolition of zamindari substantially as they are now."[2]

The Eastern Economist thought that the abolition of the zamindars, while not objectionable in itself, ignored the truly important agricultural problems. The danger in the legislation, it said, was that the need for economic holdings and for good farmers would be overlooked.[a] It commented that land reform was not a vital

---

a. *Eastern Economist*, May 9, 1952, p. 728. It also considered this the danger in Acharya Vinoba's movement for voluntary redistribution of land.

measure because incentive was not the problem. The problem was major and minor irrigation works, reclamation of waste, fallowing, manure, and other forms of investment.[3]

The U.N. group studying land tenure and the problems of economic development thought that land reform was a measure of social justice and not of development. "The changes which have recently taken place in Asia, or are now taking place, are concerned primarily with land reform in the sense of redistribution of land ownership. Widely as these laws differ in methods of execution, they possess a common aim: transfer of the ownership of land to the peasant cultivators, and abolition of the tenancy system."[4] These reforms redistribute income. As the U.N. group said, "much of what can be achieved by the change from tenancy to ownership in terms of an immediate rise in the cultivator's standard of living will clearly depend on the terms on which ownership of the holding is acquired."[5] The terms in U.P. did not really transfer ownership rights to the tenant, but rather to the state, and the terms on which the cultivator now holds are much the same as those on which he used to hold. While the U.N. group pointed out that many authorities thought the incentive of ownership would significantly raise investment, it also noted that one of the sources for possible new investment would be the additional funds retained by the cultivator.[6] In U.P. there are no such additional funds retained by the cultivator, and only a small increment in the state's income.

In summarizing the significance of land reform in countries where the ratio of population to land is "unfavorable," the U.N. group said:

> In these conditions the redistribution of land ownership involves a change in status which may lead to an improvement in the cultivator's income, and so raise his standard of living; it may also increase farm production by increasing both the cultivator's ability and his willingness to invest. But under such circumstances the redistribution of ownership will not be likely to enlarge the smaller holdings: the average farm size will still be very small, and large numbers of uneconomic holdings will still remain. Thus, land reform in these conditions will not in itself remove one of the most serious defects of the agrarian structure, the large number of excessively small farms, nor is it

likely to offer land or fuller employment to most of the landless labourers.[7]

The solution to the problem of agrarian stagnation does not lie in land reform. It lies in decreasing the ratio of people to land and capital. Since the amount of readily cultivable land cannot be increased, the solution lies in an increase in the amount of capital used by the population. Capital will help to alleviate the poverty of the rural cultivator whether it is employed in industry or agriculture. Capital employed in agriculture will directly make the cultivator's labor more productive, but capital employed in industry will indirectly make the cultivator's labor more productive, and capital employed in industry will perhaps help the cultivator more than capital employed in agriculture.

> Where the minute subdivision of land has been carried to such extreme lengths as it has in many countries in Asia, it necessarily results in a loss of productivity through millions of lost working hours. Within the framework of the existing agricultural system, this idle man-power cannot be utilized; it can only be absorbed by a diversification of the national economy through industrialization. With the absorption of surplus labour into industry, and the elimination of wasted labour in agriculture, the value of human labour in agriculture would rise, and this rise should tend to promote the introduction of agricultural machinery. The improvement of agricultural methods is thus to a large extent dependent on the absorption of abundant and consequently cheap man-power into other occupation.[8]

This argument can be expressed in a more formal way. Within the general problem of an excessive ratio of people to land and capital there is a more specific problem of the efficient combination of the three factors throughout the economy. Not only is the ratio of people to land and capital too high at present; the ratio of people to land would be too high even if there were a lot more capital. An optimum combination of resources requires fewer people with more capital working on the land, and more people with more capital employed off the land.

In developing alternatives to employment on the land there have been many suggestions for the development of cottage industries. It is regrettable that few people mean the same thing when they suggest cottage industries. In so far as cottage industries are labor-intensive industries which use more capital than is at present used by rural labor, they are valuable because they increase the amount of capital employed. In so far as they use no more capital than is now used, cottage industries will be ineffective. To a small extent they may increase rural real incomes simply because they increase the amount of labor done, but they will have no long-term effect in increasing the standard of well-being of the population. If by cottage industry is meant the farming out of industrial work throughout rural areas and the employment of capital in small lots each with a few workers, then cottage industries will make a contribution to the solution for the same reason that any industry will. But if cottage industry is to substitute for the use of increased capital resources, the cottage industries will not alleviate poverty. After all, the decline of cottage industries was due as much to the greater efficiency of capital-intensive industry as it was to the breakdown of village society. "It must be emphasized that cottage industries of the traditional type, using primitive equipment, are by reason of their low productivity no answer to the problems of surplus rural population."[9] The U.N. study recognized that some small gain would come from primitive cottage industries, and thought they might "enrich the life of the village," but would help economically only if they developed side by side with the development of factories and other large-scale industrial projects. The solution requires much more scope for development than cottage industries can supply.[10]

Once one has stated the problem of agriculture in terms of capital development throughout the economy, one is immediately faced with the problem of the source of capital. In India this has become primarily a national problem, not a state problem, under the Five Year Plans. However, the rents or revenues paid by sirdars and bhumidhars are at the reduced levels of the thirties. Rents of tenants-at-will averaged Rs. 8 per acre before abolition, while rents of sirdars are Rs. 4 to Rs. 6 per acre, and the revenue demand on bhumidhars is around Rs. 2 per acre. There is thus a margin which the government could extract if it would, and the extraction seems not nearly so burdensome when it is remembered that prices are now more than four times the pre-war level. Although the legislature has rejected a higher revenue demand as a source of investment funds by extending the settlement for forty years, it could still compel savings or investment by requiring the cultivator to invest in his own holding, in cooperatives, in industry, or in state bonds whose proceeds would be devoted to developmental projects. The administrative problem of enforcing the measure could be solved by requiring investment in government bonds bought through the revenue department, or proof that the money had been otherwise invested. The essential administrative element is that the burden of proof be on the cultivator.

In the light of the history of the market for land, and in the light of the analysis of that history and the present reforms, it can be seen that the abolition of the zamindari system will not end poverty in Uttar Pradesh or even contribute much to the solution of that problem. To alleviate the poverty of rural U.P., zamindari abolition depends upon its incentive effects, but the problems of agriculture in Uttar Pradesh stem from the vicious circle of underdevelopment and overpopulation, and from attitudes embedded in a more socioreligious than economic hierarchy. Under the stimulus of the central government and its Five Year Plans, with the development of resources being undertaken by the state government, and with the spread of Community Development Projects, the lot of the cultivator may improve and the bhumidhars, sirdars, and asamis may rise from their present impoverished state to a higher standard of living with which all can be pleased. But if this happens, it will not be because the zamindari system was bad or because the new system is good, but because capital resources have been developed and alternative employments, with higher productivities, have been provided.

APPENDIXES

Year	Event	Landowner's Position	Tenant's Position
1775	Occupation of Banaras		
1795	Permanent Settlement of Banaras	Unrestricted right of ownership subject to payment of a revenue fixed in perpetuity.	
1801 to 1818	Occupation of N.-W. Provinces	Unrestricted right of ownership to those who settle (agree) to pay revenue; revenue, however, supposed to be 90 per cent of rent receipts.	
1819	Holt Mackenzie's Minute	Discovery of the nature of Indian tenures.	
1822	Regulation VII	Revenue assessment to be only as much as needed for government expenses; revenue to be computed by finding "economic rent."	Recording of rights and interests in land.
1830s	Martin Bird's settlements	Share of produce going to revenue declines.	Occupancy rights granted to tenants of 12 years standing; tenant to hold thereafter at rent fixed by settlement officer.
1833	Regulation IX	Reduces revenue demand to two-thirds of rents; establishes system of assessing from "aggregate sum" to detailed allocation instead of trying to find economic rent.	.
1844	*Thomason's Directions to Settlement Officers*	Officers to compute rents for revenue assessment by "sound judgment" and reference to relevant information. Embodies Bird's settlement methods.	

Year	Event	Landowner's Position	Tenant's Position
1855	Saharanpur Rules	Revenue reduced to 50 per cent of rents.	
1856	Occupation of Oudh	Ineffective "zamindari" settlement of Oudh.	
1857	Mutiny	Zamindars and ryots join former talukdars.	
1858	Canning's promises	Talukdars cease helping mutineers.	
1860s	Oudh Compromise	Talukdars achieve unrestricted rights of ownership.	Tenant rights ignored except that in 1866:
1866	Act XXVI (Oudh Sub-Settlement Act)		Limited number of ex-proprietary zamindars given permanent tenure at fixed rent.
1868	Act XIX (Oudh Rent Act)	Confirms tenant-at-will status for all not covered by XXVI of 1866 unless contrary right is proved in court.	
1869	Act I (Oudh Estates Act)	Grants option of inalienability to talukdars and lists all talukdari estates.	
1870	Act XXIV (Oudh Taluqdars Relief Act)	Provides for management of indebted talukdari estates to prevent loss to talukdars.	
1873	Act XVIII (N.-W.P. Rent Act)		Creates exproprietary tenancies for proprietors who lost title at rents three-fourths of occupancy rates and with occupancy rights.
1881	Act XII (N.-W.P. Rent Act)		Forbids landlord to purchase tenant's occupancy rights.
1886	Act XIV (N.-W.P. Rent Act)		Movement of tenant from one plot to another no longer a bar to accrual of occupancy rights.

Year	Event	Landowner's Position	Tenant's Position
1886	Act XXII (Oudh Rent Act)		Rent can be enhanced only after interval of 7 years ("7-year rule") in Oudh.
1901	Act II (N.-W.P. Tenancy Act) Act IV (Oudh Rent Act, 1886 [Amendment] Act)		Brings N.-W.P. and Oudh laws closer in form; 7-year rule extended to Agra.
1903	Act I (Bundelkhand Encumbered Estates Act)	Gives zamindars in Bundelkhand area rights like those given talukdars by Oudh Taluqdars Relief Act XXIV of 1870.	
1903	Act II (Bundelkhand Alienation of Land Act)	Forbids sale or other transfer of land to non-cultivating castes.	
1921	Act IV (Oudh Rent [Amendment] Act)		Creates in Oudh "statutory tenancies" of life tenure at a rent fixed by rent officer; most former tenants-at-will qualified for these rights.
1926	Act III (Agra Tenancy Act)		Extends statutory tenancies to Agra (formerly N.-W.P.)
1932 to 1939	Series of acts	Stay executions of arrears, reduce revenue to 1901 levels, extend provisions of Acts XXIV of 1870 and I of 1903 to other landholders.	Reduce rents, stay evictions.
1939	Act XVII (U.P. Tenancy Act)		Makes statutory tenancies hereditary; forbids most subleases.
1951	Act I (U.P. Zamindari Abolition and Land Reform Act)	State assumes title to all land; owners retain sir land and khudkasht in personal cultivation as bhumidars with full rights of ownership except forbidden to let land; graded compensation for other land.	Most former tenants become sirdars with hereditary tenancy from state at pre-reform rents; full rights to manage and improve land, but must farm, cannot alienate, cannot sublet.

Year	*Event*	*Landowner's Position*	*Tenant's Position*
		Management of village lands and allocation of empty lands in hands of village assemblies.	
1954	Act V (U.P. Consolidation of Holdings Act)	Provides for compulsory consolidation of fragmented holdings under government supervision.	

Chapter 1

1. J. H. Boeke, *The Interests of the Voiceless Far East: An Introduction to Oriental Economics.* Also, his *Economics and Economic Policy of Dual Societies,* Parts I and II.

2. Sir Sarvapalli Radhakrishnan, "Indian Culture," in *Reflections on Our Age,* pp. 123–25.

3. This conception of capitalism as a culture owes a heavy debt to Karl Polanyi's *The Great Transformation,* Part II.

Chapter 2

1. M. D. Chaturvedi, *Land Management in the United Provinces,* pp. 2–3, 5, 10–11.

2. Ibid., pp. 5–7.

3. *India: A Reference Annual 1958,* p. 27.

4. Ibid., for population figures from 1951 census. O.K.H. Spate, *The Geography of India and Pakistan,* pp. 510–11, for lists of industries.

5. Spate, pp. 507–08.

6. The information in this and the following paragraphs is drawn from Spate, pp. 498–99, 513–15, 494, 501–04, 508.

Chapter 3: Section 1

1. Holt Mackenzie, "Memorandum by the Secretary Regarding the Settlement of the Ceded and Conquered Provinces, with Suggestions for the Permanent Settlement of Those Provinces, dated 1st July, 1819," in *Selections from the Revenue Records of the North-West Provinces, 1818–1820.*

2. Sir Henry Sumner Maine, *Village Communities in East and West,* pp. 190, 196.

3. Ibid., p. 178.

4. Cf. B. H. Baden-Powell, *The Indian Village Community;* W. H. Moreland, *India at the Death of Akbar: An Economic Study;* G. Slater, *Some South Indian Villages;* P. J. Thomas and K. C. Ramakrishnan, *Some South Indian Villages; A Resurvey.* There are also modern village studies by anthropologists whose findings are relevant to the issue. A partial list would include: F. G. Bailey, *Caste and the Economic Frontier* (Manchester, Manchester University Press, 1957); S. C. Dube, *Indian Village* (London, Routledge and Keegan Paul, 1955); *India's Villages* (a collection of articles originally published in the *Economic Weekly* of Bombay); Oscar Lewis, *Village Life in Northern India;* McKim Marriott, ed. *Village India: studies in the little community,* American Anthropological Association, 57, No. 3, Part II, Memoir No.

83 (Chicago, University of Chicago Press, 1955); Adrian C. Mayer, *Land and Society in Malabar* (Oxford, Oxford University Press, 1952); Charlotte Melina and William Henricks Wiser, *Behind Mud Walls* (Agricultural Missions, Inc., 1951); William Henricks Wiser, *The Hindu Jajmani System* (Lucknow, Lucknow Publishing House, 1936). The professional journals are publishing an increasing volume of reports on particular aspects of village life, while a large body, books and articles, of the anthropological literature is reviewed in Thomas O. Beidelman, *A Comparative Analysis of the Jajmani System.*

5. George Campbell, "Tenure of Land in India," in the Cobden Club's *Systems of Land Tenure in Various Countries,* p. 146.

6. B. H. Baden-Powell, *The Land Systems of British India, 1,* 220. Hereafter referred to as "Baden-Powell," with volume number and page citation.

7. The logic of the position of women in respect to family property is fully argued in Sir Henry Maine, *Ancient Law,* pp. 91–95.

8. Baden-Powell, *1,* 224–25.

9. "India: Mohammedan Law," *Encyclopædia Britannica, 12,* 236, 238.

10. *The Final Settlement Report on the Gonda District* by W. C. Bennett, p. 53.

11. *Abstract of the Proceedings of the Council of the Governor-General of India Assembled for the Purpose of Making Laws and Regulations, 4: 1865,* p. 91. Hereafter cited as *Gov.-Gen. Council,* with year and page.

12. John Strachey in *Gov.-Gen. Council, 1867,* p. 299.

13. *Report of the United Provinces Zamindari Abolition Committee,* p. 71. Hereafter cited as "*Z.A.C. Report*" with volume number only for vol. 2, which contains the statistical appendices.

14. *Report on the Settlement Operations of the Rái Bareli District,* section by Major Ralph Ouseley, pp. 83–84. This *Report* is titled as written by Major J. F. MacAndrew, but the actual report was by Maj. Ouseley, with an appendix by Maj. MacAndrew who conducted the settlement operations.

15. Bennett, p. 47.

16. Bennett, p. 48.

17. Bennett, pp. 43–44.

18. Baden-Powell, *1,* 236.

19. Bennett, p. 48.

20. *Report on the Settlement of the District of Seharunpore, 1st February 1839,* completed by Edward Thornton, submitted to Government, by the Sudder Board of Revenue, N.-W.P., October 18, 1840, p. 50.

21. *Final Report on the Revision of the Settlement in the Bara Banki District,* by C. Hope, p. 4.

22. Baden-Powell, *2,* 138–39.

23. Ibid., p. 143.

24. Campbell, p. 156.

25. Baden-Powell, *2,* 144–45.

26. Campbell, p. 155.

27. Baden-Powell, *2,* 140–42.

28. Ibid., pp. 257–58.

29. Regulation VII, Sec. XII.

30. Act XIX of 1873, Sec. 47.

31. Baden-Powell, *2,* 153.

32. Campbell, pp. 148–49.

33. Baden-Powell, *2,* 204–05.

34. Bennett, pp. 49–50.

35. Ibid., pp. 66–67.

36. Campbell, pp. 165–66.

37. Baden-Powell, *1,* 206–09.

38. For a fuller discussion of the issue, and an attempt to cast the whole problem in solvable terms, see my "Reciprocity and Redistribution in the Indian Village: Sequel to Some Notable Discussions," in Karl Polanyi, Conrad M. Arensberg, and Harry W. Pearson, eds., *Trade and Markets in the Early Empires,* pp. 229–35. This essay also contains a more detailed discussion of the formal elements in the village system in Gonda.

39. Baden-Powell, *1,* 232–33.

40. Campbell, p. 151.

41. Baden-Powell, *1,* 263–64.

42. Campbell, p. 153.

43. Baden-Powell, *1,* 369–70.

44. Moreland, *India at the Death of Akbar,* pp. 96–97, 99–100.

45. *Rái Bareli Report,* MacAndrew's Appendix, p. 31.

46. *Seharunpore Report,* p. 51.

47. Baden-Powell, *1,* 243–44; and Campbell, p. 154.

48. W. H. Moreland, *From Akbar to Aurungzeb: A Study in Indian Economic History,* pp. 269–71.

49. Baden-Powell, *1,* 264, 268, and *2,* 11.

50. *Seharunpore Report,* 1839, p. 50.

51. Campbell, p. 159.

52. Campbell, pp. 157–59.

53. *Rái Bareli Report,* MacAndrew's Appendix, pp. 23–24.

54. *Report on the Settlement of Shahjehanpore District,* by Robert G. Currie, pp. xlviii–xlix.

55. *Seharunpore Report,* p. 50.

56. *Report on the Settlement of Pillibheet,* by Elliot Colvin, p. 16.

57. *Gov.-Gen. Council, 1869,* p. 33.

58. *Gov.-Gen. Council, 1868,* p. 416.

59. Ibid., pp. 412–13.

Chapter 3: Section 2

1. Bennett, pp. 38–40.

2. Baden-Powell, *2,* 11, 211. Campbell, pp. 163–64, gives the same list, lumping adventurers and robbers with clans.

3. Z.A.C. *Report,* pp. 69, 78, 110.

4. Baden-Powell, *2,* 103–04, 106, 108–11, 124–26, 130, 133.

5. Ibid., p. 128.

6. Mazharal Huq, "East India Company Land Policy and Management in Bengal from 1698 to 1784," pp. 403–10.

7. Bennett, pp. 53–54. Nankar is an allotment from the revenue to provide subsistence.

8. Bennett, p. 55.

9. Baden-Powell, *2,* 229.

10. Bennett, p. 56.

11. Baden-Powell, *2,* 209.

12. Ibid., p. 207.

13. Bennett, pp. 66–67.

14. Baden-Powell, *2,* 207, 209–13.

15. Ibid., pp. 216–17, 228.

16. Bennett, pp. 51–54.

17. Baden-Powell, *2,* 209–13, 219, 228–29.

18. Bennett, p. 56.

19. Z.A.C. *Report,* p. 69.

20. Chaturvedi, p. 13.

21. Baden-Powell, *2,* 11–13.

22. B. R. Misra, *Land Revenue Policy in the United Provinces Under British Rule,* pp. 21–22.

Chapter 4

1. Baden-Powell, *1,* 187.

2. See Elié Halévy, *A History of the English People in 1815,* trans. by E. I. Watkin and D. A. Barker (New York, Harcourt, Brace, 1924), pp. 192–219, for a description of the English system.

3. Baden-Powell, *1,* 183–84.

4. Ibid., pp. 216–17.

5. Z.A.C. *Report,* pp. 63–64.

6. Bengal Regulation I of 1795, "The Benares Permanent Settlement Regulation, 1795," *The United Provinces Code, 1.*

7. Baden-Powell, *2,* 6–72.

8. Baden-Powell, *1*, 187–88.

9. Baden-Powell, *1*, 299, *2*, 21.

10. Chaturvedi, p. 156.

11. Misra, p. 56; also pp. 54–55, 58–59; Z.A.C. *Report,* p. 125; and Baden-Powell, *2*, 14, 16, 28, 123–24.

12. Z.A.C. *Report,* p. 95.

13. Misra, p. 68.

14. Baden-Powell, *2*, 14.

15. Misra, p. 58.

16. Baden-Powell, *2*, 160–63.

17. Ibid., pp. 122–23.

18. The chronology of this paragraph is taken from Pramathanath Banerjea, *Indian Finance in the Days of the Company,* pp. 165–69.

19. Baden-Powell, *2*, 17–20.

20. Mackenzie, "Memorandum . . . ," pp. 9–192.

21. Misra, pp. 59–60.

22. Regulation VII of 1822, in *The Regulations of the Government of Fort William in Bengal, in Force at the End of 1853, 2: Regulations from 1806 to 1834,* prepared by Richard Clarke. The quotations in the following three paragraphs are also taken from Regulation VII.

23. Baden-Powell, *2*, 158, 23–24.

24. Campbell, pp. 182–83.

25. Baden-Powell, *2*, 24, 98.

26. Z.A.C. *Report,* p. 129.

27. Ibid., pp. 133–35.

28. Regulation IX of 1833, in *The Regulations of the Government of Fort William in Bengal.*

29. Z.A.C. *Report,* p. 127.

30. Baden-Powell, *2*, 11.

31. Baden-Powell, *2*, 48. Italics in the original.

32. Baden-Powell, *2*, 47–48.

33. Baden-Powell, *2*, 47–48, *1*, 273–74.

34. Baden-Powell, *2*, 48. Italics in the original.

35. Campbell, p. 152.

36. Bennett, pp. 58–62.

37. Ibid., p. 62.

38. Baden-Powell, *1*, 207–08.

39. Baden-Powell, *2*, 48–49.

40. Campbell, p. 188.

41. Baden-Powell, *2*, 193.

42. Campbell, pp. 185–86, 211–12, 203–04.

43. Campbell, pp. 218–19.

44. *Gazetteer, 2*, 224, cited in Baden-Powell, *2*, 183.

45. Baden-Powell, *2*, 183.
46. Ibid., p. 193 n., 261, 181.

Chapter 5

1. Misra, p. 100.
2. Campbell, p. 216.
3. Baden-Powell, *2*, 201; Misra, pp. 101, 106, 113.
4. Campbell, p. 127.
5. Misra, p. 102.
6. E. Stack, *Memorandum upon Current Land Revenue Settlements,* p. 159.
7. *Gov.-Gen. Council, 1867,* pp. 283–312, passim.
8. Z.A.C. *Report,* pp. 118–19.
9. Ibid., p. 121.
10. *Gov.-Gen Council, 1866,* pp. 208–09, 212, 214.
11. I of 1869, Sec. III.
12. X of 1859, Secs. 17, 18.
13. Baden-Powell, vol. *2,* 171.
14. Campbell, p. 170.
15. XIX of 1873, Sec. 3.
16. XVIII of 1873, Sec. 3, XIX of 1873, Sec. 3.
17. XIX of 1873, Sec. 44.
18. S.N.A. Jafri, *The History and Status of Landlords and Tenants in the United Provinces (India),* p. 124.
19. XVIII of 1873, Sec. 7.
20. Baden-Powell, *2,* 175.
21. XII of 1881, Sec. 9.
22. Jafri, p. 178.
23. XXIV of 1870, Secs. 3–5, 18, 19. The manager was usually the collector or an assistant collector.
24. I of 1903, Secs. 6, 7, 10, 12–15, 17.
25. I of 1903, Secs. 20, 21, 24–27.
26. II of 1903, Secs. 2, 6, 11, 12, 14.
27. Misra, p. 238.
28. X of 1859, Secs. 6, 2, 5.
29. X of 1859, Secs. 17, 18; and XIV of 1863, Sec. 3.
30. X of 1859, Sec. 2.
31. Ibid., Sec. 8.
32. Misra, pp. 131–33, 137.
33. Z.A.C. *Report,* pp. 134–35.
34. Misra, p. 129.
35. W. H. Moreland, *The Revenue Administration of the United Provinces,* pp. 59–60.
36. Baden-Powell, *1,* 212.
37. Campbell, p. 206.

38. Misra, pp. 127–29.

39. I take the account from Campbell, pp. 208–10.

40. Misra, p. 129. He does not, however, carry through elsewhere to the conclusion that all privileged tenants were really part owners.

41. Baden-Powell, 2, 186–88.

42. XIX of 1868, Sec. 32. This proviso was carried over into XXII of 1886.

43. XIX of 1868, Sec. 19.

44. Ibid., Sec. 37.

45. Ibid., Secs. 23–25.

46. XVIII of 1873, Secs. 11, 12–15, 18.

47. XVIII of 1873, Sec. 21.

48. Ibid., Sec. 44.

49. XII of 1881, Sec. 44.

50. XVIII of 1873, Secs. 45, 46.

51. XIX of 1873, Secs. 72, 77.

52. VIII of 1879, Sec. 7.

53. XII of 1881, Sec. 29.

54. Baden-Powell, *1*, 368, quoting Government of India Resolution No. 15 R, 3 May 1882.

55. Baden-Powell, *1*, 249–50.

56. XXII of 1886, Secs. 36, 37, 45.

57. Ibid., Secs. 38, 47.

58. XXII of 1886, Sec. 69.

59. Moreland, *Revenue Administration of U.P.*, p. 64.

60. Misra, p. 162.

61. XXII of 1886, Secs. 23–25, 27.

62. Ibid., Sec. 46.

63. Baden-Powell, 2, 71–72.

63a. Misra, p. 159.

64. Moreland, *Revenue Administration of U.P.*, pp. 60–61.

65. II of 1901, Sec. 28.

66. Ibid., Sec. 13.

67. II of 1901, Secs. 67, 68.

68. Misra, p. 142.

69. II of 1901, Secs. 88–89.

70. II of 1901, Sec. 10 [5].

71. II of 1901, Sec. 53.

Chapter 6

1. Jafri, p. 181; Misra, pp. 212–13.

2. XXV of 1934, Secs. 26, 55.

3. U.P. Regulation of Sales Act, XXVI of 1934.

4. XXIII of 1934, Secs. 3, 4.

5. XXVII of 1934, Secs. 28–31.
6. Computed from Schedules II and III of XXVII of 1934.
7. XXVII of 1934, Secs. 32–36.
8. XVII of 1939, Sec. 39.
9. XVII of 1939, Sec. 97.
10. Misra, pp. 176–77.
11. XVII of 1939, Secs. 26, 27, 101.
12. XVII of 1939, Secs. 45, 50, 65, 66.
13. Ibid., Secs. 206, 158, 160.
14. Ibid., Secs. 250, 251.
15. Ibid., Sec. 252.
16. U.P. Regulation of Agricultural Credit Act, XIV of 1941,
Secs. 4, 11, 13, 16–21, 24.
17. X of 1947, Sec. 12.
18. *Eastern Economist,* Sept. 26, 1947, p. 411.
19. Ibid., Jan. 17, 1947, p. 146; March 14, 1947, p. 512.
20. IV of 1921, Sec. 6.
21. XXII of 1886, Sec. 7.
22. IV of 1921, Secs. 7, 33.
23. IV of 1921, Sec. 15, III of 1926, Secs. 45–6.
24. IV of 1921, Sec. 7.
25. Jafri, p. 130.
26. IV of 1921, Sec. 8A.
27. IV of 1921, Secs. 16, 22, 24.
28. III of 1926, Secs. 53, 54, 67.
29. IV of 1921, Sec. 33, III of 1926, Secs. 55, 56.
30. IV of 1921, Sec. 33, III of 1926, Secs. 57, 58.
31. IV of 1921, Sec. 18.
32. Misra, p. 170.
33. Jafri, pp. 181–82.
34. VIII of 1932.
35. XXIV of 1934, Secs. 2, 7, 8.
36. XVII of 1939, Secs. 104, 106, 107, 108.
37. Ibid., Sec. 110.
38. XVII of 1939, Secs. 110, 101.
39. XVII of 1939, Sec. 126.
40. Ibid., Secs. 117, 114, 119.

Chapter 7

1. Reg. VII of 1822, Secs. 20–34.
2. XIV of 1863, Secs. 8, 9.
3. Baden-Powell, *2,* 86.
4. Baden-Powell, *1,* 327–28.
5. XIX of 1873, Secs. 78, 190; XIX of 1868, Sec. 29.
6. Misra, p. 55.

7. VII of 1822, Secs. 1, 6.

8. Baden-Powell, *2*, 25.

9. Ibid.

10. Ibid.; Misra, p. 64.

11. For a full discussion of the logical problem as it has continued to this day, see my "Economic Accounting and Family Farming in India," *Economic Development and Cultural Change* 7, Part I (April 1959), 286–301.

12. Regulation IX of 1833, Sec. 2.

13. Baden-Powell, *2*, 26.

14. For a discussion of the impossibility of ascertaining the facts, see my "The Limitations of Indian Village Survey Data," *Journal of Asian Studies, 17* (May 1958), 383–402.

15. Baden-Powell, *2*, 41–42.

16. Stack, pp. 50–51.

17. Baden-Powell, *2*, 28–29, 54.

18. Ibid., pp. 49, 55–56.

19. Bennett, p. 114.

20. Stack, pp. 51–52.

21. Stack, pp. 52–55, and Baden-Powell, *2*, 54, 57–62.

22. Quoted in Baden-Powell, *2*, 92.

23. Baden-Powell, *2*, 93–94.

24. Rule 17. This rule and others were quoted in Baden-Powell, *2*, 93–96.

25. Stack, p. 143, and Baden-Powell, *2*, 260–63.

26. Stack, p. 64.

27. *Pioneer*, June 4, 1884, quoted by Baden-Powell, *1*, 333.

28. Baden-Powell, *1*, 335.

29. See Misra, p. 84.

Chapter 8

1. Z.A.C. *Report*, pp. 32–33, 49. Figures given are for 1909–13, 1924–33, and for some year or years unstated, but presumably recent.

2. Ibid., p. 33, quoting Sir Manilal Nanavati, as in footnote a in text.

3. U.P. Provincial Congress Committee, *Agrarian Distress in the United Provinces*, p. 3.

4. *Report on Agriculture in the United Provinces, prepared under the orders of the Government of the United Provinces for the Royal Commission on Indian Agriculture, 1926*, p. 117.

5. *Seasonal and Crop Reports for the United Provinces of Agra and Oudh for the Years 1923–24 to 1940–41, 1946–47*, Statements III, IV.

6. Z.A.C. *Report*, p. 33, citing W. Burns, p. 57.

7. *Eastern Economist,* 15 June 1952.

8. George Blyn, in Daniel Thorner, "Long-Term Trends in Output in India," in Simon Kuznets, Wilbert E. Moore, and Joseph J. Spengler, *Economic Growth: Brazil, India, Japan,* pp. 121–24, hereafter cited as Blyn (from Thorner).

9. George Blyn, "Crop Production Trends in India," pp. 6–9.

10. George Blyn, "A Comparison of the Crop Output Trend in India with Trends in the Underlying Determinants of Yield: 1893–1946," p. 19.

11. Thorner, "Long-Term Trends in Output in India," p. 128.

12. Culled from a logically disorganized list in Z.Λ.C. *Report,* pp. 451–56. The list numbers 13 defects but contains many more. These 11 defects are numbered 9, 10, 11, and 13 in the Committee's list.

13. Z.A.C. *Report,* pp. 451–56. See footnote b in text. These are numbers 1–4 on the Committee's list.

14. Z.A.C. *Report,* pp. 451–56. See footnote b, this chapter. These are items 6–8 and 12 on the Committee's list.

15. Z.A.C. *Report,* pp. 12–13, citing "Collection of Papers relating to the conditions of the Tenantry and the working of the present Rent-Law in Oudh," 1883, p. 277, and Bennett, p. 282.

16. Baden-Powell, 2, 154.

17. *Report of the United Provinces Provincial Banking Enquiry Committee, 1: 1929–30,* p. 22.

18. United Nations, *Land Reform: Defects in Agrarian Structure as Obstacles to Economic Development,* p. 9.

19. Z.A.C. *Report,* p. 24.

20. Royal Commission on Agriculture in India, *14: Appendix to the Report,* p. 396. The unweighted average of districts was 6.6 acres.

21. Z.A.C. *Report,* pp. 462–64. The United States was the only case where the largest farms were also the most efficient.

22. Royal Commission on Agriculture in India, *Report on Agriculture in U.P., 7,* answers to Question 7.

23. *U.P. Provincial Banking Enquiry Committee,* pp. 28–29.

Chapter 9

1. *Agrarian Distress in the U.P.,* pp. 43–79, 81–275.

2. Ibid., pp. 122–35.

3. Stack, p. 150.

4. Reg. IX of 1833, Sec. XIV.

5. Reg. LX of 1859, Secs. 10, 32, 49–53, 78, 87, 105, 112, 115.

6. X of 1859, Sec. 93.

7. XIV of 1863, Sec. 5.

8. XIX of 1868, Sec. 128; XIX of 1873, Sec. 188, and XVII of 1876, Sec. 122.

9. XVIII of 1873, Secs. 43, 48, 49, 61, 64, 82c.

10. Ibid., Sec. 157.

11. XII of 1881, Secs. 157, 171.

12. XVIII of 1873, Secs. 169, 173–77.

13. XIX of 1873, Secs. 150, 154, 156, 158, 159, 165, 166, 172, 173.

14. Baden-Powell, *2*, 96.

15. XVIII of 1873, Sec. 43, and XIX of 1873, Secs. 220–31.

16. Stack, pp. 72, 150.

17. Misra, p. 176, citing annual reports of the Board of Revenue.

18. Z.A.C. *Report, 2: Statistics,* Statement 22(ii), pp. 90–91.

19. Z.A.C. *Report,* p. 135.

20. Baden-Powell, *1*, 370.

21. Ibid., *2*, 80–81.

22. *Land Revenue Policy of the Indian Government,* published by Governor-General of India in Council, pp. 3, 28–31. See also Misra, p. 11.

23. Z.A.C. *Report,* pp. 155–56.

24. Misra, p. 224.

25. *Agrarian Distress in the U.P.,* p. 7. For similar figures for the 1930s, see Table 20, p. 238.

26. U.N., *Land Reform,* p. 68.

27. See Ragnar Nurkse, *Problems of Capital Formation in Underdeveloped Countries,* pp. 32–37.

28. Nurkse, p. 35.

29. I am indebted to Professor Warren E. Adams of the University of Texas for suggesting this case.

30. The anthropological evidence for the survival of the village system is summarized in Beidelman, *A Comparative Analysis of the Jajmani System.* Other evidence, both of the vitality of the system until recently and of its decline, may be found in Lewis, *Village Life in Northern India,* pp. 55–84; S. C. Dube, *India's Changing Villages,* pp. 29–31; Oscar Lewis, "Peasant Culture in India and Mexico: A Comparative Analysis," pp. 145–70 in McKim Marriott, ed., *Village India,* pp. 151–54; McKim Marriott, "Social Structure and Change in a U.P. Village," pp. 96–109, in *India's Villages;* McKim Marriott, "Western Medicine in a Village of Northern India," pp. 239–68 in Benjamin D. Paul, ed., *Health, Culture and Community,* pp. 245–250. *Village India* and *India's Villages* contain a number of other articles showing that the village system is still found over wide areas of India.

31. *Agrarian Distress in the U.P.,* p. 8.

32. Z.A.C. *Report,* pp. 365–66.

33. Vera Anstey, *The Economic Development of India,* p. 551.

34. Computed from figures in *Agrarian Distress in the U.P.*, p. 5.

35. *Seasonal and Crop Report, 1930–31*, p. 4.

36. *Agrarian Distress in the U.P.*, p. 6, citing "Young India."

37. The figures in this paragraph are computed from the *Annual Reports of the Working of Cooperative Societies in the United Provinces for the years 1921–22 to 1941–42*, Statement B.

Chapter 10: Sections 1 and 2

1. *Report of the Administration of the Registration Department*, United Provinces, 1923–25, para. 5.

2. Z.A.C. *Report*, p. 4.

3. Harvey Leibenstein, *Economic Backwardness and Economic Growth*, p. 51.

4. Nurkse, p. 9.

5. Gunnar Myrdal, *Rich Lands and Poor*, p. 84.

6. W. Arthur Lewis, *The Theory of Economic Growth*, pp. 23, 201.

7. Maurice Dobb, *Some Aspects of Economic Development: Three Lectures*, p. 7.

8. Ibid.

9. Lewis, *The Theory of Economic Growth*, p. 23, and passim.

10. Ibid., p. 201.

11. W. Arthur Lewis, *Aspects of Industrialization* (Cairo, National Bank of Egypt, 50th Anniversary Commemoration Lectures, 1953), p. 14.

12. Nurkse, pp. 9–10.

13. Moses Abramovitz, "Resource and Output Trends in the United States Since 1870," *American Economic Review, 46* (1956), 11, 8 (Table 1), 10.

14. Robert M. Solow, "Technical Change and the Aggregate Production Function," *Review of Economics and Statistics, 39* (1957), 316, 320, 317 n.

15. Seymour Melman, "Higher Wages Raise Efficiency—By Forcing Mechanization," *Manchester Guardian Survey of Industry, Trade and Finance 1953* (Manchester), p. 80.

16. Z.A.C. *Report*, p. 43.

17. *Reports of the Registrar of Cooperative Societies*, 1920–21 to 1940–41, Statement B, and Reserve Bank of India, *Review of the Cooperative Movement in India, 1948–50* (Bombay, 1952), p. 9.

18. *Reports of the Registrar of Cooperative Societies*, 1920–21 to 1940–41, Statement B.

19. Eleanor M. Hough, *The Cooperative Movement in India: Its Relation to a Sound National Economy*, p. 80.

20. H. Calvert, "Prevailing Types of Rural Credit Societies," in R. B. Ewbank, ed., *Indian Cooperative Studies*, p. 41.

21. Anstey, pp. 195–96.

22. Planning Commission, Government of India, *The New India, Progress Through Democracy*, p. 29.

23. Lewis, *The Theory of Economic Growth*, pp. 201–02.

24. George Rosen, "Capital : Output Ratios in Indian Industry," *Economic Trends* (Bombay, Dec., 1956).

25. Wilfred Malenbaum, "India and China: Contrasts in Development Performance," p. 15.

Chapter 10: Section 3

1. *Report of the U.P. Panchayat Raj Amendment Act Committee*, pp. 8–10.

2. Oscar Lewis and Harwant Singh, *Group Dynamics in a North Indian Village: A Study of Factions;* and Lewis, *Village Life in Northern India*, pp. 82, 113–54, 312–13, 318. Dube, *India's Changing Villages*, pp. 31–58, 79, 120, 126, 129–30, 166, 174, 178; Albert Mayer, McKim Marriott, and Richard L. Park, eds., *Pilot Project, India*, pp. 79–81, 222–224; *India's Villages;* Marriott, "Social Structure and Change in a U.P. Village," pp. 96–109.

3. Sir Cecil Walsh, *Indian Village Crimes*, p. 101.

4. Bernard S. Cohn, "Some Notes on Law and Change in North India," *Economic Development and Cultural Change, 8* (1959), 82–88, 90, 91.

5. Marriott, letter of July 19, 1958.

6. Cohn, "Law and Change . . .," p. 91.

7. Cf. V. M. Dandekar and G. J. Khudanpur, *Working of Bombay Tenancy Act, 1948: Report of Investigation.*

8. R. Carstairs, *The Little World of an Indian District Officer*, p. 15.

9. Penderel Moon, *Strangers in India*, pp. 39–40.

10. Moon, p. 39.

11. Moon, p. 38.

12. Walsh, p. 68.

13. Walsh, pp. 37–38.

14. Moon, pp. 42–45.

15. Walsh, p. 13.

16. Carstairs, p. 28.

17. Walsh, pp. 149–51.

18. Ibid., p. 151.

19. Carstairs, pp. 18–20.

20. Carstairs, p. 91.

21. H. D. Malaviya, *Land Reforms in India*, p. 103, quoting Porter's settlement report for Allahabad District, 1877.

22. Ibid., pp. 104–05, quoting Major Grigg, Deputy Commissioner of Partabgarh, quoting a subordinate, Mr. Baillie.

23. Ibid., pp. 103–04.

24. Cohn, "Law and Change . . .," pp. 80–81.

25. Daniel Thorner, *The Agrarian Prospect for India,* p. 10.

26. Ibid., p. 11.

27. Cohn, "Law and Change . . .," pp. 90–91.

28. Ibid., p. 87.

29. Ibid., pp. 87–88.

30. Walsh, pp. 212–23.

31. Ibid., passim, and pp. 64–84.

32. John T. Hitchcock, "Leadership in a North Indian Village: Two Case Studies," in Richard L. Park and Irene Tinker, eds., *Leadership and Political Institutions in India,* p. 397.

33. Carstairs, p. 98.

34. Cf. Thorner, *The Agrarian Prospect,* pp. 29–53; Malaviya, *Land Reforms,* passim; Dankekar and Khudanpur, passim.

Chapter 11

1. Z.A.C. *Report,* p. 481.

2. Ibid., pp. 490–91.

3. Ibid., p. 54.

4. Ibid., p. 452.

5. Ibid., p. xi, citing Assembly resolution of Aug. 8, 1946.

6. Ibid., pp. 59–60.

7. Ibid., pp. 338–39.

8. Ibid., p. 340.

9. Ibid., pp. 342–43. See also Table 16, p. 216.

10. Ibid., pp. 343–44.

11. Ibid., p. 58.

12. Ibid., pp. 254–55.

13. Ibid., pp. 488–92, 486–87, 472–73.

14. Ibid., pp. 461–67.

15. *Eastern Economist,* Jan. 3, 1946, p. 339.

16. Ibid., June 22, 1951, p. 1004.

17. Ibid., Feb. 21, 1947, pp. 367–68.

18. Z.A.C. *Report,* p. 55.

19. See U.N. *Land Reform,* pp. 40–41, 74–77; *Eastern Economist,* April 30, 1948, p. 807; and ibid., "Cooperative Farming (contributed)" July 18, 1947, pp. 99–100.

20. *Cooperative Farming,* Ministry of Agriculture, Govt. of India, New Delhi, 1949, p. 19.

21. Z.A.C. *Report,* pp. 514–18.

22. Ibid.

23. *Eastern Economist,* June 28, 1946, p. 1071.

24. Z.A.C. *Report,* pp. 261, 219, 493–504.
25. Ibid., p. 504.

Chapter 12

1. *Eastern Economist,* Aug. 19, 1949, p. 285; June 1, 1951, p. 884; May 9, 1952, p. 728.
2. I of 1951, Secs. 142, 152, 154–57, 163, 165.
3. I of 1951, Secs. 15, 18(2).
4. X of 1949, Secs. 3, 7, 8.
5. I of 1951, Secs. 134, 137.
6. I of 1951, Secs. 146, 156–57, 166–68.
7. I of 1951, Secs. 19, 10, 131. Groveholders were deleted by XVI of 1953, Sec. 12.
8. Ibid., Secs. 21, 133, 11.
9. I of 1951, Secs. 143, 156–57, 166–68, 213–16, 212, 199, 210, 206, 212, 149.
10. Ibid., Secs. 241–44.
11. I of 1951, Sec. 245.
12. I of 1951, Secs. 251, 246–47.
13. Ibid., Secs. 252–53.
14. I of 1951, Secs. 254–55, 265–67.
15. Ibid., Secs. 20, 235.
16. XX of 1954, Sec. 55, inserting Secs. 240A–240M in I of 1951. New Sec. 240B(a) is the relevant clause.
17. I of 1951, Secs. 295, 298, 314, 316.
18. I of 1951, Sec. 318.
19. Ibid., Secs. 106–12.
20. XXVI of 1947, Secs. 3–32, 34–113.
21. I of 1951, Secs. 113–14, 117–19.
22. I of 1951, Secs. 120–28.
23. I of 1951, Secs. 194, 195, 197, 198.
24. I of 1951, Secs. 275–76, 279, 281, 283–86, 289, 291.
25. Z.A.C. *Report,* p. 529, 537–39.
26. Ibid., p. 603.
27. I of 1951, Sec. 264.
28. Z.A.C. *Report,* pp. 198, 211–13, 395.
29. Z.A.C. *Report,* pp. 395, 430. See also Peshotan Nasserwanji Driver, *Problems of Zamindari and Land Tenure Reconstruction in India,* p. 127.
30. Z.A.C. *Report,* pp. 199–200.
31. Z.A.C. *Report,* pp. 395–96, 405–10. Rs. 1 lakh is Rs. 100,000.
32. I of 1951, Sec. 28.
33. Z.A.C. *Report,* pp. 411–12, recomputed to account for changes made in the Committee's Recommendations by Act I of 1951.

34. Z.A.C. *Report,* pp. 438–44.
35. Computed from Z.A.C. *Report, 2,* Statement 21, p. 87.
36. Z.A.C. *Report,* pp. 405, 409–10, 605.
37. I of 1951, Secs. 73–74, 76–77, 80, 86, 89, 93–96, 99, and Schedule I.

Chapter 13

1. Thorner, *Agrarian Prospect,* pp. 47–50.
2. Interview with Shri A. B. Lal, Assistant Registrar of Cooperatives for Farming, U.P., August 23, 1955.
3. Baljit Singh, *Next Step in Village India,* p. 33.
4. S. C. Gupta, *An Economic Survey of Shamaspur Village,* pp. 29–34.
5. P. K. Mukerjee and S. C. Gupta, *A Pilot Survey of Fourteen Villages in U.P. and Punjab,* p. 29.
6. Z.A.C. *Report,* p. 218.
7. *Eastern Economist,* Sept. 9, 1949, p. 431; March 31, 1950, p. 515; June 16, 1950, p. 913; and August 11, 1950, p. 206.
8. Bhowmani Sen, *Indian Land System and Land Reforms,* p. 90.
9. Interview with Shri A. B. Lal.
10. Thorner, *Agrarian Prospect,* pp. 48–49.
11. *Agricultural Situation In India,* Nov., 1955, p. 602.
12. Thorner, *Agrarian Prospect,* pp. 49, 48.
13. Ibid., p. 24.
14. Dobb, pp. 45–46.
15. Ibid., p. 72.
16. *Eastern Economist,* Jan. 2, 1948, p. 31.
17. Z.A.C. *Report,* p. 29.
18. Daniel and Alice Thorner, "Agricultural Manpower in India: Labourers," *Economic Weekly* (Nov. 9, 1957), pp. 1446–47.
19. Daniel Thorner, "India's Agrarian Revolution by Census Redefinition," *Indian Economic Review, 3* (1956), 1–21.
20. Z.A.C. *Report, 2: Statistics,* Statement 5, p. 6.
21. Ibid., p. 64.
22. Mukherjee and Gupta, *A Pilot Survey of Fourteen Villages in U.P. and Punjab,* p. 17.
23. Gupta, *An Economic Survey of Shamaspur Village,* pp. 21, 23, 24.
24. Thorner, *Agrarian Prospect,* p. 12.
25. Ibid.
26. Doreen Warriner, *Economics of Peasant Farming,* p. 163.
27. Ibid., pp. 140, 147–48, 154, 163–67, 157–59.
28. Bernard S. Cohn, "Madhopur Revisited," *Economic Weekly* (July 1959, Special Issue), pp. 965, 966.

29. Thorner, *Agrarian Prospect,* p. 82.
30. Myrdal, p. 84.
31. Thorner, *Agrarian Prospect,* pp. 49–50.
32. H. D. Malaviya, *Village Panchayats in India,* pp. .325, 323–24.
33. Cohn, "Madhopur Revisited," pp. 963, 965–66.
34. N. Gangulee, *The Indian Peasant and His Environment,* p. 95.
35. Malaviya, *Village Panchayats,* p. 324.
36. Carstairs, pp. 21–24.

Chapter 14

1. *Cooperative News Digest,* Reserve Bank of India, Bombay, private circulation only, No. 11, 1952, citing *The Hindu,* Nov. 5, 1952.
2. Z.A.C. *Report,* p. 494.
3. U.N., *Land Reform,* p. 11.
4. Ibid., p. 67.
5. Baden-Powell, *1,* 225.
6. F. G. Bailey, *Caste and the Economic Frontier* (Manchester, Manchester University Press, 1957), pp. 47–173.
7. III of 1926, Secs. 38–39.
8. VIII of 1939, Secs. 3, 7, 8, 12, 13.
9. XVII of 1939, Sec. 53.
10. *Report of the Registrar of Cooperative Societies,* 1923–24, para. 32, 1935–36, para. 38.
11. Ibid., 1930–31, to 1940–41, Statement B.
12. Ibid., 1931–32, para. 47.
13. Ibid., 1940–41, para. 41.
14. Ibid., 1931–32 to 1940–41, Statement B.
15. *Eastern Economist,* Nov. 28, 1947, p. 784.
16. Reserve Bank of India, *Cooperative Farming,* Bombay, 1949, pp. 50–51.
17. U.N., *Land Reform,* pp. 13–14.
18. U.P. Consolidation of Holdings Act 1953 (U.P. Act V of 1954) as amended by Acts XXVI of 1954 and XIII of 1955, with illustrative and explanatory notes by Badri Bishal Tripathi; Allabahad, Ram Narainlal, Law Publisher, 1955. Sec. 2 repeals VIII of 1939.
19. V of 1954, Sec. 4.
20. V of 1954, Secs. 5(2), 7, 8, 10–A (enacted by XXVI of 1954), 11, 12.
21. V of 1954, Sec. 14(1).
22. V of 1954, Secs. 11, 14(2), 17, 43, and I of 1951, Sec. 121.
23. V of 1954, Sec. 15(1) a.

24. V of 1954, Sec. 15(c), (d), (h).
25. V of 1954, Sec. 15 (i).
26. V of 1954, Secs. 30, 31, 25–27, 33.
27. Singh, *Next Step in Village India,* pp. 33–34.
28. Act I of 1951, Sec. 176.
29. Ibid., Secs. 169–71.
30. Ibid., Secs. 183–86, 189–90.
31. Z.A.C. *Report,* p. 19.
32. U.N., *Land Reform,* p. 6.
33. *U.P. Prov. Banking Enquiry Committee,* pp. 24–26.
34. U.N., *Land Reform,* pp. 8–9.
35. *U.P. Prov. Banking Enquiry Committee,* pp. 27–28, 22, 26–27.
36. Z.A.C., *Report,* pp. 19, 21.
37. Ibid., pp. 385–86.
38. Ibid.
39. Ibid., pp. 503–04.
40. Ibid., pp. 502–03.
41. *Statistical Abstract, India, 1950.*
42. Chaturvedi, pp. 30–31.
43. *Seasonal and Crop Report,* 1946–47, Statement II.
44. Chaturvedi, pp. 45, 46, 60, 95, 96.
45. Z.A.C. *Report,* p. 536.

Chapter 15

1. Thorner, *Agrarian Prospect,* p. 80.
2. Z.A.C. *Report,* pp. 457, 509.
3. *Eastern Economist,* Aug. 11, 1950, pp. 206–07.
4. U.N., *Land Reform,* p. 51.
5. Ibid., p. 69.
6. Ibid., p. 63.
7. Ibid., p. 91.
8. Ibid., p. 84.
9. Ibid., pp. 85–86.
10. Ibid., pp. 86–87.

GLOSSARY

Abadi—The village site.

Abwab—Minor taxes and dues; also school and road rates under the British.

Adhivasi—Temporary tenant during land reform.

Amil—A collector of revenue under pre-British governments.

Amin—An Indian officer in the British administration, often a subordinate revenue officer.

Anna—One-sixteenth of a rupee.

Asami—A holder of rights in shifting cultivation.

Assessment—The fixing of the revenue demand.

Batai—Division of the produce between those having rights in it.

Begar—Labor or duties owed by a tenant or one of the lower orders in the hierarchy to the landlord or powerful people in a village. Now often called "forced labor."

Bhabar—Porous and hence waterless land north of the tarai.

Bhaiachara village—A village owned by a group of independent persons whose shares were based on some ancient custom, not on ancestry.

Bhatta—Village deductions from the grain heap before division between cultivator and raja.

Bhumidhar—A holder of all rights to land except the right to rent.

Bigha—Indian measurement of land area. Varies in size from place to place. Standard revenue bigha in North-Western Provinces was five-eights of an acre.

Birt—A grant or endowment for maintenance, often with religious or charitable purposes.

Birtya—Holder of a birt.

Biswa—Right of a cultivator to cut one-twentieth of a bigha before the harvest division.

Bundh—A low dike.

Cesses—See *Abwab*.

Chak—A plot of land.

Chakladar—A revenue official.

Chamar—One of the harijan (untouchable) castes.

Chowkidar—A watchman.

Circle—Subdivision of a tehsil having roughly uniform characteristics of soil and productivity. The smallest revenue assessment area above a village. The circle area is composed of villages on similar soils of roughly equal productive capacity.

Collector—A British jack-of-all trades revenue officer of a district.

Crore—10,000,000, written 1,00,00,000.

Diwan—Chief revenue officer of a province or area under the Mughals and kings of Oudh.

Doab—Land lying between the Ganges and the Jumna.

Gaon—Village.

Gaon Panchayat—Council of the local government established by the Panchayat Raj Act XXVI of 1947.

Gaon Sabha—Local village government.

Gaon Samaj—Corporate body of all tenure-holders in a village, established by the Zamindari Abolition and Land Reform Act I of 1951.

Gram—A millet.

Headman—Political chief of a village. Responsible for land revenue before British rule. Often recognized as landlord by the British.

Jagir—The rights to the revenue held by a jagirdar.

Jagirdar—A person granted a portion or all of the revenue of a village in reward for service to the king or raja. He was also the local political chief.

Jaziya—Mohammedan head tax.

Kamin—Village artisan or servant who receives a share of the harvest in kind.

Kanungo—Revenue, records, and legal officer of a district. Indian assistant to collector under British rule. In charge of the *patwaris.*

Kans—A deep-rooted weed.

Khaliyan—A granary.

Kharif—Autumn crop.

Khas—A chief officer under the Mughals; therefore collection of revenue by officers without intermediaries between them and cultivators; and later lands cultivated by the zamindars.

Khiraf—Tribute levied by Muslims on non-Muslims.

Khudkasht—Land cultivated by the landowner.

Kisan—Cultivating peasant.

Lakh—100,000 written 1,00,000.

Lakhiraj—Land held free of rent and revenue.

Lambardar—Village headman or person responsible for turning over revenue collections to the government.

Lekhpal—New name for patwari or village record-keeper.

Mahajan—Village merchant and money-lender.

Mahal—Landed estate belonging to one or several co-sharing zamindars. Assessed as one unit at settlement. May be one or more villages or parts of one or more villages. Spelled "mehaul" in earlier years.

Malikana—Allowance paid to a zamindar who refuses a settlement.

Mazdoor—Landless agricultural laborer.

Mukaddam—The representative of a village.

Munsif—Judicial officer.

Mustajir—A revenue officer.

Nawab—Senior official representing emperor or king in a province.

Naya paisa—One-hundredth of a rupee in new coinage.

Nazim—Pre-British governor of a province. Frequently included the office of Diwan.

Nazrana—A gift from a tenant to his landlord; in the nature of a bribe in more recent years.

Pahikasht—Cultivation of land by a person not a resident of the village in which the land lies.

Panchayat—Traditional village council, supposedly of five members. Now the local council.

Panchayati Adalat—Local council in new system of local government.

Pargana—Third subdivision of the Mughal administration: subas were divided into sirkars (districts) and sirkars into parganas. Parganas were replaced by tehsils under the British.

Patta—A lease or written settlement of the land revenue.

Patta dawami
 Patta istamrari } A lease in perpetuity.

Pattidar—Co-sharer in a written settlement of the land revenue.

Pattidari village—One owned by a group of co-sharers who together constituted the equivalent of a zamindar and whose shares were based on descent rather than custom.

Patwari—The village accountant. Usually hereditary.

Pie—One-twelfth of a rupee.

Pice—One-fourth of a rupee, or 3 pies.

Rabi—The spring crop.

Raja—Hindu king of a small kingdom. Not to be confused with the Mughal emperor at Delhi or the Mohammedan kings of Oudh at Lucknow.

Rajput—Warrior caste of North India.

Ryot—A peasant or cultivator.

Ryotwari—Areas originally settled directly with the cultivator individually, mostly in Madras and Bombay provinces. Over the past century differences in complexity between ryotwari and zamindari areas have tended to disappear.

Sanad—Written grant of rights.

Sayar—Income from forests, pastures, and waste.

Settlement—The assessment of the revenue and the agreement with the owner to pay the revenue.

> *Permanent Settlement*—Settlement in perpetuity. Land revenue never to be changed.

> *Regular Settlement*—Settlement for about 30 years.

> *Temporary Settlement*—Settlement for a few years; i.e., one to five.

Singhara—A fruit that grows in ponds and lakes.

Sir—Land cultivated by the owner. Variously defined and limited by legislative enactment. Tenant rights did not accrue on sir if it were let.

Sirdar—Holder of a perpetual tenure under the Zamindari Abolition Act I of 1951.

Sirkar—An official.

Siyaha—Record of rents submitted by zamindars.

Suba—Large administrative district under Mughals.

Sudder Malguzar—Village headman or headman–proprietor of a village.

Takavi—A loan in kind, especially by the government to cultivators.

Tarai—Swampy, malarial lands at the foot of the Himalayas.

Taluka—A revenue collection area of one or more villages before British rule. See *Talukdar*.

Talukdar—A revenue farmer of a taluka. He also possessed judicial authority, frequently engaged in general management of the land, and wielded political power independent of any formal grants. Often reduced zamindars to status of occupancy tenants. In North-Western Provinces was usually removed from authority by the British. In Oudh was recognized as landlord by the British.

Tehsil—Subdivision of a district under the British. There are from three to six tehsils in each district of Uttar Pradesh.

Tehsildar—Revenue official in charge of a tehsil.

Thakur—Rajput caste in Uttar Pradesh, often landlords.

Thekadar—The lessee of a landowner's rights.

Usar—Alkaline or saline soil.

Waqf—A religious or charitable trust.

Zamindar—In North-Western Provinces and Oudh was individually, or as one of a group, the local authority in the village, managing its economy and frequently cultivating the soil himself. He possessed varying amounts of power delegated by the raja, including minor judicial causes, local government, and often control of land revenue even to the exclusion of the raja. In North-Western Provinces the British generally recognized him as landlord. In Oudh he had often lost so much power to the talukdars that he was recognized frequently as a subproprietor or even an occupancy tenant. Where he had kept his power in Oudh, the zamindar became landlord.

Zamindari village—A village owned by a single zamindar or owned undivided by several co-sharing zamindars.

BOOKS, PAMPHLETS, PERIODICALS, AND ARTICLES

Abramovitz, Moses, "Resource and Output Trends in the United States Since 1870," *American Economic Review, 46,* 1956.

Anstey, Vera, *The Economic Development of India,* 4th ed. London, Longmans, Green, 1952.

Baden-Powell, B. H., *The Land Systems of British India, 1* and *2,* Oxford, Clarendon Press, 1892.

——*The Indian Village Community,* London, Longmans, Green, 1896.

Banerjea, Pramathanath, *Indian Finance in the Days of the Company,* London, Macmillan, 1928.

Beidelman, Thomas O., *A Comparative Analysis of the Jajmani System,* Locust Valley, N.Y., J. J. Augustin, 1959.

Blyn, George, "A Comparison of the Crop Output Trend in India with Trends in the Underlying Determinants of Yield: 1893–1946" (private paper).

——"Crop Production Trends in India" (private paper).

Boeke, J. H., *Economics and Economic Policy of Dual Societies,* Parts I and II, New York, Institute of Pacific Relations, 1946.

——*The Interests of the Voiceless Far East: An Introduction to Oriental Economics,* Leiden, Universitaire Pers, 1946.

Campbell, George, "Tenure of Land in India," in the Cobden Club, *Systems of Land Tenure in Various Countries,* London, Macmillan, 1870.

Carstairs, R., *The Little World of an Indian District Officer,* London, Macmillan, 1912.

Chaturvedi, M. D., *Land Management in the United Provinces,* Allahabad, Supt., Printing and Stationery, U.P., 1946.

Cohn, Bernard S., "Madhopur Revisited," *Economic Weekly,* July 1959, Special Issue.

——"Some Notes on Law and Change in North India," *Economic Development and Cultural Change, 8,* 1959.

Dandekar, V. M. and Khudanpur, G. J., *Working of Bombay Tenacy Act, 1948: Report of Investigation,* Poona, Gokhale Institute Publication No. 35, 1957.

Dobb, Maurice, *Some Aspects of Economic Development: Three Lectures,* Occasional Papers No. 3, Delhi School of Economics, Delhi, Ranjit Printers and Publishers, 1951.

Driver, Peshotan Nasserwanji, *Problems of Zamindari and Land Tenure Reconstruction in India,* Bombay, New Book Co. Ltd., 1949.

Dube, S. C., *India's Changing Villages*, Ithaca, N.Y., Cornell University Press, 1958.

Eastern Economist, The (Delhi), dates as cited.

Economic Weekly, The (Bombay), dates as cited.

Ewbank, R. B., ed., *Indian Co-operative Studies*, Bombay, Oxford University Press, 1920.

Frankel, S. Herbert, *The Economic Impact on Underdeveloped Societies*, Oxford, Basil Blackwell, 1953.

Furnivall, J. S., *Colonial Policy and Practice*, 2nd ed. New York, New York University Press, 1956.

Gangulee, N., *The Indian Peasant and His Environment*, Oxford, Oxford University Press, 1935.

Griffiths, Sir Percival, *The British Impact on India*, London, Macdonald, 1952.

Gupta, S. C., *An Economic Survey of Shamaspur Village*, Bombay, Asia Publishing House, 1959.

Hitchcock, John T., "Leadership in a North Indian Village: Two Case Studies," in Richard L. Park and Irene Tinker, eds., *Leadership and Political Institutions in India*, Princeton, Princeton University Press, 1959.

Hough, Eleanor M., *The Cooperative Movement in India: Its Relation to a Sound National Economy*, London, P. S. King, 1932.

Huq, Mazharul, "East India Company Land Policy and Management in Bengal from 1698 to 1784," Typescript of doctoral thesis deposited at the London School of Economics, 1932.

"India: Mohammedan Law," *Encyclopaedia Britannica, 12*, Chicago, University of Chicago Press, 1945.

India's Villages (A collection of articles originally published in the *Economic Weekly*, Bombay), Calcutta, Development Department, West Bengal Government Press, 1955.

Jafri, S.N.A., *The History and Status of Landlords and Tenants in the United Provinces (India)*, Allahabad, Pioneer Press, 1931.

Leibenstein, Harvey, *Economic Backwardness and Economic Growth*, New York, John Wiley, 1957.

Lewis, Oscar, *Village Life in Northern India*, Urbana, Ill., University of Illinois Press, 1958.

——and Singh, Harwant, *Group Dynamics in a North Indian Village: A Study of Factions*, Programme Evaluation Organization, Planning Commission, New Delhi, 1954.

Maine, Sir Henry Sumner, *Ancient Law*, London, Dent, 1954.

——*Village Communities in the East and West*, 3rd (author's) ed., New York, Henry Holt, 1876.

Malaviya, H. D., *Land Reforms in India*, New Delhi, All-India Congress Committee, 1954.

——*Village Panchayats in India*, New Delhi, All-India Congress Committee, 1956.

Malenbaum, Wilfred, "India and China: Contrasts in Development Performance," M.I.T., India Project mimeograph D/58–6, Cambridge, Mass., 1958.

Marriott, McKim, "Western Medicine in a Village of Northern India," in Benjamin D. Paul, ed., *Health, Culture, and Community*, N.Y., Russell Sage Foundation, 1955.

Mason, Philip (pseud: Philip Woodruff) *Call the Next Witness*, New York, Harcourt, Brace, 1946.

Mayer, Albert; Marriott, McKim; and Park, Richard L., eds., *Pilot Project, India*, Berkeley, University of California Press, 1958.

Misra, B. R., *Land Revenue Policy in the United Provinces under British Rule*, Benares, Nand Kishore, 1942.

Moon, Penderel, *Strangers in India*, New York, Reynal and Hitchcock, 1945.

Moreland, W. H., *The Agrarian System of Moslem India*, Cambridge, Eng., W. Heffer, 1929.

——*From Akbar to Aurungzeb: A Study in Indian Economic History*, London, Macmillan, 1923.

——*India at the Death of Akbar: An Economic Study*, London, Macmillan, 1920.

——*The Revenue Administration of the United Provinces*, Allahabad, Pioneer Press, 1911.

Mukherjee, P. K. and Gupta, S. C., *A Pilot Survey of Fourteen Villages in U.P. and Punjab*, Bombay, Asia Publishing House, 1959.

Myrdal, Gunnar, *Rich Lands and Poor*, New York, Harpers, 1956.

Neale, Walter C., "Economic Accounting and Family Farming in India," *Economic Development and Cultural Change, 7*, Part I, April 1959.

——"The Limitations of Indian Village Survey Data," *Journal of Asian Studies, 17*, May 1958.

——"Reciprocity and Redistribution in the Indian Village: Sequel to Some Notable Discussions," in Karl Polanyi, Conrad M. Arensberg, and Harry W. Pearson, eds., *Trade and Markets in the Early Empires*, Glencoe, Ill., Free Press, 1957.

Nurkse, Ragnar, *Problems of Capital Formation in Underdeveloped Countries*, New York, Oxford University Press, 1953.

O'Malley, L. S. S., *Modern India and the West*, London, Oxford University Press, 1941.

Park, Richard L. and Tinker, Irene, eds., *Leadership and Political Institutions in India*, Princeton, Princeton University Press, 1959.

Planning Commission, Government of India, *The New India: Progress Through Democracy*, New York, Macmillan, 1958.

Polanyi, Karl, *The Great Transformation*, New York, Rinehart, 1944.

Radhakrishnan, Sir Sarvapalli, "Indian Culture," in *Reflections on Our Age*, London, Allan Wingate, 1948.

Rosen, George, "Capital : Output Ratios in Indian Industry," *Economic Trends*, Bombay, December 1956.

Sen, Bhowani, *Indian Land System and Land Reforms*, Delhi, People's Publishing House, 1956.

Singh, Baljit, *Next Step in Village India*, Bombay, Asia Publishing House, 1960.

Singh, Tarlok, *Poverty and Social Change, A Study in the Economic Reorganization of Indian Rural Society*, Calcutta, Longmans, Green, 1945.

Slater, G., *Some South Indian Villages*, London, 1918.

Solow, Robert M., "Technical Change and the Aggregate Production Function," *Review of Economics and Statistics, 39*, 1957.

Spate, O. K. H., *The Geography of India and Pakistan*, New York, E. P. Dutton, 1954.

Thomas, P. J. and Ramakrishnan, K. C., *Some South Indian Villages: A Resurvey*, Madras, University of Madras Press, 1940.

Thorner, Daniel, *The Agrarian Prospect for India*, Delhi, University of Delhi Press, 1956.

———"Feudalism in India," in Rushton Coulborn, ed., *Feudalism in History*, Princeton, Princeton University Press, 1956.

———"Long-term Trends in Output in India," in Simon Kuznets, Wilbert E. Moore, and Joseph J. Spengler, eds., *Economic Growth: Brazil, India, Japan*, Durham, N.C., Duke University Press, 1955.

———"India's Agrarian Revolution by Census Redefinition," *Indian Economic Review, 3*, 1956.

——— and Thorner, Alice, "Agricultural Manpower in India: Labourers," *Economic Weekly*, Nov. 9, 1957.

Tiwari, Shri Gopal, *The Economic Prosperity of the United Provinces*, Bombay, Asia Publishing House, 1951.

United Nations, *Land Reform: Defects in Agrarian Structure as Obstacles to Economic Development*, New York, United Nations, 1951.

U. P. Provincial Congress Committee, *Agrarian Distress in the United Provinces,* Allahabad, Sri Prakasa at the Allahabad Law Journal Press, 1932.

Walsh, Sir Cecil, *Indian Village Crimes,* London, Ernest Benn, 1929.

Warriner, Doreen, *Economics of Peasant Farming,* London, Oxford University Press, 1939.

OFFICIAL PUBLICATIONS

Abstract of the Proceedings of the Council of the Governor-General of India, Assembled for the Purpose of Making Laws and Regulations, 4: 1865, 5: 1866, 6: 1867, 7: 1868, 8: 1869, Calcutta, Office of Supt. of Government Printing.

Agricultural Situation in India, New Delhi, Economic and Statistical Adviser to the Ministry of Food and Agriculture (Monthly, dates as cited).

Annual Reports of the Working of Cooperative Societies in the United Provinces for the Years 1921–22 to 1940–41, Allahabad, Supt., Printing and Stationery, U.P.

Co-operative Farming, Ministry of Agriculture, Government of India, New Delhi, 1949.

India: A Reference Annual, 1958, Delhi, Publications Division, Old Secretariat, 1958.

Land Revenue Policy of the Indian Government, published by Governor-General of India in Council, Calcutta, Supt. Govt. Printing, India, 1920.

Mackenzie, Holt, "Memorandum by the Secretary Regarding the Settlements of the Ceded and Conquered Provinces, with Suggestions for the Permanent Settlement of Those Provinces, dated 1st July 1819," in *Selections from the Revenue Records of the North-West Provinces, 1818–1820,* Calcutta, Military Orphan Press, 1866.

Papers Relating to Land Tenures and Revenue Settlement in Oude, Calcutta, Military Orphan Press, 1865; "Minute" by Sir C. E. Trevelyan, 23 August 1864.

Proceedings of the Legislative Council of India, 3, Calcutta, J. Thomas, Baptist Mission Press, 1857 (?).

Report of the Administration of the Registration Department, United Provinces, Triennial Reports, 1920–22, 1923–25, 1926–28, 1929–31, 1932–34, 1935–37, Annual Reports 1938, 1939, 1940, 1941, Allahabad, Supt., Printing and Stationery, U.P.

Report of the U.P. Panchayat Raj Amendment Act Committee, Lucknow, Supt., Printing and Stationery, U.P., 1954.

Report of the United Provinces Provincial Banking Enquiry Committee, 1: 1929–30, Allahabad, Supt., Govt. Press, U.P., 1930.

Report of the United Provinces Zamindari Abolition Committee, M. G. Shome, Allahabad, Supt., Printing and Stationery, U.P., 1948.

Reserve Bank of India, *Review of the Cooperative Movement in India, 1948–50,* Bombay, 1952.

———*Cooperative News Digest,* No. 11, Bombay, 1952.

Royal Commission on Agriculture in India, *Report on Agriculture in the United Provinces,* prepared under the orders of the Government of the United Provinces for the Royal Commission on Indian Agriculture, 1926, Naini Tal, Govt. Branch Press, 1926.

———*14: Appendix to the Report,* London, H.M.S.O., 1928.

———*Abridged Report of the Royal Commission on Agriculture in India,* London, H.M.S.O., 1928.

Seasonal and Crop Reports for the United Provinces of Agra and Oudh for the Years 1923–24 to 1940–41 and 1946–47, Allahabad, Supt., Govt. Printing, Dept. of Land Records.

Selections from the Revenue Records of the North-West Provinces, 1818–1820, Calcutta, Military Orphan Press, 1866.

Stack, E., *Memorandum upon Current Land Revenue Settlements,* Calcutta, Home, Revenue, and Agricultural Department Press, 1880.

SETTLEMENT REPORTS

Final Report on the Revision of the Settlement in the Bara Banki District, by C. Hope, Allahabad, N.-W.P. and Oudh Govt. Press, 1899.

The Final Settlement Report on the Gonda District, by W. C. Bennett, Allahabad, N.-W.P. and Oudh Govt. Press, 1878.

Report on the Settlement of Pillibheet, by Elliot Colvin, Allahabad, N.-W.P. Govt. Press, 1873.

Report on the Settlement Operations of the Rái Bareli District, by Maj. J. F. MacAndrew, Lucknow, Oudh Govt. Press, 1872. Actual Report by Maj. Ralph Ouseley, Appendix K by Maj. J. F. MacAndrew.

Report on the Settlement of the District of Seharunpore, 1st February 1839, completed by Edward Thornton, submitted to Government, by the Sudder Board of Revenue, N.-W.P., October 18, 1840.

Report on the Settlement of Shahjehanpore District, by Robert G. Currie, Allahabad, N.-W.P. Govt. Press, 1874.

REGULATIONS AND ACTS

Bengal Regulation I of 1795, "The Benares Permanent Settlement Regulations, 1795," *The United Provinces Code, 1,* 6th ed. Allahabad, Supt. Govt. Printing and Stationery, U.P., 1943.

Regulation VII of 1822, *The Regulations of the Government of Fort William in Bengal, in Force at the End of 1853, 2: Regulations from 1806 to 1834,* prepared by Richard Clarke, London, J. and H. Cox, 1854.

Regulation IX of 1833, *The Regulations of the Government of Fort William in Bengal, in Force at the End of 1833, 2: Regulations from 1806 to 1834,* prepared by Richard Clarke, London, J. and H. Cox, 1854.

Act X of 1859, "The Bengal Rent Act, 1859," *Bengal Code, 1,* 5th ed. Alipore, Bengal, Supt. Govt. Printing, 1939, p. 377.

Act XIV of 1863, "North-Western Provinces Rent Act," William Theobald, ed., *The Legislative Acts of the Governor General of India in Council, 4: 1862–1865,* Calcutta, Thacker, Spink, 1868.

Act XXVI of 1866, "The Oudh Sub-Settlement Act, 1866," *The United Provinces Code, 1,* 6th ed. Allahabad, Supt., Printing and Stationery, 1943.

Act XIX of 1868, "Oudh Rent Act," *A Collection of the Acts Passed by the Governor General of India in Council in the year 1868,* Calcutta, Supt. of Govt. Printing, 1868.

Act I of 1869, "The Oudh Estates Act," William Theobald, ed., *The Legislative Acts of the Governor General of India in Council of 1869,* Calcutta, Thacker, Spink, 1870.

The following Acts are published in the series *A Collection of the Acts passed by the Governor General of India in Council,* each volume published in the year following the Acts, at Calcutta, Superintendent of Government Printing, until 1900, then at Allahabad, Superintendent, Government Press, U.P. (Exception: Act XX of 1890).

Act XXIV of 1870, "Oudh Taluqdars' Relief Act."

Act XXII of 1872, "North-Western Provinces Rent Act."

Act XVIII of 1873, "North-Western Provinces Rent Act."

Act XIX of 1873, "North-Western Provinces Land Revenue Act."

Act XVII of 1876, "Oudh Land Revenue Act."

Act VIII of 1879, "North-Western Provinces Rent Act."

Act XII of 1881, "North-Western Provinces Rent Act."

Act X of 1885, "The Oudh Estates (Amendment) Act."

Act XIV of 1886, "North-Western Provinces Rent Act."
Act XV of 1886, "North-Western Provinces Rent (Amendment) Act."
Act XXII of 1886, "Oudh Rent Act."
Act XX of 1890, "The North-Western Provinces and Oudh Act, 1890." *The United Provinces Code, 1,* 6th ed. Allahabad, Supt., Government Printing and Stationery, U.P., 1943.
Act II of 1900, "The Oudh Settled Estates Act, 1900."
Act II of 1901, "The North-Western Provinces Tenancy Act, 1901."
Act IV of 1901, "Oudh Rent Act, 1866, Amendment Act, 1901."
Act I of 1903, "The Bundelkhand Encumbered Estates Act, 1903."
Act II of 1903, "The Bundelkhand Alienation of Land Act, 1903."
Act IV of 1921, "The Oudh Rent (Amendment) Act, 1921."
Act II of 1922, "The U.P. Land Revenue (Patwaris Amendment) Act, 1922."
Act III of 1922, "The Bundelkhand Encumbered Estates (Amendment) Act, 1922."
Act V of 1922, "The U.P. Land Revenue (Amendment) Act, 1922."
Act I of 1923, "The Oudh Rent (Amendment) Act, 1923."
Act IV of 1923, "The U.P. Land Revenue (Amendment) Act, 1923."
Act VIII of 1923, "The Agra Pre-Emption (Amendment) Act, 1923."
Act III of 1926, "The Agra Tenancy Act, 1926."
Act V of 1926, "The Oudh Rent (Amendment) Act, 1926."
Act I of 1929, "The U.P. Land Revenue (Amendment–Settlement) Act, 1929."
Act II of 1932, "The U.P. Land Revenue (Amendment) Act, 1932."
Act VIII of 1932, "The U.P. Assistance of Tenants Act, 1932."
Act XII of 1932, "The U.P. Land Revenue (Amendment) Act, 1932."
Act VII of 1934, "The Agra Tenancy (Amendment) Act."
Act IX of 1934, "Oudh Rent (Amendment) Act."
Act XVIII of 1934, "The Bundelkhand Alienation of Land (Amendment) Act, 1934."
Act XXIII of 1934, "The Usurious Loans (U.P. Amendment) Act, 1934."
Act XXIV of 1934, "U.P. Temporary Regulation of Execution Act, 1934."
Act XXV of 1934, "The U.P. Encumbered Estates Act, 1934."
Act XXVI of 1934, "U.P. Regulation of Sales Act, 1934."
Act XXVII of 1934, "U.P. Agriculturalists' Relief Act, 1934."
Act X of 1937, "Temporary Postponement of Execution of Decrees Act, 1937."

Act VIII of 1939, "U.P. Consolidation of Holdings Act, 1939."
Act XI of 1939, "U.P. Encumbered Estates (Amendment) Act, 1939."
Act XIII of 1939, "U.P. Tenancy Laws (Amendment) Act, 1939."
Act XVII of 1939, "U.P. Tenancy Act, 1939."
Act I of 1940, "U.P. Tenancy (Amendment) Act, 1940."
Act II of 1940, "U.P. Encumbered Estates (Amendment) Act, 1940."
Act XIII of 1940, "U.P. Debt Redemption Act, 1940."
Act XIV of 1941, "U.P. Regulation of Agriculture Credit Act, 1941."

The following Acts were published by the Superintendent, Government Printing and Stationery, U.P., Allahabad, as separate pamphlets in the years in which the Acts were passed.
Act X of 1947, "U.P. Tenancy (Amendment) Act, 1947."
Act XXVI of 1947, "U.P. Panchayat Raj Act, 1947."
Act X of 1949, "U.P. Agricultural Tenants (Acquisition of Privileges) Act, 1949."
Act I of 1951, "The Uttar Pradesh Zamindari Abolition and Land Reforms Act, 1950."
Act XVI of 1953, "U.P. Zamindari Abolition and Land Reform (Amendment) Act, 1952."
Act V of 1954, as amended by Acts XXVI of 1954 and XIII of 1955, "U.P. Consolidation of Holdings Act, 1953," ed. by Badri Bishal Tripathi, Allahabad, Ram Nanaia Lal, 1955.
Act XX of 1954, "U.P. Land Revenue (Amendment) Act, 1954."

Index